HOW TO UNDERSTAND MUSIC

BY

OSCAR THOMPSON
Author of " Practical Musical Criticism "

1936 · *The Dial Press* · NEW YORK

PRINTED IN THE UNITED STATES OF AMERICA
BY VAN REES PRESS, NEW YORK

JOHANN SEBASTIAN BACH

TO KEITH

whose fresh interest in old problems has helped
me to feel that this effort was worth while.

Sept. 1, 1935

CONTENTS

LIST OF ILLUSTRATIONS

AN AVOWAL OF AIMS

THE aims of this book are practical and realistic. The author addresses adults, not children. There are contained within these covers no elementary lessons in rhythms, scales, chords, key relationships. The adult who knows something of what the professional calls "essentials" does not need such lessons. The adult who is completely lacking in this knowledge will rarely learn anything about them from reading a book. They require study, not mere perusal and reflection. With few exceptions, the musically unlettered adult is in no position (and no mood) to attend a musical kindergarten. If he can enjoy an opera or a symphony, he does not relish being talked to as a musical ignoramus; and he has no intention of going to a piano stool and poking out, in one-finger drudgery, little examples of the kind that prove useful for six-year-olds. For him, it is not musicianship that is at issue, but musical understanding.

Without reflection on much valuable work that has been done and is now being done in the elementary schools, the high schools, and colleges, a question may be raised as to whether the time has not come to retire to the shelf the term "Musical appreciation." Inevitably, it has acquired a certain odium for the adult mind. There have been too many bedtime stories circulated in its name. To "appreciate" is one thing, to "understand" is another. The dint of much talk may convince the most unmusical layman that it is his duty to "appreciate" good music; though, for the life of him, he cannot see why it is "good." He can *appreciate* the importance of what every one around him *understands*—or pretends to understand—and go away from a concert in a worse muddle than when he arrived.

There is an ugly smack of obligation about that word "appreciate." A man appreciates a kindness, a favor done him, a birthday gift, a little commiseration and sympathy when he is in trouble or pain, the extension of a loan. He may appreciate the good qualities of an individual he avoids as a pest or a bore. His appreciation of any of the arts may be primarily a form of acknowledgment of his own limitations; he may appreciate and *dread*; appreciate and *resent*; appreciate, the while his approach is that of the youth to the woodpile or the girl to the kitchen sink; appreciate in the spirit of getting done with a chore. The professional appreciators have done their share in discrediting the term. Such strictures as are here implied have to do not so much with those who have talked to children about trombones as if they were rabbits, or of fugues as a species of tricycle with green handle-bars and yellow tires, as with the bookmakers, broadcasters and lecturers of every sort and description who have sought to make children of grown men and women by feeding them fairy tales about music. To appreciate music, in all too many instances, has been to know so many things that are not so; it has been to substitute all manner of verbal interpretations, literary, sentimental, emotional, imaginative, for the plain speech of the music itself. Often, it has been a farrago of *everything but music*, save as some baby-talk about essentials might find a place with dubious biographical or other factual data; smothered, whether right or wrong, in a cloud of insupportable opinion as to what the music "means."

If there are errors of fact in this book, they are just that. If descriptions or definitions are faulty or inconclusive, that, regrettably, is what they are. But an earnest effort has been made to face the facts and not to build romances. One such fact, and an inescapable one, is this: the layman, in numbers beyond count or even conjecture, *begins his listening at the top.* He may have studied in childhood, or he may never have studied, the rudiments of music. In either case, he is not going to study them now. Neither is he going to put off hearing a symphony until he is sure he knows all there is to know about a suite, an overture, a string quartet or the compass of a bassoon. His great need is to know what he is hearing, not how it was made. This is a book of what and not of how. It construes music as for the ear and not the eye. It relies on the practical proof of everyday experience that music in its most complex forms, as well as its most simple, is understood by multitudes who depend entirely on the ear and not the eye. And it contends that the understanding of music of necessity *begins with the music itself*—whatever the perspective in which it may be viewed by reason of a broader or a narrower cultural outlook—and that this is not to be confused with the play of individual or collective imagination, or the accumulation of extra-musical data, in an effort to determine what was behind its composition or what (in the terms of human experience) the music "means." In italicizing the word *begins,* the writer trusts he has left himself elbow room in which to move in his discussions of program music, music of the theatre and all music that has an avowed, or otherwise obvious, literary, pictorial, imitative or dramatic purpose. To *begin* otherwise, is to deal with something else than music. To *understand* otherwise, is not to understand music.

THE NATURE OF MUSIC

To generalize about music is dangerous. What is true of most music is not true of some music. What is particularly true of some music may be anything but true of most music. To begin with, even a definition of music is difficult. One man of the acquaintance of the author has made a collection of such definitions, ranging from a phrase or a sentence to a chapter or an essay, each purporting to say what music is. Only an occultist could have evolved some of them. Every conceivable religious, ethical, mathematical, physical, psychical, emotional and naturalistic basis has been found for music, aside from the acoustical and vibrational qualities that enter into production and recognition of sound. And as sound itself does not exist aside from an impact upon an ear mechanism—the vibrations that cause a sound being as silent as any void, whatever the disturbance they create—even a workaday and completely realistic definition of music as "an ordered sequence of sound, forming a design," opens the way to valid

[5]

objections. The listener has only to regard this sequence as unpleasant, or the sounds themselves as
unmusical, and for an individual, at least, there is no
music.

Whether any so-called law of music is actually
a law or only a recipe remains a battleground. So
far as man is concerned, there can be no doubt that
music came first; any and all laws of music afterward.
There are folk melodies that no twist of definition-
making could rob of their right to be called music;
some of these probably are older than anything that
has come down to us as a law of music; they blos-
somed in the blood of primitive peoples, as innocent
of musical laws as any jungle denizen of today. Laws
that come after the fact, that are deductions from
what already has been done, that prescribe for the
present and the future on the basis of what has been,
may be no laws at all. Music can be made in such
and such a way. Music so made gratifies the human
ear. Here, as elsewhere, the proof of the pudding has
been in the eating. But puddings are made, not by
law, but by recipe. The possibility of an altered
recipe, or a new recipe entirely, resulting in a better
and tastier pudding is not to be overlooked. Much
of the mistaken judgment that has plagued musical
criticism in the past undoubtedly was due to mistak-
ing recipes for laws. Good music had been made in
certain ways. Time proved that those ways could be
altered and good music still come out of the making;

unless one is to accept the laments of those few and scattered individuals who believe that music stopped short with Palestrina, or Mozart, or Brahms or Debussy.

Vibrations can be stated in mathematical terms. That done, relations between one set of vibrations and another, and combinations thereof, will take the form of mathematics when written out on paper. But if mathematics ever really proved anything about the nature of music—much as it has been applied in efforts to rationalize what has needed no rationalization for the human ear—the mathematicians either have kept their secret to themselves or so buried it in calculations like those of a piano tuner bent on providing some new equalization of the scale, as to leave music precisely where it was before their lucubrations began. Again, let us hasten to repeat, to generalize is dangerous. But although much has been said and written on the scientific aspects of music, as represented by acoustical considerations and the measurement of vibrations, the theory of music is pre-eminently an accumulation or distillation of *practice*, reasoned about *retrospectively* rather than *predetermined* by the application of scientific principles. This is not to deny that there may be laws of music— physical, mathematical, God-given, what you will. But the man, woman or child who is building an understanding of music has no need of them, or of the controversies that can so readily be engendered by any attempt to prove their validity. Neither, in the belief of this writer, has an intelligent and properly attuned listener any crying need to know that moiety of theory which can be recognized without difficulty as recipe—in that it is primarily the established way of arriving at certain results. Craftsmanship is for the worker. It is by no means certain that the worker is always the best listener. A smattering of knowledge of the way things have been done is not infrequently the cause of unfortunate convictions as to the way they *must* be done. As the most fluid of all the arts, it is music that demands the greatest fluidity, the least of fixity, in the receptivities of those who would take it to their hearts.

Generalities are dangerous—still, the opinion will be ventured here that most of the obstacles to straightout understanding of music are man-made—self-made —rule-made. It is not alone the pedant, intent upon preserving inviolate what he himself may have been taught, who raises barriers to understanding in the form of rules. The most untutored listener may have his rules, the dictates of his own predilections, and of his own limited experience; his own convictions as to what should or should not be true of the music he consents to hear. If, to begin with, he has misconceived the nature of music, and stubbornly endeavors to apply to *all* music what is applicable only to *some* music, or to *some* music what may very well be true of *most* music, without an understanding and

[8]

grasp of music's infinite variety of means and ends, he has erected a wall between himself and one or many works of the musical art; and either he has no one to blame but himself or he shares the responsibility with others like himself, in or out of the musical profession, who have made it their business to help him put up the wall.

The number of persons fit for treasons, stratagems, and spoils may be assumed to be infinitely greater than the number of those who have no music in their souls. Indeed, many a great rogue has had a love for music and it is not too much to say that there are those who would resort to treasons, stratagems and spoils of the most nefarious order, *for music's sake.* It is the nature of music to suggest the ideal, to refine, sensitize and in a sense to glorify all that it expresses or shadows forth in the messages it conveys to humanity. But man is too complex a character to be made saintly by that alone. He can respond to this ideality in music one moment and rob his neighbor the next. Quite probably, he could do both in one and the same moment were the circumstances favorable, although the police records do not reveal many instances of pockets being picked at symphony concerts. What happens to the umbrellas left under the seats when the program is finished is another matter!

We stray afield, but it is one of the truisms of the musical art that it cannot, of itself, embody evil. With the aid of words, or the dance, or pictorial representation of some kind, music may find ways of heightening the effect of subversive forces, but the power of association invariably is necessary; left to go its own way, about the worst that music can do to man is to bore him by being dull or irritate him by being ugly. Vulgarity is possible to it; obscenity must be assumed.* Composers have found ways to represent revels and orgies of sensuality. These do not appear to have corrupted the morals of church-goers, or even of backsliders, anywhere. To the contrary, they have had in their most glamorous moments the appeal of the ideal, as in the voices of the sirens in the "Tannhäuser" Bacchanale—a call certainly not to the stews, with or without a Teutonized Venus, but to a far land of poetic beauty which the fleshy spirit enters ill at ease. Man's inhumanity to man is something for words or the pictorial arts to deal with, not music. Alban Berg has striven heroically to be merciless toward his soldier subject in the psychopathic "Wozzeck." The outcome, for those who can abide the music, is sympathy for the maltreated soldier; surely one of the least criminal of possible reactions! There is always the possibility that some theory professor of the old school will start shooting up the opera house, because of new music's many heinous offenses against his holy harmony. But would it be the music

---

* The trombone slurs of Shostakovitch's "Lady Macbeth of Mzensk" have not caused the author to change this opinion. They are obscene only by association with the stage action. They represent musical clowning. Audiences are not shocked: they laugh.

[10]

that was to blame?—or his theory books, like the romances that warped the brain of Don Quixote de la Mancha and set him astride his steed, a barber's basin for his helmet, to tilt with windmills and charge flocks of sheep in the holy cause of Dulcinea and Richard Strauss? As for theft, our music may be full of it, conscious or unconscious. It would be a rare tune that could identify its own composer. But the effect on the listener is not that of go thou and do likewise. He refrains from plucking his neighbor's watch and chain. He may lie glibly as to how much he enjoyed the music—but he is no more apt to commit perjury in court or to falsify his income tax report than he was before he discovered one composer in the act of using another's ideas. When music is diverted to the expression of petty meanness or backbiting, as with Beckmesser in Wagner's "Die Meistersinger," it amuses, as no doubt it was intended to do; but although all the world knows that the Vienna critic, Hanslick, was the prototype for Wagner's querulous scrivener, no one really holds that against Hanslick—or against Wagner—or against whatever party happens to be in power in our national capital.

If music is limited in its powers of subversion or perversion (whatever the Puritanically-minded may have had reason to think of some of its past associations), its burden of ideality also circumscribes its humorous possibilities. An indefinite language, it cannot perpetrate a pun or any specific play on words.

All it can do is, resort to quirks of sound and oddities of interval or rhythm. Some of it may suggest a boy making faces. Again, there may be something in music like a practical joke—the equivalent of a chair being pulled from under someone about to sit down. Gaiety and high spirits come as naturally to music as melancholy and intense sorrow. There is a lilt that is like laughter, as there are melodic sequences that are like sighs and tears. All human attributes of the more heroic or the more tender persuasions—courage, nobility, fortitude, faith; gentleness, sweetness, naïveté, resignation—have found ready expression in music and at the beck of a multitude of composers. Folk-songs, indeed, comprehend them all. But only a few great masters, by the employment of all the craft of which they have been masters, have been able to devise music that was appropriate for the depiction of any species of villainy—and almost the same can be said for humor. Love, in every form, tempestuous or pleading, tragic or ecstatic, impassioned or brooding, love requited or love denied, but almost invariably colored with an ideality by no means the rule in literature or the graphic arts, has been the food of music. The love of lovers, of fathers, of sons and daughters, of sisters, of brothers, of friends; the love of priest and prophet, acolyte and thurifer; the love of a maid or the love of God, the love of a cause or the love of home—all of these music has made its own; but not the love of money. Beethoven's rondo, "Fury Over a Lost Penny," to the whimsical contrary!

Music is a creature of moods and there are angry moods as well as tranquil ones. But anger, too, lends itself readily to idealization. If music flames, the fire is still the refiner's fire. It may sear and wound, but it purifies. If there is bitterness in music, even that bitterness is mostly something of association with a text, a legend, a dramatic situation or some other extra-musical element with which it has been linked. It may be said that the reason for much of this is the vagueness of music, its generalized rather than specific character; its lack of recognizable symbols for concrete ideas such as are conveyed by words or by the painter's brush. But why, if the old terms of "good" and "bad" still have something of their traditional moralistic or ethical meaning in the affairs of mankind, why is there so obviously in music a generalized "good" and so debatably a generalized "bad?" If, instead of seeing music as a reflection of life, we were to try to see life as a reflection of music, how would we account for a multitude of things? Perhaps the musical conservative of any age, not to exclude our own, already has accounted for them; murder, mayhem, arson, kidnaping, forgery, embezzlement, cheating, bad table manners, wise-cracking and all other high crimes and misdemeanors may be summed up in one infamous general classification dubbed *atonality* —with lesser offenses like miscegenation or trumping your partner's ace regarded as unresolved dissonances.

But we are likely to come back to the notion that the only "bad" music is music that is dull or banal or music that has been botched in the writing, and find it rather difficult to agree that this same thing is precisely all that is wrong with the world we live in.

The vagueness of music, its lack of definite symbols, its dependence on moods rather than specific ideas, may be taken for granted here as one of the generalities in which the danger of pointed contradiction is relatively slight; but the human tendency to give to music definite meanings that may or may not have had any parallel in the composer's mind when he shaped a work in question, has to be recognized, guided and guarded against at times, harmless as most of these imaginings are as long as they are not broadcast by someone of supposed authority. That some music may have almost as many meanings as there are listeners is thinkable. That *one* listener's conception of that meaning, possibly as arbitrary and purely personal as any other person's, even though founded on greater knowledge, study and experience—should be imposed on many, may be deplorable. The author has ventured the belief that what passes for the theory of music is not necessary to the understanding of music. But comprehension and acceptance of one cardinal fact —that *music is a language of itself* and can and does convey its message *without translation into some other language*—is fundamental to any broad-gauged and fruitful understanding of the art. Music has resemblances to architecture, to painting, to sculpture, to the visual movement of the dance—but it is none of these things. If the terms of the sister arts are borrowed to describe music, this is because their imagery, dealing with more concrete subjects, is more definite and thus more easily understood than the more purely arbitrary terms that serve a technical purpose in the description of music. If music sometimes tells a story with almost the force of words, the music is still neither the story nor the words. It is music and nothing else. And when that is realized, the music that has a universally recognizable story to tell (as well as the music that can mean one thing to one listener, something quite different to another, and something remote from either to a third), is that much nearer its goal of direct speech—untranslated, untranslatable, but none-the-less intelligible to the understanding human mind and heart.

THE LANGUAGE OF MUSIC

MUSIC is a language in and of itself. As the letters of German, or Russian or Arabic are not the language, so the notes that appear on the staves are not the language. They are the letters of music and, like the letters of all other languages, they came into existence long after the language was spoken, shouted, moaned, whispered, sobbed and sung. Something like a universal literature in the verbal languages is a relatively recent development in the occidental world. If musical literacy, today, is much more restricted, it yet is more common than verbal literacy was in Chaucer's time in England, less than six centuries ago. Only a little further back and only the priesthood could read and write in those countries of our Western world that today have the least illiteracy. But let us not pursue the musical parallel too far. The practical necessities of daily life are largely responsible for the universal teaching of the three R's. To read, to write, to figure simple sums were essential to the earning of a livelihood, once the world had become a place

of barter rather than of spoliation and once the trades-
man had replaced the serf and man-at-arms. No such
necessity for widespread knowledge of the letters of
music has arisen or is likely to arise in our time. Those
whose livelihood has depended in any degree on their
knowledge of music's symbols have always been
few in comparison to the multitude who could eat,
sleep, keep a roof over their heads and go about ade-
quately clad, as ignorant of musical notation as they
were of Sanskrit or Choctaw.

It would be pleasant to view the world as quite
otherwise, with every reasonably well-educated person able to play or sing at sight; and a great many,
rather than a scattered few, equipped to peruse a
complicated orchestral score and hear it, so to speak,
from the examination of the printed page. One
feels that the English may take a reasonable pride
in those gentlemen and ladies of the late Tudor period
who could sit about the table of their host in some
manor house and unite their voices in madrigals,
ballets and glees, singing from some manuscript they
had never seen before, each with his own part wend-
ing its own way, sometimes in a complication of
strands that would trouble experienced groups of
sight-readers today. A gentleman rode, a gentleman knew the uses of the rapier, and a gentleman
sang. He knew notes as he knew the stirrups and
as he knew thrust and parry. One may view with
like satisfaction a later era in Austria and the Ger-

man lands when study of the string instruments was common enough to provide little ensembles among neighbors or within the family; trios, quartets, miniature orchestras for street and garden serenades. The daughter of a pastry cook and the son of a game warden were as likely to scrape away on fiddle or 'cello as the children of the burgomaster or the count. It was the pleasanter side of an era in which musicians, however gifted, were quite generally regarded as servants. Liveried, or no, they were the literates who taught their masters.

We contrast, a little ruefully, this personal music-making—however raucous much of it must have been—with today's tendency to substitute radio and phonographic music in the home, and realize that not all that has happened in the intervening years has made for greater literacy in music. At the same time we know that there is a much more widespread comprehension of music in its larger and more important forms in the world today than at any time in its past; and note, as one of the reasons for this, that opportunity to hear music has far outstripped opportunity to perform music; and that the average human being can go much further in hearing than he can with performing. His limitations with respect to reading music do not seriously handicap him as a listener. Undoubtedly there are times when any lay listener would be a more intelligent auditor if he could visualize, as some few musicians may visualize, the letters of the language they hear. But we are brought back to the consideration that these letters are not the language. They are the symbols, by means of which the language is made available. They have become necessary in the complicated state of our highly developed art music, but they were not always essential even to the musician. Folktunes were passed on from generation to generation, and sung and played through long periods of time, without the symbols existing for their preservation. Mozart, Rossini and Mendelssohn, in a day when music had been elaborated so as to require a written record, proved that they were able to reproduce what they had heard without ever seeing the notation. The world is full, today, of persons who can play by ear more or less correctly music that is complex enough to trouble a fairly good sightreader. That many others who do not play at all have ears equally quick to grasp and retain what is heard, also is common experience. To say that such an individual is musically illiterate may be to state the narrow truth. But to deny that he *understands* music on that ground alone would be equivalent to stating that a peasant who could not read or write but could carry on conversation by the hour did not understand his language.

But if it is not a knowledge of the notation of music that determines the understanding of music, what is it? The question becomes the more perplexing when we recall what already has been said of the wide variety of meanings that can be given a single composition; since, after all, it is the meaning of the words that matters in the conversation of the illiterate peasant. It is only when that word "meaning" is bereft of its precise, literal and *unmusical* aspect that it comes properly within the musical scheme. It has to be reconciled with that vague and generalized quality that is the characteristic of music; as a specific representation of an object or an idea is the characteristic of words. Emotional reaction to music does not of itself give that music a meaning. There can be emotional reaction to the beauty of design in music, as in scrollwork or the architecture of a building; a reaction in which the question of meaning can scarcely arise. A single sound, like the clang of a bell or the note of a bird, can stir an emotion and nothing of meaning be implied. The exhilaration of motion may have behind it nothing of meaning and yet be a kind of emotional experience. It is so with the language of music. At one and the same time it may express far less than words and far more. It may stir by profundities and exaltations that words are powerless to utter. It also may stir by mere sound, by mere motion and by mere design.

In sound, motion and design we have the true essentials of the musical language. To comprehend the sound, the motion and the design of a composition is to comprehend much more than the notes, save as the notes are transmuted back into sound, motion and design. There is no music without these three attributes, unless we are to concede that a single detached sound, like a bell stroke, can stand alone as music. If there are even two successive tones there is motion and there is design. To pass from one sound to a second is motion. To follow one tone with another is design. Comprehension of music, then, would seem to resolve itself into a grasp of its combinations of sound, its successions of sound, the patterns into which these combinations and successions are woven. It is by means of these that whatever meaning the music may have, (whether it is a meaning intended by the composer or one read into the music by the interpreter or the listener,) is evoked or conveyed. This meaning is the *idea* the language has been used to express, but it is *not the language*. The sounds, the motion, the design constitute the language, as words, phrases and sentences constitute a spoken language, whatever the sense or nonsense uttered in their use.

The language of music is the language of melody, harmony, time values, rhythms and musical form. All of these are only variations on the theme of sound, motion and design. A melody is a succession of sounds pleasing to the ear. It cannot escape having motion and design and remain a melody. Harmony is a combination of sounds and acquires motion and design the moment one harmony follows another. Time values and rhythms have to do with motion. A single note may have time but not rhythm. Every melody, whether there is harmony or not, has both time and rhythm. Musical form is another word for design, but of larger scope, in that the design of a single phrase, passage, section or movement of a work may be only a contributing part to the form of the composition as a whole. There is no more apt expression than the time-honored one, which construes form as the bottle into which the composer's music has been poured. Yet the contents have largely shaped the bottles in innumerable instances. In either case, the bottle, of itself, is something of art, or it has been bungled in the making. There is art, unquestionably, in the shaping of a folksong or a country dance; most of what is true of advanced musical forms is true, in some respect, of the most elementary ones. The complex is derived from the simple. The symphony, the opera, the quartet, the sonata, the aria are all growths from the tunes to which early peoples danced or marched; the tunes they used ceremonially in their worship, or sang or played for entertainment or consolement in much the same spirit as the music-making of today. Without notation, there has existed from earliest times this language, with its melody, its harmony, its time values, its rhythms, its forms. To grasp the most complex art music of today is thus the same problem that confronted any one who heard the most elementary music in primitive times. The language has been greatly extended, it has an infinitely

SCENE FROM A VERDI OPERA, SIMONE BOCCANEGRA

richer and more varied vocabulary, but its elements are the same.

No distinction can be drawn here between the elements of folk music and art music; or between art music and so-called popular music. The language is the same for all music, good, bad, simple, complex, dull or palpitant with genius. To understand *some* music is to understand, at least to that extent, *the language of all music.* Some melody is making its effect, some harmony is in some degree comprehended, something of time and rhythm is grasped, some species of musical form is seen for what it is. Sound, motion and design have spoken, not with the meaning of words, or any other form of factual communication, but in the language that is the language of music and of music alone. The listener who can thus think of music in its own terms, rather than through eternal translation into something of words or mental images, is the one who most readily can approach the greatest of art products in substantially the same spirit of understanding that is brought to the folk dance or the popular song.

BARRIERS TO HEARING MUSIC
AS IT IS

W HAT do we mean by hearing music as it is? Precisely what the phrase implies. The greatest single barrier to the enjoyment and the comprehension of music is to be found in the insistence on the part of multitudes of listeners that the music be something else. Nor is the untutored layman, frank to confess his lack of technical knowledge but sure of one thing, that he knows what he likes, the only one hemmed in by such a barrier. The professional musician, the musical pedagogue, the tonal aesthete, quite as often permits preconceptions as to what the music ought to be, to cut him off from a sound response to what it is. Most of the historic mistakes of music criticism, as they have been exposed to us by the passing of time, were the result of similar preconceptions— of predilections for or biases against certain types or forms of musical expression, which resulted in condemnation or praise on grounds that must seem largely irrelevant to us today. The violence attributed to the modulations of Beethoven presents a case in point. As compared to those of some of his illustrious predecessors, these modulations were abrupt. But why should they not be abrupt, if thereby they were expressive of Beethoven's powerful musical thought? There was an underlying stream of violence in the music of Beethoven, as there was in his everyday personality. To have denied that violence its inevitable place in the musical upwellings of this personality would have been to have bound, gagged and stifled one of the most fruitful geniuses of all time. But many an heir of a more courtly era, seeking only elegance where he found much storm and stress, could only protest at that which seemed unmannerly or uncouth. The orthodox looked for, not a Beethoven, but another Mozart, another Haydn. The experience of Verdi presents a parallel case. After Rossini, Bellini and Donizetti, the greatest of all Italian opera composers was, for many, the proverbial bull in the china shop. With Beethoven, Verdi, Wagner and others who were centres of controversy in their day, the great public responded sooner than the musical clerisy. The uninitiated had fewer barriers to be swept away.

Music, we know, is every man's domain, in-so-far as he is fitted by the responses of his nature and the cultivation of these responses to dwell within it. In probably a vast majority of instances, the individual who is responsive to one form of music will, when sufficiently experienced, prove responsive to all. There is little reason save that of inexperience, for the layman to dedicate his listening to one type of music—the song program or the violin recital, the symphony or the opera—to the exclusion of others. The professional musician who has undergone a hardening of the musical arteries and enjoys only chamber music, or a piano recital, or a concert of experimental works fresh from the laboratories of the ultraists, presents quite another problem. Often he is a fanatic, a bigot or a man musically sick. Or he may be no real lover of music, as such; but a mathematician, a tonal mechanic, an acoustical engineer who has happened to concern himself with sound-patterns instead of with metal alloys or methods of indirect lighting.

That many laymen are fundamentally more musical than many musicians needs no argument. There can be no confusing *musicality* with *musicianship*. To listen well requires the one; to perform well, the other. When they are united in one individual, he is likely to be a better listener, as he is certain to be a better performer. But for sound listening, give us the layman with musicality and little or no musicianship in preference to the professional with his measure of musicianship and, if this must be, little or no musicality. The music that endures, the music that contributes something tangible to the heritage of men, the music that justifies and, in justifying, often glorifies all this dabbling in apparently useless consortiums of sound, is the music that is written for the ear and not the eye; the music that conveys a sense of pleasure or an emotional stimulus that often is more melancholy than happy; but in either event has in it something of that cleansing of the spirit, that catharsis, which all art has a tendency to bring on. This is the music that matters, as distinct from the music that may be interesting enough in paper dissection, but which, when sounded, has little of human significance to convey. As already touched on in these pages, there are art emotions that spring from contact with the purely decorative or the purely architectural, as there are sensory emotions that may arise from mere concords or clashes of sound; but they come as readily within the reactions of human musicality as do the emotions born of the associations, direct or indirect, which much of the finest music has with the inner life of humankind.

The musician who has permitted his responses to be warped by too zealous a cultivation of certain musical types, forms or mediums, to the virtual exclusion of others, may serve a purpose as a specialist, in that he may find it in his power to go beyond his fellows in some chosen sphere. There may be a gain for the world; if there is a loss, it is most likely to be his own. He need trouble us no more, since we are occupied here with the tilling of a far more fertile soil, as found in the receptivities of the millions of men, women and minors who know and love some music, but who find in their way barriers that shut them off from the knowing and the loving of much other music as rightly theirs to possess and to enjoy. Their problem, in all too many instances, is their inability to hear music as it is, for what it is, once they have stepped out of the confines of elementary tune. They strive to hear in the music what is not there, and, missing the essential, they miss all. It is peculiarly the problem of adults who approach good music with the background of the popular song or the dance orchestra. They listen for what they will not hear. Their preconceptions as to what constitutes a tune, what has "life" or "swing," what "gets somewhere," what is singable or capable of being hummed or whistled, are just so many bolts and bars against the natural responses they otherwise might have. There is a reason for utterly untutored children taking more readily than adults to music of widely divergent types; and this, in spite of the child's instinctive (and pampered!) liking for jingle and sing-song. Often it is when the first rudiments of musicianship enter in—the drudgery of those introductory piano lessons—that native musicality flies out of the window.

The number of once-prospective good listeners who may remain convinced to the end of their days that they will never like the so-called "classical music," and whose hostility or dread can be traced to their childhood horror of finger exercises and teaching pieces, is beyond all calculation. Let us not stop to argue here where the fault was to be found—in the child, the teacher or the method. It is enough to concede that among the unhappy preconceptions that act as barriers to the natural and instinctive love of good music, are those that have grown out of ill-timed or wrongly directed preliminary studies; studies that have served chiefly to convince the unfortunate beginner that in the world of his choice he wants none of the sort of music he forever-after associates with his own weary hours at the piano or the violin.

Often one hears it said that no music study is wasted. This is a luxurious euphemism, squarely contrary to the obvious fact. Most music study plays its part in creating better listeners. But *some* music study makes enemies for music—and for life! Back of innumerable instances is probably this general condition: there is too much drudgery of accomplishment, too little enjoyment of listening. Music is for the listening ear, the listening heart, the listening spirit. The boy or girl who has opportunity to hear much fine music, and music in all of its forms, with the drudgery of personal accomplishment so contrived as to be incidental to the hearing, is much less apt to be oppressed by the musical chores that constitute the beginnings of musicianship, than the one whose musical horizon is that of the practice room, the teacher and sundry allied taskmasters in the family. Of all preconceptions, the one perhaps most difficult to overcome in after years is that which had its origin in a revolt against the relentless tyranny of rows of black and white keys.

To hear music as it is, a living message of beauty and vitality to mankind, involves ridding the mind of all such incumbrances as may have been loaded upon it by continual association with the more obvious types of popular music, on the one hand; and early misadventures with study pieces, on the other. Of all the forms of musical entertainment, in the best sense of that easily cheapened term, the piano recital is the last place to expect the person with such associations, predilections and aversions to feel comfortable or other than annoyed. Many a child who has practiced under duress will have to work back in adult life to an eventual appreciation of the benison of beauty there can be—and so very often is—in a piano recital, by first having come under the spell of the opera or the symphony. To hear opera as it is, and not as it might be if it were something other than opera; to hear the symphony as it is, without attempting to convert it into a potpourri of hymn tunes, musical comedy "hits" and jazz dance rhythms; to hear oratorio, chamber music, the violin recital and the song program each for what it is, is to have mastered the art of listening; and small, indeed, will be the number of such listeners who will not find in the treasury of piano music, as disclosed to them by artists of subtlety, imagination and power, one of the richest of their musical heritages. To listen thus—and not for what, in accordance with the biases of limited experience, the listener would *like* the music to be—is the layman's problem. The man who "knows what he likes" is too often the man who has given himself little opportunity either to know or to like. In trying to listen to an opera air as if it were "Mother Machree" or "Silver Threads among the Gold," he misses the effect of a melody quite as direct and more spontaneous; misses, because the air does not correspond to his conception of what constitutes a tune. Or he flounders through a symphony, waiting for the dance rhythms that never come, the while he misses the pulsation and the élan of other rhythms quite as positive and vigorous. And if he has learned to listen to opera or symphony, he is balked by the art song, as represented by a Wolf Lied or a Duparc chanson, or by a string quartet; why?—because the one has not the high notes and the excitement of the opera aria and the other no such sumptuosities of sound and no such emotional climaxes as, for example, the Tchaikovsky "Pathetic" symphony. This does not mean that he is lacking in musicality. It may very well be that he only is diverted from intelligent and responsive listening by pre-established notions as to *what he wants to hear* and, therefore, as to what the music he hears *ought* to sound like and *ought* to be.

This man does not need technical studies. In many instances, what he needs is a little clearer picture of the fortunate diversities of music, the different types, forms and mediums, to the end that in listening to each he no longer is groping vainly for what he will not find; but, instead, has attuned himself to the music that comes to him so as to hear it, not in the terms of something else, but as it is.

OPERA AND MUSIC–DRAMA

TWO extreme positions commonly are taken about opera. One is that of the relatively inexperienced layman who thinks of it as the most "highbrow" form of music and something he really would like to understand if only he could. The other is that of the "pure" musician who scoffs at it as a hybrid form of "popular" entertainment. For the one, opera is something upon a remote pinnacle and therefore to be admired, whether comprehended or not; for the other it is only to be tolerated, the black sheep of the family that has far worthier sons and daughters in the symphony, the sonata and the string quartet. Approached by way of the theatre, the ascent from musical comedy to opera is one to give the non-musical person pause. In contrary motion, for so he would regard it, the descent of the "pure" musician from his Bach partita, his Mozart symphony, his Beethoven quartet, to the theatricality of opera is something to make him feel very superior, indeed. He (the "pure" musician) may imagine that Bach, himself, felt very much that

[33]

way when he used to invite his son Friedemann to go with him from Leipzig to Dresden, where there was opera, and "hear the pretty tunes."

Bach wrote no operas, though his cantata, "Phoebus and Pan," has sometimes been given in operatic dress. But Mozart expended much of his genius on opera; so much so that one distinguished American critic, the late Henry T. Finck, was wont to treat the symphonies and chamber music as by-products, asserting that Mozart saved his best melodies for his operas. As for Beethoven, the opera-scoffer has to be much more high-minded, musically, than this man whose final string quartets may be that scoffer's summa summarum of what music should be. This self-same Beethoven wrote "Fidelio"; and for many years he had it in mind to make another opera of Goethe's "Faust." Few, indeed, of the great geniuses of composition were able to resist the fascination of the lyric stage. Brahms is pointed to as a shining example of the "pure" musician. He, too, schemed to write opera. His correspondence shows he had several plans; considered several libretti. But he was timid and hesitant. Mendelssohn, too, was always on the lookout for the libretto he never found. The "pure" musician cannot claim Schumann or Schubert, although the world does not know them as opera composers. Schumann wrote his unsuccessful "Genoveva"; and Schubert, so erudite an authority as Edgar Istel tells us, spent more days of his short life on his virtually unknown operas, "Alfonso und Estrella," "Fierrabras" and several equally obscure operettas, than on all his other works. So few, indeed, are the really first rank composers who considered opera beneath them, that the "pure" musician who disdains it of necessity finds himself much "purer" than his own chosen idols; he affords us cause to wonder how he possibly can associate with them or their music!

Generalities are dangerous—but the belief may be hazarded that *more of the world's musical genius has gone into opera than any other form of the musical art—the symphony, the string quartet, the sonata not excluded.*

The layman who thinks vaguely of opera when he hears talk of "good" or "classical" music, in differentiation from the popular music or the hymn tunes that he is familiar with in his everyday life— or at least on Sunday—and who has only the haziest notions about music of the concert room, has at least the advantage of ignorance. That can be overcome. Experience may give him the needed new light. He may learn to put opera in its place.

Of the two, the pedant with his nose in the air, scornful of what he considers a bastard art, may go on to the end closing the door on magnificent achievements of the human spirit, masterworks of an inspiration that could only have been liberated in this form.

Opera, as truly as symphony or chamber music, or

any form of music for the solo instrument or voice, speaks the musical language. The circumstance that it embodies simultaneously other appeals than those of music does not alter the fundamental that its music is music, not something else. And the long retrospective vista that opera presents leaves little doubt on one score: *it is by virtue of its musical appeal that an opera lives on.*

The layman and the pure musician alike have reason to survey that vista. Within it is to be found a struggle for supremacy that supplies what may be termed a philosophy of operatic history. No less a critic than Ernest Newman in England has pointed out that most so-called musical history is not history, but mere chronicle. To record names, dates, eras, epochs, changes, new elements, salient achievements, is to chronicle. To become history, this chronicle must embrace a theory, such as that of a conflict between the monodic and the polyphonic, the melodic and the harmonic, the vocal and the instrumental, to explain the progress music has made. The circumstance that there may be several such theories and that no one of them would preclude the others would not alter the validity of the one chosen for the purposes of the history. This may be regarded as something particularly applicable to opera.

From the first there has been a struggle between the word and the note, the poem and the melody, the drama and the music. The perfect mating of these two complementary elements of the opera is an old and still roseate ideal. Here and there in the three-and-a-third centuries that opera has held its sway, it has been assumed that something like that perfect mating has been achieved. But has it? Time has a way of upsetting critical verdicts; a new generation finds a new relation in applying a new set of values; the old equality as between text and musical setting is no more an equality; usually either the music has dwarfed the words or the opera is sung no more. For music is a jealous jade. Second fiddle is not for her. She dominates or she sulks. That is why so little "incidental" music (so-called) to dramas and other festivities is music of importance. To be "incidental," with music, is to be just that—incidental. Music has wings and would soar. The clipped eagle is not an inspiring bird.

Turn, then, to the backward vista, the long road that leads back to the Florentines of the final fifteen hundreds, and see how our philosophy of operatic history begins to apply. To scholars and experts may be left further delving into "the opera before the opera." If there is curiosity in this direction, it can be satisfied handily with W. J. Henderson's admirable volume, "Some Forerunners of Italian Opera." It is enough to begin with the first public performances of opera as an avowed art form, while taking for granted that opera had ancestors in various church and secular entertainments, ranging in character from miracle

plays to the frottole that were sung in the streets of
the Italian cities of the fourteen and fifteen hundreds.
There may be occasion to hear Vecchi's "L'Amfiparnasso," given in concert form, and to meditate, if
meditation is the listener's habit, on a "madrigal
opera," with the parts sung not by soloists but by
groups of voices in the old polyphonic style; but that
too, for the convenience of our story, can be regarded
as belonging to the era of the opera before the opera.

The first operas of our particular vista were those
written by the group of Italians for public performance at the beginning of the seventeenth century with
the definite intention of providing musical plays in
a particular form; the form which, in spite of all subsequent developments, was recognizably that of what
today is known as opera. Jacopo Peri's "Eurydice"
(1600) if sung today is definitely opera, though it
could find its place in the present-day répertoire only
as a devoir to the past. The musical antiquarian may
love its music; the public would not be likely to consider that it possessed dramatic interest. Yet, strangely
enough—and characteristically for our philosophy
of history—dramatic interest was what brought it into
being. Those Florentines who gave a definite stamp
to the operatic form were interested first of all in re-
viving the spirit of the old Greek drama. These men
of the closing days of the Renaissance had come to
the conclusion that the Greek drama must have been
sung, a natural enough notion in view of the prom-

WOLFGANG AMADEUS MOZART

inence given the Greek chorus in the classic plays.
So, in attempting to duplicate for their era the plays
of the ancients, they called in music—not for music's
sake but to give the words the added expressiveness
and emotional beauty they believed the Greeks had
given them by means of music. There is still plenty
of room for argument as to whether they were historically so misguided as they once were believed to
have been; the fact that interests us is that they
thought of music as a means to make the poetic texts
more eloquent and moving, rather than of music as
an end in itself. So opera may be said to have begun
as *music for the play's sake*. There had been plenty
of musical entertainment for *music's* sake before this.
There was to be plenty of it after this. What the
Florentines had devised was a stately undulating recitative, distinct from the street tunes of the day on
the one hand, and the polyphonic writing of the
church and the madrigalists on the other. Here was
in truth a beginning on which dramatic music was to
build.

Along came Claudio Monteverdi. He had written
church music and madrigals. He was a master of his
craft. The world credits him with having introduced
the violin tremolo and pizzicato. Inevitably he turned
to opera. The Florentine recitative did not suffice
for this early genius. He craved more elbow room for
music. To enhance the emotional expressiveness of
the words was not enough. Spectacle invited the use

of music for purposes other than heightening the effect of words. In operas such as his "Coronation of Poppaea" (1642) there is music for its own sake. Already within a few decades of its Florentine beginnings, opera was a battleground between music and words. In the operas of Monteverdi was clearly something of that synthesis of all the arts of which Wagner dreamed two centuries later—indeed, it was present in the first operas of the Florentines, in the miracle plays, in "L'Amfiparnasso" and the other examples of "the opera before the opera."

Once given its head, music came to exert an imperious and even a contemptuous sway over this early synthesis that was opera. The long day of Opera Seria, which retained the external aspects of the Florentine opera in that it dealt with classic stories derived from the Renaissance, but so corrupted as often to be more a matter of the names of the characters than anything else, gave music its complete hegemony. The same stilted texts were set to music over and over again, particularly those of the poet Metastasio (1698–1782), and the libretto became primarily an excuse for music; so that in the great day of the Handel operas in London (1711–1741) there was some basis for the charge that opera had degenerated into a form of concert in costume. Today we know, from some recent revivals of the Handel operas, that they did possess dramatic interest of a kind, as we know that they contained much of the most glorious music

ever written for the theatre. But there can be no
questioning that in this era it was *music* that came
first; great singers triumphed in solo airs that dis-
played their amazing vocal gifts; the composer of
opera had first of all to be a melodist; like Handel, he
could set the words of a foreign tongue he barely
understood—there was then no question of music for
the drama's sake. Parallel to Opera Seria had developed in Italy another form of musical entertainment, Opera Buffa; and in it, quite as much as in
Opera Seria, melody was king. The texts of Opera
Buffa were amusing or vulgar, or both. But it was the
tunes, either as solos or concerted numbers, that really
mattered—they had to be composed; the jokes could
be improvised.

Where, then, were the ideals of the Florentines?—
where the restoration of the Greek drama?—where
the principle of music for the poem's sake? None of
these was dead. The pendulum had swung to its limit
but it had not stopped. Already it was swinging back,
as it has been swinging, first one way, then the other,
in all subsequent years. Without that swing, where
would the progress of opera have come from? The
Austrian, Gluck (1714–1787), who had occupied
himself with amusing little operas in the Italian and
French spirit, as well as with Opera Seria, and who
looked up to Handel as the greatest genius of the time,
was troubled in his soul. He came to think of opera
in a way to link him to the ideals of the Florentines.

He may have known little about them or their operas
but he declared himself in his famous Preface to the
opera "Alceste" (still the old Greek stories!) as believing that music must be the handmaiden of the
text. He became the first great reformer of opera.
His historic role was to redeem it from the concert
in costume. Today, there may seem to be less difference between a Gluck opera like "Iphigénie en Tauride" (1779) and a Handel opera like "Giulio Cesare"
(1723) than there was when "Iphigénie" was new.
The passion for the ballet which ruled the Paris for
which Gluck wrote resulted in a form of stage spectacle that seems to align Gluck with Monteverdi quite
as much as with the Florentines. Some latter-day
Frenchmen, like the composer, Claude Debussy, have
insisted that Gluck never sensed the true flow of the
French language, thereby upsetting Gluck's own
choicest theory. But it is only fair to assume that
Gluck really believed his music was the handmaiden
of his text, in spite of his ballets (for which, of course,
no text was to be considered) and his Austrian approach to his French words. In principle, then, Gluck
was a reversion to the Florentines; he was a champion
of music for the drama's (e.g., the poem's) sake. His
triumph over Piccini in the famous operatic war that
produced "Iphigénie en Tauride" for Paris may very
well have been something more of music than of
theory; but that did not belie the theory.

After Gluck, what happened? Opera Seria died

out, and with it the much perverted stories of Orpheus, Daphne, and sundry Persian, Roman and Greek potentates. The young Mozart, who had been present in Paris at the time of the Gluck-Piccini contest, wrote like Gluck in his "Idomeneo" (1781). But when he found his stride, first in the German Singspiel, "The Escape from the Seraglio", and then in his "Marriage of Figaro," he was singularly free of theories. There is nothing to indicate that he was haunted by ghosts of the Florentines. Gluck's reforms did not keep Mozart from taking as models earlier Italian and German works that were primarily operas of tune. Music was an eternal spring within him and he could write a "Don Giovanni" to order, song on song, concerted piece on concerted piece, while members of the company, already in rehearsal, waited for him to give them the music they were to sing. Here, certainly, was nothing to be likened to the Florentine recitative. Here was no music for drama's sake, though it was music full of characterization, rich in appropriateness to the dramatic situation, to the word, often even to the syllable. It was music for music's sake, with its aptness to the text a musical by-product and not the governing consideration of its composition. Free of any such basic consideration as influenced the Florentines and Gluck, Mozart yet stands as one of those who most perfectly mated his musical material to the words given him to set. To go further is to realize that the music clearly transcends the text in every one of his major operas. The mating was not one of equality. The text was hand-maiden to the music, not the music handmaiden to the text.

Meanwhile the Italians, developing Opera Buffa, ridding themselves of the last sterilities of Opera Seria, were writing operas as melodious as those of Mozart, without, however, his by-products of characterization and of dramatic aptness. As in Handel's day, great singers again excited the applause of multitudes concerned much less with textual meanings than with vocal fireworks. Rossini, at his best akin to Mozart, and then Bellini and Donizetti made vocal melody supreme. In France, spectacle had the place of primacy in the time of the ascendancy of Halévy and Meyerbeer (1791–1864), but not to the exclusion of music for music's sake. Here, again, was more of Monteverdi than of the Florentines, though there remained some of the externals of Gluck. The pendulum once more had reached the limit of its swing. The day was ripe for another reformer concerned primarily with the word.

So came Richard Wagner, who as a boy thought first of being a poet; then, when he went to the theatre, of being a dramatist, because poetry was more effective as drama; and, later, as a third and last choice, of being a composer, because the drama in turn was more effective as opera. He began with the word. Music came last. His stage works were written that way. He was his own librettist and completed the texts before he composed any music. A great publicist for his own ideas, he gave to the world a flood of opinions on what opera should be; opinions that in their far more complex and grandiose form corresponded, at least in basic principle, with the ideal of the Florentines, the ideal of Gluck. But, as no other had done, he stressed the idea of a synthesis of all the arts, in which music was merely to play an important part. In this synthesis, he began, of necessity, with the word. With Wagner, came the term music-drama to dispute the place of the word opera. The Florentines might have used that word; so might have Gluck. But opera, either as a word or as a form, was not doomed. Wagner built upon all that had gone before, including the more distant composers of opera, as well as on Beethoven (1770–1827), Marschner (1795–1861) and Weber (1786–1826), who prefigured in their lesser ways some of his most characteristic achievements. His "Rienzi" (1842) was Meyerbeerian. After his succession of masterpieces, culminating in "Parsifal" (1882), half the new music of the world was imitatively Wagnerian. His principles were widely avowed, his reform as widely recognized.

But Italy and France went on producing melodists who wrote music for music's sake. The young Verdi (1813–1901), capable of the sort of tune that gave its own variety of vitality to "Ernani" and "Trovatore" changed with the years to the master craftsman of "Otello" (1887) and "Falstaff" (1893) but he never went over to Wagnerian theory. Opera and music-drama existed side by side. France had Gounod with his "Faust" (1859), Bizet with his "Carmen" (1875), and, later, Massenet with his "Manon" (1884), to offset the plentiful charge that French composers had forsaken Euterpe for strange gods worshipped across the Rhine. Music for drama's sake had not halted the production of operas in which the music was an end in itself. The French artist might be dubbed "Mademoiselle Wagner," but with the passing of time he was found to be more "Mademoiselle" perhaps than "Wagner"; what latter-day French operas most lack being the virility of composers like Berlioz and Bizet.

Though music-drama, as represented by the works of Wagner and his imitators, overwhelmed the older form of opera in Central and Northern Europe and strongly influenced the form of opera in Italy and France, it could not wipe opera from the boards; any more than the Gluck reformation could stop the production of Opera Buffa in the more limited and localized opera world of the century before. On the later Verdi was built a new period of Italian opera, no less melodious than the old and basically on the same principle of opera for the music's sake, though the choice of the story and the character of the libretto became increasingly important, lest the composer discover he had wasted his music on a book that was lacking in theatrical appeal.

The distinction involved in this care over the choice of a libretto, to the end that the work should prove good "theatre," as compared to a professed purpose of using music to enhance the effectiveness of a poem or a drama—music in the Gluck rôle of handmaiden —may be a fine one; but, nevertheless, it needs to be drawn. In the first instance, the care over the choice of a book was care for the music's sake. Music was not being asked to play a secondary rôle. Music was the *raison d'être* of the opera. The composer's great concern was not to heighten the effect of the drama but to have a proper vehicle for his music, lest he throw it away on an unsatisfactory subject. The difference in conception was perhaps greater than that of practical results. Many an opera-goer gives no thought as to whether the work to which he is listening is opera or music-drama; and he has more than a wisp of something on his side when he accuses the analytical of splitting hairs. Where opera ends and music-drama begins is no easy matter to determine. Suffice it to note that the lyric stage has found room for both of them, side by side, and that certain old works which Wagner held in contempt have remained in high favor, the while a further swinging of the pendulum has made it possible for new works to come into existence that have little regard for Wagnerian reforms and proclamations.

Wagner changed the face of opera, it is true—but in the Latin lands he never changed its heart. Verdi, Boito, Ponchielli, Leoncavallo, Mascagni, Catalani, Giordano, Puccini, Montemezzi; these have been singers all, melodists to the manner born, as truly as Rossini, Bellini and Donizetti or their ancestors of the Handelian sunset and the Gluckist dawn. The same era that produced Strauss's music-dramas, "Salome" and "Elektra", produced the Puccini operas, "La Bohème" and "Madama Butterfly." The France that produced Massenet's "Manon," beyond cavil an opera, brought into being Debussy's "Pelléas et Mélisande," the perfect type of music-drama. Our own day could produce Berg's "Wozzeck" in Austria, as a challenging example of music for the drama's sake; and, across the line in Czechoslovakia, Weinberger's "Schwanda," in which the story is as much an excuse for the music —though ingenious and amusing in its own right— as were the plots of the old Italian Opera Buffa. But this is not surprising when Richard Strauss, the composer of "Salome" and "Elektra," could write "Rosen-kavalier"—as the Wagner of "Tristan" and "Götter-dämmerung" could write "Meistersinger"; each of the comedy operas named representing in many of its details a contradiction of the principles of music-drama as Wagner avowed them and as Strauss accepted them.

What then, has come of this struggle of the word and the note, the poem and the setting, the music and the drama? A vast enrichment, through a greatly increased variety, of the musical art itself, as well as of that repertory of entertainment which for the public is part music, part play and part spectacle; a mixture of the ludicrous and the deeply felt. The upshot is, indeed, a stunning paradox, in that those men who were the great contenders for music for the drama's sake, are the men most loved—or among the most loved—for their music as music, without thought of their drama. Wagner, for instance, because he wrote in a symphonic style that permits of performance of his music by the great orchestras, is heard in the concert hall, away from drama and stage trappings, more often than any or all of the composers who wrote music for music's sake, with little thought of the drama. Today, Gluck is more often to be heard in concert than in an opera house —a whole work like his "Orféo" withstanding nobly the transference from the theatre to the hall, sans action and with nothing of drama save that inherent in the music and the text; and, sung in any one of the three languages, perhaps without the majority of the audience understanding a dozen words!

If the Florentines figure at all in the professional music of our times—as distinguished from an occasional antiquarian revival on the part of a college or musical society—it is in some concert singer's program, when an air is included in an old Italian group for its own sake as classic melody, with scarcely a suggestion of the dramatic or poetic context from which it has been removed.

The paradox is that those who wrote music for drama's sake in these notable instances wrote better music than those who wrote music for music's sake. It is explainable; the music-dramatists hitched their musical wagon to a higher star. Their subjects compelled an ideality in their approach (if the subjects themselves were not, in fact, chosen because of a pre-existing ideality) that would not permit them to write cheaply or carelessly or merely for public acclaim. It is when music is pandered to that she turns courtesan. So many of the little men—and some with more talent than ideals—really wrote, not music for music's sake, but music for the crowd's sake. Their vocal melodies, though of no dramatic significance, and hence certainly not music for drama's sake, were confections to melt in the consumer's mouth; banalities to flatter the lazy ear. They were caterers, not composers.

This, of course, refers only to the less worthy representatives of their school. Here and there a genius, writing in much the same manner as these lesser men, gave to opera an inspiration as lofty and as lasting as anything in the music of the Florentines, of Gluck, or Wagner. Mozart, who had no theories, Bellini, whose "Norma" was greatly admired by Wagner, Bizet, whose "Carmen" could as little be spared as any Wagnerian work, and Verdi, who began like a

[50]

hurdy-gurdy and ended in one of the most exalted spheres of craftsmanship that the lyric stage has known—these four, and doubtless others, remind us again how dangerous it is to generalize, even for the sake of stating a paradox.

But, so far as the Florentines, Gluck and Wagner are concerned, the paradox remains. They live on because of their music and because it is superior music. Their drama is quite another story and subject to no end of argument—little of which is of interest or profit to the opera or concert patron who loves their music. The poems could not keep the Florentine operas on the stage for a later world. Either as poems or dramas, the libretti of the Gluck operas would never draw audiences to an opera house today. Wagner dealt with momentous material, but a Ring cycle as spoken drama, or drama with secondary music, would be a decidedly stodgy affair. To go once would be enough—to go back, year after year, even several times a year, as audiences go back to hear the music of these works, when the stories have become utterly familiar, would be almost out of the reckoning. Either the music of an opera or a music-drama builds affection in its own right or that opera or music-drama dies. The story cannot save music that lacks appeal. Operas like "Trovatore" and "Forza del Destino" are proof enough that the music, to the contrary, will perpetuate an opera the story of which perhaps a majority in a typical audience does not fully comprehend—or care to comprehend.

What then of the post-Wagner works that have been illustrations of the principle of music for drama's sake—"Pelléas et Mélisande" for instance? Here is a setting of a Maeterlinck play, with few changes in the words (one scene always is omitted in performance) which seemed, at the outset, to have no musical life of its own; to be merely a conversion into sung speech of what before had been for actors to recite; the notation following the undulations of the speaking voice but enhancing it through the emotional timbres of the singing tone, and surrounding the action with an envelope of "atmosphere," as produced by an orchestra playing music too insubstantial to have other than a scenic purpose. So much for those first conceptions of a play made more effective by means of music; music that really was what Gluck's music was not, a handmaiden to the poem; music that was what Wagner's music was not, the equivalent of the word.

How is it that, as a play, "Pelléas et Mélisande" has all but disappeared from the boards, while the Debussy music-drama holds its place and has steadily increased in the number of its annual performances? What has happened? Only what happened with Gluck and with Wagner; the music eventually asserted a power that was its own; it built affection in its own right. Affecting as the play may be (whether spoken or sung) it is not the play that draws the same listener back to three or four performances in a season. That is not the way of plays; or of the patrons of plays. But it is the way of music and of the lovers of music. To hear once is to rejoice in the opportunity to hear again. To hear a third or a fourth or a fifth time is often to feel that one is really hearing for the first time. That is what happens with "Meistersinger" for an ever-increasing multitude. That is what is happening, slowly but surely, for those who have been drawn back to "Pelléas et Mélisande." The music of Debussy is in the blood, as that of Wagner is in the blood, play or no play. "Pelléas," like the works of Wagner, like those of Gluck, like the little that we hear of the operas of the Florentines, lives on because its music transcends its drama.

Berg's "Wozzeck" is too recent for us to say of it precisely what has just been said of "Pelléas et Mélisande." Those who have most vigorously championed it, have done so on much the same grounds as "Pelléas" was championed in its first days—as a marvelous enhancement of the play. Like Debussy, Berg took a drama already successful and devised music which permitted it to be sung almost as if spoken, without materially altering the text. In view of what has happened in the entire progress of opera and music-drama, the question now very well may be, not does the effectiveness of the music-drama *as drama* wear off with repetitions, but does the *music build affection in its own right?* A masterpiece of word-setting will not live without that affection, whether it be the affection of the many or the affection of a scattered but influential few. To the extent that music-drama meets opera on its own ground as music *and surpasses it*, music-drama is a higher form; but not because of its theory, because of its music. Let us consider then, by way of differentiation rather than of belittling the one to elevate the other, some typical aria operas that may be regarded as operas of music for music's sake, and some typical music-dramas which may have begun on the basis of music for drama's sake, but which live on today as examples of drama *and* music—*also for music's sake.*

A MOZART ARIA OPERA—
"THE MARRIAGE OF FIGARO"

IT has been said of Mozart (1756–1791) that he had no theories; he took opera as he found it and wrote it with the same readiness that he wrote symphonies, sonatas, concertos, serenades, string quartets, church music and oddities such as compositions for glass harmonica and mechanical clock. One of two operas written at twelve, "Sebastian und Sebastienne," is still performed occasionally and in Europe is a familiar puppet show. Mozart's early models were Italian ones. Three of the five great operas of his maturity were settings of Italian texts and in the Italian manner. The Austrian Mozart, like the German Handel, had no compunctions about writing music for words in a language not his own, and, also like Handel, it was in the theatre that he hoped to make his fortune and career. Undoubtedly, as a boy, he learned much about opera from still another German engaged in writing Italian opera, John Christian Bach (son of Johann Sebastian), who was Handel's successor in London. To this Bach, Mozart is said to have attributed much of his vocal style—learned while sitting on Bach's knee, or beside him at the piano, playing duets, when he was a child prodigy on a visit to the English capital with his father.

Mozart wrote aria operas and wrote them divinely well. His "Idomeneo" conformed to the Gluck pattern. His "Escape from the Seraglio" came closer to German Singspiel, as was fitting for a work written in the German language. "Idomeneo" possesses magnificent choruses. The choral writing in "The Escape from the Seraglio" is negligible. The solos for the former are in the set forms of the old Opera Seria. Those for the latter, though they contain some brilliant numbers that plainly derive from Italian forerunners, come closer to the German Lied.

It is with "The Marriage of Figaro" (1786) that we reach the typical Mozart of what must be regarded as his Italian aria operas. Its companions, "Don Giovanni" and "Così fan Tutte," are quite as typical. Differ as they do in detail, they are musically of close kin. "The Magic Flute," again, is more German, though it contains airs that might have found place naturally in one of the Italian operas.

"The Marriage of Figaro" presents for latter-day audiences an interesting contrast with Rossini's "Barber of Seville," which was not staged until a quarter of a century after Mozart's early death. Both derive their plots from Beaumarchais. But Mozart's opera, the earlier of the two in point of composition and production, would have to be considered in the light of a sequel to "The Barber of Seville" if they were linked together. Its story begins some little time after the ending of the "Barber". Together, the two works present the picture of before and after—marriage. Rossini's opera deals with youthful romance; Mozart's with the philandering of subsequent years. But in youth and romance, "The Marriage of Figaro" certainly is no second to "The Barber of Seville." There is a freshness in its music that is like Spring winds. That, to be sure, is only Mozart. The same freshness is in symphonic and chamber works where a clever artisan of the theatre like Rossini could not have hoped to follow him. Great as are the symphonies, however, the opinion once ventured by an American critic, Henry T. Finck, is not easy to put aside: Mozart, he said, saved his best melodies for his operas. This, of course, is debatable; but of those "best melodies," the operas alone considered, many undoubtedly are to be found in "The Marriage of Figaro." It is possible to prefer "Don Giovanni," "Così fan Tutte" or "The Magic Flute" to "The Marriage of Figaro"—and to advance this or that reason therefor—but the most devout lover of any one of these is likely to concede that this is a purely personal choice. All are works of genius; to be ready for the delight of one is to be in a position to experience delight from all.

Fortunate, indeed, the listener who could begin his

opera-going by hearing—and hearing rightly—a performance of "The Marriage of Figaro." That he will
hear rightly is by no means a foregone conclusion.
Hearing Mozart is not the same thing as hearing
Verdi, Puccini, Wagner or—closer in time and manner—Rossini. But as no operas are more melodious
than the Mozart operas, there can be no barrier to
ready comprehension on that score. What the listener needs is an open ear to a kind of melody that
is no longer in the world, save as it has come down
from a vanished era. This music must be heard with
an ear sympathetic toward the past. It is music for
all time, if any music is, but it perpetuates another
day. It is melody no less human for being aristocratic,
no less warming to the human heart for suggesting
the rococo architecture, the courtly dances, the white
wigs and satin garments of the eighteenth century.
It sings as only the rarest melody sings; and the
magic of the singing is in the countless felicities of
Mozart's orchestral writing quite as much as in the
human voices, though nowhere in all opera have the
voices greater play or less interference in making their
beauty felt.

Let us attend, then, if we can, a performance of
"The Marriage of Figaro." An ideal place would be
the little Residenz theatre in Munich, a theatre of Mozart's own time ("Idomeneo" had its first performance there) or perhaps the Redoutensaal of the Burg
in Vienna. But the opera should be heard in Italian,

not in German. If there must be a translation, it might as well be English. "Figaros Brollop," which the author of this volume heard in Stockholm, sounded quite as near the original "Nozze di Figaro" as any of many performances of "Figaros Hochzeit" heard in Germany and Austria. There is in the rococo decoration of the Residenz, however, the counterpart of much of the decoration of Mozart's music. And a small theatre, not an opera house on a grand scale, is the place to hear "The Marriage of Figaro."

With the first notes of the orchestra, any patron of symphony concerts is likely to be on familiar ground. Radio and the phonograph similarly have acquainted a multitude of persons who have never seen a Mozart opera with this brilliant and characteristic introduction. Its liveliness, its plunging gaiety, its crisp melodies attune the ear and the spirit to what is to follow. The effect of spontaneity and vitality, of aristocracy and bubbling mischief, is never lost. Of the entire opera can be said what has been said of the overture, that "it is compounded of sparkle and sigh"—though the sighing is, indeed, more obvious elsewhere in the opera than in the overture. With the stage disclosed, Figaro and Susanna are discovered in the room of the Count's palace they expect to occupy after their marriage. Figaro is taking some floor measurements; Susanna is admiring herself in the glass as she tries on a hat intended for her mistress, the Countess. Susanna enlightens Figaro on the true reason for the Count having assigned them this particular room, so near his own; in his philandering, his eye has fallen on the pretty servitor. But this Figaro is a resourceful chap and, valet though he is, quite ready to match wits with his master. In the gay melody, "Si voul ballare," he assures the Count —though not in the Count's hearing—that if he is of a mind for dancing, Figaro will play him a tune.

But Figaro already has difficulties enough. These begin to take an acute form with the entry of Don Bartolo and his housekeeper, Marcellina. Don Bartolo has not forgotten that Figaro helped to hoodwink him at the time the Count wooed and won his ward, Rosina, now the Countess. He would like to be rid of Marcellina, who long ago had borne him a son. Marcellina, in her turn, has her eye on Figaro, who borrowed money from her with a promise to marry her if he did not repay. There is no love lost between Marcellina and Susanna, as is delectably shown in a duet between them, during which each entreats the other to precede her through a door.

In the succeeding scene we make the acquaintance of the page, Cherubino. The boy's reactions to his not very circumspect surroundings are such that he is in love with every petticoat. His countess is no exception. In a breathless, impetuous air, "Non son piu cosa son, cosa faccio" he reveals the ardor of the latest of his grand passions. Susanna listens indulgently; she, too, is an object of Cherubino's adorations. The Count's step is heard. Cherubino hides himself behind a great chair and thus becomes an eavesdropper on the advances that the Count now makes toward Susanna. A voice is heard outside— the voice of the music master. Now it is the Count who seeks to hide; he in turn stoops behind the chair, Cherubino having meanwhile contrived to slip around into the seat of it, where he conceals himself under a dress that has been thrown there. Basilio, the music master, entering and thinking himself alone with Susanna, begins to make all manner of malicious remarks about the goings-on in the palace, naming the Countess as well as Cherubino and Susanna. The angry Count discloses himself, and without knowing of the presence of Cherubino, pulls the dress from the chair. In his anger, the Count decides to send the page away as an officer in his regiment. Whereupon Figaro, returning to the scene of these misadventures, twits Cherubino with his famous martial air, "Non piu andrai," telling the lad that this is the end of his career as a lover.

The second act introduces us to the lonely Countess. In her apartment, she calls upon holy love to restore to her the wandering affections of the Count; her air at the opening of this act, "Porgi amor" is one of the loveliest in all music, though matched, if not surpassed, by "Dove Sono," another air for the Countess later on. Figaro and Susanna are perturbed over the Count having still withheld his consent for their marriage. The Countess is ready to aid them in a scheme of Figaro's to bring his master to his senses; they can make common cause. Figaro gone, Cherubino enters with a song for his mistress, the favorite "Voi che sapete." Though, on the stage, Susanna goes through the motions of accompanying this air on a guitar, the listener's eyes will scarcely deceive his ears. In the orchestra are twining woodwinds achieving those delicate figurations and flushes of color that distinguish the scoring of Mozart, for all time, from that of any other composer. Not that others did not write in the same way. They simply never achieved the delicacy, the variety, the grace, the charm that is in this music. Elsewhere, quite as much as during this particular air, the instrumentation has this distinction and this beauty. The rarest qualities of the orchestral writing in the Mozart symphonies, the serenades and the chamber music are found in profusion in the operas; and nowhere more so than in "The Marriage of Figaro."

Cherubino has his army commission, but the Count has forgotten to affix the seal. The boy tries on one of Susanna's dresses. Consternation replaces merriment as a knock is heard. Again, the Count! Cherubino flees into the Countess's private room and bolts the door from the inside. Susanna hides behind a curtain. Convinced that there is some one in the inner room, the Count goes after tools to force the lock and requires his wife to accompany him. In their absence, Cherubino, responding to Susanna's signal, unlocks the door and escapes by leaping out a window. Susanna then takes his place in the inner room. The Count is scarcely more astounded than the Countess when the door is opened and Susanna responds from within. The Count, convinced against his will that his suspicions were unfounded, is asking his wife's forgiveness when Antonio, the gardener, enters. He has a complaint. Some one who jumped from a window broke one of his flower pots. The handy Figaro happens in. Quick-witted as usual, he says it was he who leaped from the window. The gardener is not convinced. He has with him a paper he found, dropped by the person who broke the flower pot. The Count recognizes it as Cherubino's commission. How can Master Figaro explain possession of that? The two women by signals and whispers convey the hint that Figaro needs. Cherubino, he says, gave him the commission to take to the Count so as to have the missing seal affixed. Again the Count has been outwitted.

The amazing manner in which all of this is worked into a musical ensemble of rare beauty excites no less wonder today, a century and a half after "The Marriage of Figaro" was written, than when it achieved its first success in Vienna in 1786. This, however, is but one of a half dozen or more such ensembles in "The Marriage of Figaro." If we are justified in styling this an aria opera, because of the many beautiful

[63]

solos, we could, with equal justification, term it an "ensemble" or "concerted" opera because of the number and the supreme art of the ensembles or concerted numbers. What is true of "The Marriage of Figaro," in this respect, is equally true of "Don Giovanni" and "Così fan Tutte." The ensemble, quite as much as the air, is the glory of Mozart; and whether the set numbers are for solo voice, for two voices, or three, or five, or eight, the orchestra has its own delicious music to assert the witchery of his genius.

To resume our story. Figaro has still to settle with Marcellina. A birthmark saves him from the marriage the Count would like to see forced upon him. It proves him to be the long-missing son of Marcellina and Don Bartolo. He cannot marry his mother. Even this, however, does not even scores with the Count. That worthy has still to be cured of his designs upon Susanna. She, in connivance with the Countess, sends him a note, making an appointment at night in the park. This brings us to the celebrated letter duet, one of the most hauntingly lovely of Mozart's melodies, sung by the Countess and Susanna. But one such melody has followed another —among them the Countess's "Dove Sono," in which she again laments the love lost to her; the duet "Crudel! Perchè Finora," in which the Count urges his case and Susanna dissembles.

The scheme now is for the Countess, dressed in Susanna's clothes, to keep the appointment in the park made for Susanna. But Figaro has not been consulted. Misled, he is now the jealous one. The final scene in the park puts all straight, but not before Figaro has pretended to make love to the supposed Countess, whom he has recognized as Susanna in her mistress's clothes. The Count, discovering that he has wooed his own wife, accepts the situation and begs forgiveness. The gardener's daughter, Barberina, solves (for the time being at least) the problem of Cherubino, and with Marcellina and Don Bartolo no longer intent upon making trouble for their own son, Susanna and Figaro at last are free to make their own little nest in the palace of their master.

"The Marriage of Figaro" is aria opera in its highest estate. But it is opera of a type that no longer is written. Within a generation after it appeared, melody had assumed other shapes; the airs of Bellini, of Donizetti, of Meyerbeer, and subsequently of Verdi, have a very different character from those of Mozart. Even more marked was the change in the treatment of conversational passages, connecting the set numbers. Mozart, and Rossini after him, employed a variety of rapid patter, supported only by piano chords, with here and there an expansion into an orchestral accompaniment. From the time of Bellini on, the Mozartean sort of recitative was obsolete. Chords and figurations were played by strings, woodwinds or brass, no matter how inconsequential these accompaniments might be. Eventually recitative was to disappear in Italian operas of the arioso character of Puccini's—a century after Mozart had been buried in a pauper's grave.

A VERDI ARIA OPERA—
"LA TRAVIATA"

IN "La Traviata" (1853), the aria opera of the last century may be considered at its most typical. Many another work would have served quite as well as an example from which to expound the similarities and the differences existing between opera and music-drama. Verdi's own "Rigoletto," "Trovatore," "Forza del Destino," "Don Carlos," or "Aïda"; Bizet's "Carmen," Gounod's "Faust," Meyerbeer's "Huguenots" or "Le Prophète," Halévy's "La Juive"—these are but ten of twenty or thirty works in the continuing répertoire of the opera houses of the world that would illustrate the case almost equally well. Rossini's "Barber of Seville" is closer to the Mozart type, as is also Donizetti's "Don Pasquale." The former's "William Tell" or the latter's "Lucia" might have been as satisfactory for the purpose as "La Traviata," but no more so; so, too, Bellini's "Norma." The last Verdi operas, "Otello" and "Falstaff," while perhaps the culmination of the operatic form, are less typical; and it is a simpler thing to view a Puccini opera in the light of "Traviata," a Massenet opera in the light of "Faust," than the reverse. "Faust" may be regarded as a French equivalent for Italian "Traviata." Other countries similarly have their equivalents. "Traviata" is fairly representative of all. In quality of inspiration as well as in the continuing hold it has exerted on the operatic public in many lands, it is a work to do honor to all.

Giuseppe Verdi (born at the village of Le Roncole, near Busseto in the Duchy of Parma, Oct. 10, 1813; died Milan, Jan. 27, 1901) was forty years old when he wrote "Traviata," midway in the long career that found him still able to produce a masterpiece in "Falstaff" when he was eighty. A glance at the table of composers in the back of this volume will enable the reader to place the work, not only in Verdi's career, but in relation to what was being produced contemporaneously by Wagner and other composers. The libretto of "La Traviata," by Francesco Piave, derives from Dumas's "La Dame aux Camélias" and represents for the Verdi of that period a departure from the melodramatic stories, filled with violence, gloom and horror, that seemed to exert a first appeal not only to him but his public. As compared to "Il Trovatore" or "Rigoletto," "Traviata" has a modern story; though one that finds its proper setting in the first or second quarter of the last century, rather than in a later or earlier time, as sometimes given it. For the Verdi of 1853, it was a tale of the Paris of his

own day. Adventure, cruelty, revenge, the malignity
of fate here give way to a simple human story of
everyday life as it then was lived; a life of other
manners and other clothes, but in its human relations
not very different from our own. The contemporary
costumes, indeed, seem to have been one of the
reasons for the public's failure to respond heartily
to the work at its world première in Venice; much
the same prejudice exists today against opera in the
clothes of our own time; but, of course, it is no longer
difficult for us to accept opera in the clothes of
Verdi's time. In one particular detail, "Traviata"
was peculiarly of its era; the heroine is consumptive.
Those were the days when "the white plague," since
so widely controlled, was as romantic as it was de-
structive. Many the romance shattered by the dread
cough of pthisis. And many the romance built about
the shattering. "As on consumption's waning cheek,
'mid ruin blooms the rose."

Let us take our seats in the theatre for a performance of "Traviata," ready to be transported back
into the world of which Dumas, Piave and Verdi
were denizens. The orchestral prelude tells us that
Verdi, too, knew the uses of divided strings, a device
of scoring ordinarily associated with Wagner, Strauss
and the later symphonic writers, though Berlioz had
used it before "Traviata." The curtains part on a gay
supper party. The hostess is Violetta, a Parisian demi-
mondaine. Among the guests is Alfredo Germont, a

[69]

youth whose infatuation touches Violetta although she is not of a mind to take such things seriously. He sings a toast to pleasure in which she joins. All this is music of a gaiety a little unlike any that Verdi had written up to that time, concerned chiefly as he had been with vengeance, wretched partings, broken lives and sudden death. It is his first "social" music, so to speak, and (always excepting "Falstaff," which was a compendium of his entire career) almost his last. In this connection, it is well not to overlook certain dances and court episodes, such as that at the opening of "Rigoletto," though they scarcely achieve the same purpose as the waltz at the outset of "Traviata." Alfredo's toast, "Libiamo ne'liete calici," a song of the wine-cup, is straight-out Italian tune. It is not necessary to the drama, but it does not impede it. It represents the operatic theory that the story should supply opportunity for set numbers, for music's sake; it probably would seem out of place in an avowed music-drama with music for the drama's sake. It is of such that "La Traviata' is made, and beautifully made, as the opera discloses as it moves on.

Spells of coughing give the hint from the first as to what Violetta's tragedy is to be; but the merriment goes on about her, with Violetta the gayest of the gay. Alfredo's infatuation is disclosed in a duet with Violetta, "Un di felice," containing a melody that is to recur a moment later in the soliloquy

PORTRAIT OF VERDI, BY BOLDINI

of Violetta, when she is left alone. This is the famous air, "Ah, fors' è lui," one of the most haunting and caressing of all opera; a pensive and poetical recollection of something about Alfredo that has touched her heart. But Violetta is resolved not to be melancholy. She must live her kind of life. She summons back her gaiety in a brilliant and ornate second air, or pendant to the first, the equally famous "Sempre libera," which brings to the music of the rôle various coloratura embellishments that do not appear elsewhere in it, thus requiring of the singer a mastery of the technique of the voice beyond that of ordinary lyric attainments. Perhaps no soprano air of the last century has played a more important part in the careers of the foremost women singers of Italian opera than "Ah, fors' è lui," with "Sempre libera" as its sparkling conclusion.

The first act having ended thus with Violetta's musing and her artificially stimulated abandon, the second reveals to us at the outset that she and Alfredo are living together, making the most of a situation not likely to end in marriage. Alfredo discovers that it is Violetta who has been footing the bills, selling her possessions to meet expenses of their country house in ·the outskirts of Paris. Tenor-like, Alfredo is filled with remorse, but not before he has sung an air, "De' miei bollenti spiriti," If scarcely one of Verdi's inspirations, this is music nevertheless agreeable in its exercise of the tenor voice. Violetta, expecting her lawyer, is called upon, instead, by Alfredo's father, the elder Germont. In one of the most pathetic, and, at the same time, one of the most frankly melodious scenes of all opera, the father impresses on Violetta the consequences of the liaison. She is particularly affected by what he tells her of the effect a public scandal would have on the future of Alfredo's young sister. Violetta rises to the sacrifice. She will leave Alfredo. The beauty of Germont's air, "Pura siccome un angelo," in which he tells of Alfredo's sister, is surpassed by that of "Dite alla giovine," with which Violetta replies. There is a duet-close for the scene, as the elder Germont, much moved by the sacrifice, leaves Violetta to fulfill her resolution. Alfredo, entering inopportunely, surprises her in the writing of a farewell note. This she hides in her dress and when he tells her he is expecting his father who has come in an effort to separate them, she leaves him, pretending that this is merely so as not to be present at the interview, though her emotional manner betrays the stress under which she is laboring. Almost immediately, Alfredo receives her note from a servant; she is returning to her old life in Paris and will look to Baron Douphol as her "protector." Alfredo reels in excitement and distress, to find himself confronted by his father. The elder Germont, endeavoring to soften the blow, appeals to his son's memories of home. His air, "Di Provenza" is certainly opera and not music-drama; it harks back to the earlier Verdi of

[72]

"Ernani" in its barrel-organ repetitions; it is a tune that can be whistled after a single hearing; but it remains the joy of baritones with the ringing upper notes essential to the singing of virtually all Italian opera of the period—and, sung as it can be sung, it seldom fails of precisely the effect that Verdi must have had in mind. But Alfredo is not reconciled. It is with the thought of vengeance that he hurries out—followed by his father,—intent upon a certain fête to be given by Flora, friend of Violetta, which the latter had promised to attend.

The scene changes to this fête. It affords opportunity for a ballet and for a gambling scene in which Alfredo, sneering at Violetta, participates. Insult leads to insult. He hurls bank notes at her. The Baron Douphol challenges him to the inevitable affair of honor. The elder Germont arrives in search of his son. He sees the tragedy and injustice of what is happening but for the sake of his own daughter he must be silent. The scene ends in a dramatic ensemble, "Alfredo, di questo core," that is one of the supreme achievements of Verdi in utilizing the voices of his principals and chorus for melodic part-writing of great vitality and emotional force. This finale is as much a set number as any solo or duet in the score; the orchestra plays its part but it is to the singers that Verdi turns for his effect; this is not the way of the writers of what may be termed "symphonic opera"; yet, in the last analysis, where-in lies the musical or the dramatic difference between the employment of voices and that of instruments for the achievement of an illusion that in neither instance can be confounded with reality?

In the last act, there is reconciliation, along with revelation of Violetta's sacrifice, but too late. The coughing that has been a recurrent detail in each of the preceding acts is now the symptom of a dying invalid. The scene is Violetta's bedroom. There is music of a carnival outside as the doctor arrives. The medical man tries to cheer his patient, but whispers to her maid that Violetta has only a few hours to live. In a speaking voice, Violetta reads a letter from the elder Germont, in which he tells of having apprised his son of her sacrifice. Alfredo is coming to see her; but will he arrive in time? Her "Addio del passato" is an air of lingering sadness. But soon she is in her lover's arms and the approach of death is crowded from their thoughts. Alfredo is resolved to take her to Paris; "Parigi, o cara," they sing; never again will they be parted. The doctor returns with the elder Germont. There is nothing that can be done; Violetta expires in her lover's arms to music as wistful as it is melodious. Death has here a tender hand. There is no escaping the compassion of the last pages of this score. They make out a strong case for opera in the face of everything that can be said against it and in favor of some other form. Granted that illusion, not reality, is opera's goal,

"Traviata," with its solo airs, its duets, its stirring
third act ensemble and this pathetic close, must be
considered to have fulfilled its mission for humanity
and art. It must be recognized as quite a different
manifestation of genius, in spirit as well as in style
and manner, from the Mozart "Marriage of Figaro,"
already described; and an equally different manifestation from the examples of music-drama that are
here to follow. Wise the listener who will avoid
trying to understand one in the light of preconceptions based on another.

A WAGNER MUSIC–DRAMA—
"DIE WALKÜRE"

To understand the difference between music-drama and opera it is only necessary to hear and comprehend any one of the later works of Richard Wagner, with some reservations made for "Die Meistersinger," which contrives to retain more of the set forms of opera than its fellows, yet has the intent and effect of music-drama. The earlier works, "Rienzi," "Fliegende Holländer," "Tannhäuser" and "Lohengrin" represent a compromise between the two forms; the earliest, "Rienzi," being the closest to opera as it was known before the term music-drama came into use; the latest, "Lohengrin," approximating more nearly the maturer works that can be taken to represent Wagner's ideal. "Die Fliegende Holländer" and "Tannhäuser" have as much to connect them with the German operas of Weber and Marschner, Wagner's immediate predecessors, as they have with the Italian and French works that Wagner, as a young man of the theatre, conducted in his formative years. That "Lohengrin" and "Tannhäuser" should be re-

ferred to now as his "Italian operas" does not mean
that they are any less German in the character of
their melodies than the later works; the term has its
meaning chiefly as something to distinguish the early
Wagner, still following in enlarged outlines the general pattern of opera as it existed before his day, from
the later Wagner, who worked out his own pattern in
conformity with his theories of music-drama.

The gulf between "Rienzi" (1842), with its Meyerbeerian formulas, and "Parsifal" (1882), which would
have been beyond the conception of any composer
before Wagner, is, indeed, an amazing one; but the
more the listener hears of Wagner's music-dramas
the more he must realize that the points of contact
with opera as written by Italians, Frenchmen, Rus-
sians, Bohemians and other Germans before him, far
outnumber and far outweigh those of departure and
differentiation. "Meistersinger" (1867), written in
Wagner's fullest maturity, merely exposes more
generously and openly the presence in all the later
Wagner scores of those same features of opera that
cause "Lohengrin" and "Tannhäuser" to be considered in the light of compromise. There is compromise in plenty in the Ring, in "Tristan und Isolde,"
in "Parsifal." All these works have the *equivalent* of
the aria, the set number, interwoven in their texture.
These lyric exfoliations are less easily excerpted from
their surroundings than in Italian or French opera,
but it can be and often is done. Music-drama, then,

is much less a separate form than it is a modification of opera in the direction of a structure in which the drama shall be less subservient, if not to the music, at least to the singers. Inevitably, since the drama must be expressed by means of music, the lessening of the dominance of the singer results in an increased importance for the composer's other musical means, namely, the orchestra. So, irrespective of any theory as to the hegemony of the word, music-drama has largely resolved itself into what might justly be styled *symphonic opera* to distinguish it from the older type of *singers' opera.*

Here is the beginning of a proper understanding of Wagnerian music-drama. The listener must have more than half an ear for the orchestra. Indeed, he may well end in devoting to what goes on in the pit something more than equality of attention; it is the vocal line that, much of the time, may have to proceed with half an ear. Many listeners of an elder day revolted at this precedure. Either the voice was in its heaven or opera was no opera. The tremendous growth since those times of popular appreciation of symphonic music has altered all this. A great multitude of listeners now find their kind of melodic stimulus in the symphonic surges of the Wagnerian orchestra rather than in the vocal embroidery of a Rossini. For them the former possesses more, not less, of music; it expresses more, not less, of personal emotion; it says more and means more; it with-

stands continued repetition better. In all too many
instances, the easily grasped vocal melody loses its
freshness with continued familiarity; the gleaming
strands of a many-voiced orchestral score are forever
presenting new glints of beauty heretofore undis-
covered by the ear.

But none of this is any justification for the notion,
too widely held, that the Wagner music-dramas are
not for singers; that they are to be shouted, screamed,
barked and croaked, on the assumption that the vocal
melody is negligible and all the beauty in the orchestra. Many of the most beautiful of the orchestral
motives have their place in the vocal parts; they are
no less melodies when assigned to the tenor or the soprano, the contralto or the bass, than they are when
voiced by the 'cellos, the trumpets or the oboe. Nowhere else in all music, unless it is in Bach, are more
salient melodic ideas to be found, or in greater profusion, than in these scores. In the many reappearances
of these melodic ideas, transformed, combined, re-
stated with many changes of color and in varying harmonic surroundings, the characters on the stage do
their full share of singing; they, quite as much as the
orchestra, justify for Wagner the description "continuous melody."

In this late day, few lovers of music can have failed
to hear or read of the Wagner system of "leading
motives." In a sense, these motives correspond with
the basic themes of a symphony, or would so cor-

[79]

respond if their purpose were purely a musical one. They are relatively brief musical phrases, most of them of a striking melodic character, that serve as building blocks for the musical edifice, or strands for the musical fabric. With them the structure is erected, of them the texture is woven. They represent, quite as much as the thematic ideas of a symphony, the principle of repetition, development, transformation, variation, combination, recapitulation. If there were no drama, no stage action, no purpose but a musical purpose, they would be the melodic basis of a symphony, or whatever this music would have to be called.

But the purpose is only partly a musical one. The Wagner *Leit-motiv* serves also its dramatic purpose. It embodies ideas, it attaches itself to individuals, it becomes a symbol of forces, it is in itself a participant in the play. Of Wagner's music it has been said that its special mission in the music-dramas, as the composer conceived it, was to place the spectator in direct communication with the very spirit of the characters, to reveal their secret thoughts, and to render these transparent to their hearers. But this applies not merely to the characters. The world in which they move, the aura of the night, the awakening of a wood, the fateful powers that shape the destiny of man—all these come as naturally within the scope of the music as the human revelations and the dramatic disclosures in which the motives play

a significant and revelatory part. The leading motive may be described as the musical equivalent of
an idea, so far as it is possible for a composer to
represent a mental conception by a musical contour;
it may be suggestive in its sound, it may remain purely
arbitrary, but in either case it has an extra-musical
function that is almost hieroglyphic.

Wagner did not create the idea. In some rudimentary form, other composers before him employed
repetitions of phrases to represent and recall ideas,
chiefly a matter of reminiscence for the sake of
reminiscence. There is as much of this in Meyerbeer
as there is in "Rienzi," which Wagner wrote in the
Meyerbeerian way. But there had never been anything
like the elaborate machinery provided by Wagner
in his mature writing, when entire works—and, in the
Ring, a series of four works—were constructed of
an interplay of motives almost too numerous to
recognize and name. At the outset, only bewilder-
ment can result from the attempt of a listener who
is hearing his first Wagner music-drama to identify
these motives in their multiplicity of forms. It may
be questioned whether Wagner, himself, had in mind
that the auditor should study and tabulate in advance
his symbolizing or representative phrases. He had his
own plan for making the motives felt, irrespective
of whether they signified precisely to others what
they signified for him. This was the plan of fore-
shadowing and recollection. Many times his use of

motives or fragments of motives is to acquaint the ear with something that is still to come, so that it will have a familiar ring, even though never fully stated before. In many more instances, the motives come back as reminders of what the ear already has heard but might have forgotten completely but for hearing it again. More than eighty leading motives have been found and labeled for the Ring—the titanic tetralogy that embraces "Rheingold," "Die Walküre," "Siegfried" and "Götterdämmerung"—some of which, like that of "The Sword," are to be met with in virtually every act and scene of the entire cycle; others like "The Incantation of Thunder" in "Rheingold" pass out of the picture entirely after a few statements; still others, like "Murder" and "The Call to Marriage," appear only in the closing episodes of "Götterdämmerung."

The second and probably the most universally beloved work of this colossal cycle, "Die Walküre" (and, incidentally, the work which in practical theatre experience seems to stand best alone) may be taken as thoroughly representative of Wagnerian music-drama. It is first of all an opera of melody. In music such as that with which Siegmund greets the Spring night and Wotan bids farewell to Brünnhilde there are vocal exfoliations at no great remove from the airs of Italian or French opera. They are none-the-less closely interwoven parts of the symphonic fabric and serve as legitimate and essential a dramatic purpose as any other music, whatever its type or character, conceivably could do. "Die Walküre" abounds in lyric scenes. Indeed, it points strongly to the lyric scene as the essential of Wagner and, arguably, of all opera or music-drama. Where the aria, the duet, the quartet or other set number ends and the lyric scene begins, is a question not to be answered too confidently.

"Die Walküre" contains first statements of fully a fourth of the total of the motives of the Ring, more than "Siegfried" and many more than "Götterdämmerung." It repeats in richer, more rewarding form many of the musical ideas which are shadowed forth in "Rheingold" and which, by the time they reach "Siegfried" and "Götterdämmerung," have undergone transformations from their basic melodic stuff. It is for this reason, perhaps, that with many listeners the second of the series possesses the most easily grasped melodic line; though the occasional listener is likely to lose this line in two of the scenes—that of the supper in the first act and that of Wotan's narrative to Brünnhilde in the second—only to discover, if he is persistent about it, that vocal melody abounds in both these scenes, with a play of those motives that elsewhere take their place as among the most salient of the "Ring". Perhaps "Götterdämmerung" is more consistently symphonic; but even that is arguable. Suffice it that the "Ride of the Valkyries" and the "Magic Fire" music have played as extensive a part in concert programs, away from the opera, as any other music from the Ring. Like the "Meister-singer," "Flying Dutchman" and "Tannhäuser" overtures, the "Lohengrin" and "Parsifal" preludes, the "Forest Murmurs," of "Siegfried," the "Rhine Journey" and "Death Music" of "Götterdämmerung," and, even more notably, the Prelude and "Liebestod" of "Tristan und Isolde," these excerpts from "Die Walküre" have enriched the symphonic répertoire un-til, in America at least, Wagner has become almost as much a figure of the concert room as of the theatre. Nowhere is the beauty of his orchestral scoring more inescapable than in "Die Walküre"; nowhere fresher, more youthful in spirit, more tender; the orchestra of "Die Walküre" sings as few orchestras ever have sung—a perpetual challenge to those on the stage whose business it also is to sing.

What, then, is "Die Walküre" like, in the listening and the seeing? With the conductor's first beat in the darkened house, a storm rages. Through its blasts is a sound as of some one running, and as the curtain rises and the tempest abates Siegmund stum-bles into the rude abode of Hunding. Fleeing for his life, he has unwittingly sought refuge in the house of his enemy. The music grows tender as Sieglinde enters, to find a stranger stretched out, exhausted, before the hearth of the savage Hunding. She gives him a refreshing drink and at her behest he abandons his intention of going out again into the storm. A succession of beautiful motives, affectionate, sorrow-

ful, lead up to the first sounding of the musical
symbol for Hunding, a motive harsh, threatening,
rudely powerful. Sieglinde is at once Hunding's
prisoner and his wife. With her master's entrance,
she explains to him the stranger's presence. Hunding
will not shed blood in his home. He breaks his fast,
while Siegmund narrates his desperate adventures.
Hunding, on retiring for the night, warns Siegmund
that at daybreak he will show him no mercy. Sieglinde,
forced to retire first, has mixed for Hunding a sleeping potion and has tried vainly to call Siegmund's
attention to something that glimmers in the trunk
of the great tree that is the central support of the rude
dwelling.

Left alone by the hearth, Siegmund fails to notice
the sword hilt in the tree as the firelight plays upon
it, though he recalls his father's promise that there
would be a sword for his defense in the hour of his
supreme need. Sieglinde returns and tells how an
old Wanderer drove a sword into the tree for the
use of the hero who would come and how all the
efforts of others to withdraw it from the trunk have
been vain. In the intoxication of awakening love they
gaze at one another; then of a sudden the door of the
hut is blown open and the room is flooded with the
radiance of the Spring night. Siegmund sings of
Spring and the orchestra of love. In music of great
tenderness, recognition comes to these two lonely
souls that they are children of the same father; they

are Walsungs, and Siegmund must be the hero for whom was placed the sword in the tree. Triumphantly, to music of great splendor in which the motive of the sword has a brilliant part, Siegmund withdraws the weapon from the tree and Sieglinde flees with him into the night. Few scenes in all opera have greater beauty of sound—purely as sound—than the last third of this act, devoted to the rapturous singing of the lovers and that of an equally enraptured orchestra. But as details of the score become more familiar, not even the splendor of the sustained melody here can be more welcome than fleeting moments like that of the first statement of the motive known as "The Heroism of the Walsungs" in the grim supper scene.

The orchestral prelude to the second act of "Die Walküre" presents in vigorous and powerful accents a typical instance of Wagner's upbuilding of music which is at once recollective of what has gone before and prefigurative of what is still to come, yet has its own life and entity. The "sword" motive, one of the outstanding few that have already been referred to here, reappears at the outset, though in altered form; the "flight" motive from the first act is another recollection; and, looking forward, are what may be described as advance quotations of "The Shout of the Valkyries" and "The Ride of the Valkyries," the former to be heard in expanded form as the battle cry of Brünnhilde when the curtains part,

RICHARD   WAGNER

the latter to be developed into the prelude to the third act with such completeness and mastery as to supply an extended composition for the concert repertory.

The scene represents a rocky passage in mountains. There, Wotan, the master of Walhalla, is discovered in godlike converse with his favorite daughter, Brünnhilde. Her "Battle Cry" is followed by his announcement that she has been intrusted with the fate of Siegmund, fleeing before the wrath of Hunding. But Fricka, goddess of the hearth and guardian of the proprieties, arrives to combat her husband's will to aid Siegmund. Outraged by the guilty love of Siegmund and Sieglinde, she puts her case so strongly that Wotan surrenders; Siegmund must die. The "Fricka Scene," as this is called, is one of the loftiest in all Wagner. Through it moves a procession of motives already heard, culminating in a new figure, called "Wotan's Rage," which will be met with many times as the music-drama proceeds. But the Fricka scene, like so many others throughout the Ring, develops broad melodies, aside from these combinations of motives. The term "aria" is even applied sometimes to one of Fricka's adjurations. This is music for the voice, quite as much as for the orchestra; music that must be sung, and beautifully sung, to have its true effect.

In a long scene between Brünnhilde and her father, Wotan recounts all that has gone before in the history

of the Ring, virtually reviewing for her the plot of
"Rheingold"—so much so that a celebrated English
critic once wittily suggested that it would have been
better to give Brünnhilde a libretto of that work to
read. Here again is a procession of motives, musical
phrases that go back to the very beginnings of
"Rheingold," each with its idea to represent—"Love,"
"The Treaty with the Giants," "Love's Regret," "The
Power of the Ring," "Valhalla," "The Norns," "The
Ride," "The Ring"; ideas readily identified in performances of the Ring, but unnecessary to explain
individually in presenting this brief summary of
"Die Walküre." This scene, like that of the supper
in the first act, often seems to the person hearing
"Die Walküre" for the first, second or fifth time, a
musically barren one. Orchestrally, it is one of the
recessions, as compared to the climaxes, of a score that
must ascend and descend, and have its valleys as well
as its mountains, rather than remain perpetually on
some high plateau. Eventually, the play of motives
becomes a fascinating one. Some beautiful melodic
phrases are given to Brünnhilde. Wotan's cry, "Das
Ende, das Ende!" is of great tragic effect.

Brünnhilde, having brought on her head the anger
of the embittered god by making a further plea for
Siegmund, is left saddened as Wotan strides into the
mountains. She retires into a grotto as Sieglinde stum-
bles, exhausted, into view with Siegmund. Here the
motive of flight, repeated from the first act, becomes

the basis of some amazing orchestral writing, intertwined with other motives that recall the meeting of the lovers, Hunding, the sword and the heroism of the Walsungs. Sieglinde faints in Siegmund's arms. From the grotto comes Brünnhilde to tell Siegmund he must die. In one of the most affecting scenes in all Wagner, and one of the most inspired, musically, old and new motives form the basis of a colloquy of the loftiest melody. Sombre and dark of color, it has a richness and depth of scoring only hinted at in some passages of the Mozart, Gluck and Beethoven operas that went before. Yet, as all music echoes the past, the motive of death which appears in Brünnhilde's announcement to Siegmund will be found in the earlier "Hans Heiling" of Marschner, one of the German works that in some small way presage Wagner. So the motive of Fate, which also is heard for the first time in this scene, served César Franck in his cherished symphony and appears more than once in the music of Brahms, remote from the theatre. Wagner's reminiscences of other composers, if in a few instances of surprising similarity, remain singularly infrequent. But many the echoes of Wagner!

Leaving the sleeping Sieglinde, Siegmund takes his position high in the rocks to combat Hunding. The Walsung is slain, but not before Brünnhilde has attempted to interfere in his behalf and thus brought about the intervention of Wotan himself, to uphold the promise to Fricka. Brünnhilde, with the fragments of Siegmund's shattered sword, leads Sieglinde away. With a lightning glance Wotan strikes Hunding dead; then he bursts into a wild fury over the disobedience of Brünnhilde, as a tempestuous orchestra ends the act.

"The Ride of the Valkyries," thunderous, exultant, filled with a clamor as of neighing and prancing steeds, gives to the orchestra the center of the stage, so to speak, at the opening of the last act, where are revealed the Valkyries, daughters of Wotan, sisters of Brünnhilde, calling their battle cry, one to another. Brünnhilde enters with Sieglinde in flight before the fury of Wotan. The music throughout this scene is tumultuous, fateful, portentous of direful things to come. Sieglinde, overwhelmed by grief, reproaches Brünnhilde for having saved her from the same fate as her lover. But Brünnhilde tells her that she is to be the mother of the great hero to come, Siegfried, and with this there appears in its full splendor a motive foreshadowed but once in the preceding act that is as outstanding as any in the Ring, that of "Siegfried, Guardian of the Sword." Sieglinde, exalted by what Brünnhilde has told her, takes the broken pieces of the sword and sings a motive well worth remembering—that of "Redemption by Love"—which has not appeared before and will not appear again in "Die Walküre," or all of "Siegfried," or in "Götterdämmerung" until the final scene, where it will assume a dominating place in the superb orchestral peroration that is the end of the cycle.

Sieglinde is hidden away and Brünnhilde attempts to hide under the protection of her sisters. But the raging Wotan summons her forth, drives the others away and tells her of the punishment she must undergo. The remainder of the act is at once great symphony and gloriously vocal. Brünnhilde must lose her godhood. She shall be put to sleep on her rock and the first man who finds her and wakes her shall claim her for his wife. Her noble plea for a more honorable conquest causes Wotan to consent that the rock shall be surrounded by fire, so that only a great hero may reach her and fulfill the edict of his will. The god's love for his daughter overrides his anger. There is a great orchestral phrase, one of Wagner's sublime inspirations, to signify "The Awakening to a New Life." Drifting, mysterious, mesmeric music weaves a spell of sleep. Wotan, with Brünnhilde in his arms, sings his "Farewell", an extended melody or succession of melodies of the highest beauty, with the sleep music and reminiscent motives interwoven in magical instrumentation that moves parallel to the voice in long-breathed, sustained, exalted song. The father tenderly kisses Brünnhilde's godhood away. Sleeping, she is placed recumbent on a rock under a great tree. Wotan covers her with her shield, places her helmet on her head, her spear at her side.

Then, striding from her, he summons Loge, the

god of fire, in a sonorous incantation of great power and majesty. As the rock is surrounded by flames the orchestra paints the scene with a leaping, tingling musical figure of rare descriptive aptness; interwoven with this is the spell of sleep, the mutter of fate, the melody of farewell, the magnificent motive of "Siegfried, Guardian of the Sword"—and finally, as the curtain falls, a great peace, surrounded by its ring of fire.

A DEBUSSY MUSIC DRAMA—
"PELLÉAS ET MÉLISANDE"

IN 1902, when Claude Debussy's "Pelléas et Mélisande" was first produced in Paris, music-drama, as distinguished from the aria opera, arrived at a new milestone in its development. Here, far more than in Wagner, was music for the play's sake. This was a work apparently not open to the charge often leveled against the Bayreuth master's music-dramas that what really had been accomplished was merely to substitute the orchestra for the voice and have opera for symphony's sake in place of opera for singing's sake. Debussy (1862–1918) took the successful play by Maurice Maeterlinck and set it as it was, almost without a change of word or syllable, though with some omissions. Instead of suspending his dialogue above orchestral writing that, with Wagner, often provides the momentum and the chief substance of the score, he gave his text the clear right-of-way, treating it as if it were spoken, so far as pace of sentences and duration of words and syllables were concerned. Wagner had no hesitation in prolonging the word, or the syllable, when this conformed with the musical effect he desired; nor did he hesitate to let the singers wait for their entrances if there was something of importance to be said by the orchestra. "Pelléas et Mélisande" approximates conversation in the writing for the voice as no work intended to be sung had done before. This is something of the intervals of the notes quite as much as of normal speed of utterance.

The composer was passionately French. Almost an obsession with him was the belief that the French language had been persistently mis-set by French composers since the heyday of Gluck (a German-born, though he composed for the Paris public), because they had taken alien models; had, in fact, imitated the heavy accents of the Germans, in violation of the simple fact that French is a language of inflection, not of accent. The undulating character of the vocal line of "Pelléas et Mélisande" in the quest of a new degree of naturalness, in an approximation of spoken French, remains one of the outstanding characteristics of "Pelléas et Mélisande." It is not more marked than the reserve—reticence, even—of the orchestra, which, instead of building great climaxes as in Wagnerian music-drama, serves a purpose chiefly atmospheric by providing a murmurous and misty background, fragile and evanescent. That the score eventually builds musical interest and affection in its own right is an experience now so widely verified, however, as

to make untenable a contention that "Pelléas et Mélisande" is merely the Maeterlinck play decked out
with some nebulous arabesques and intoned on varying pitches that have no melodic effect. The score
not only is one of subtle coloristic appeal but one
that is an intricate mesh of motives, though the character of these does not permit them to stand forth
in the manner of the Wagnerian motives; they are
melodious, in the sense that the basic thematic material of Debussy's other orchestral music is melodious;
but they are merged into the tissue of the music so
delicately that repeated hearings of the work may
leave the most alert listener unconscious of their
presence. Nor is it necessary that he should begin
his experience with "Pelléas et Mélisande" by going
out on a hunt for these motives. Their symbolic and
representative character is of no such import as that
of the Wagnerian motives. They color more than
they characterize; they influence more than they
signify.

The opening scene presents to the onlooker an
autumnal forest of old time, in an unknown land. The
stern Golaud has been hunting and has lost his way.
A sound attracts him to the prostrate form of a young
woman, little more than a child, whose appearance is
that of a princess, though her dress has been torn by
briars. He learns her name but little to explain her
presence there; she has fled, she says, from far away.
Golaud persuades her to follow him out of the wood.

The tale has begun in strangeness; it is to remain enveloped in mystery until the close. Though on the surface all is simple, always there is something unexplained, enigmatic, inscrutable beyond.

Scene follows scene: twelve scenes in all, divided among five acts. From the forest, the spectator is transported to the hall of a castle near the sea. A letter that Golaud has written to his half-brother, Pelléas, is read by Genevieve, Golaud's mother, to the aged Arkel, Golaud's father. Golaud is coming home. Six months have passed since he married Mélisande but he knows as little of her past now as on the day he found her in the wood. The scene changes to a wood where Mélisande and Genevieve are joined by Pelléas. Saddened by the lot of a dying friend, Pelléas is going away. The faint sound of sailors singing on the ship that brought Mélisande gives to the scene one of the many curious touches difficult to explain; something uneasy, prophetic, ominous. Pelléas and Mélisande are next discovered together at a fountain in the park. "One can hear the water sleep" says Pellèas. Mélisande, toying with her wedding ring, accidentally tosses it into the water. "What shall we say if Golaud asks where it is?" she asks Pelléas in distress. "The truth," he replies. But when, in the succeeding scene, Golaud, confined to his bed as the result of a hunting accident, harshly puts the question on discovering that Mélisande is not wearing the ring, she is confused and dissembles; she must have lost the ring in a grotto by the seashore. Golaud demands that she go at once and look for it; Pelléas shall go with her.

Mélisande and Pelléas are next discovered in the grotto. Why should they have gone there? They know the ring is not there. It is dark, the scene has about it something eerie, something of foreboding. A ray of moonlight reveals the vague forms of three old beggars asleep. Again, something strange, fateful. Mélisande is tremulous as they depart. With another of the many changes of scene, the exterior of one of the towers of the castle is presented, with Mélisande singing from a window as she combs her long and luxuriant hair. This is almost a set number, though its character is archaic and unlike any operatic tune. In the orchestra is the breath of the starlit night. Pelléas ascends the winding stair under the window. He waxes lyrical over Mélisande's hair, which streams down to him from the window above. Again the music is close to song. Golaud comes down the stair; Mélisande's hair has caught in the branches of a tree beneath the window. "What children!" says Golaud, nervously, as he and Pelléas depart together. With a shift of scene, Golaud and Pelléas are in the deep vaults under the castle, an uncanny place. Golaud calls the attention of his half-brother to the stagnant water below them and the "death-odor" that arises from it. He holds the lantern while Pelléas bends far over. "Let us go!" says Pelléas. Nothing has happened. But there is no escaping the sense of warning the scene conveys. The pair re-appear in the sunlight on the terrace above the vaults. Golaud then tells Pelléas that he has observed his friendship for Mélisande and he instructs Pelléas to avoid her as much as possible, though not too pointedly. She is perhaps with child.

Before the castle again, Golaud is seen with little Yniold, his son. The lad is questioned, first cautiously, then harshly, about what he has seen when Pelléas and Mélisande were together. A light shows in Mélisande's room. Golaud lifts the boy to the window, and learns that Pelléas is there with Mélisande. But Yniold is frightened at the questions rained upon him. The scene is characteristic of the entire effect of the work. It suggests so much more than it discloses; it mystifies the listener as it mystifies the personages of the play. The music colors and at times intensifies, but it never impedes. The characters sing as they would speak; the orchestra provides an aura of sound through which they move.

Meeting in an apartment in the castle, Mélisande and Pelléas arrange for a farewell meeting by the fountain; Pelléas is going away. A moment later, Mélisande is with old Arkel, when Golaud enters, distraught and savage in his demeanor. He repulses Mélisande and turns fiercely to his father. Intimating deceit, he asks the patriarch what he sees in Mélisande's great eyes. "Only a great innocence," the old man replies. Golaud loses self-control. He seizes Mélisande and when she falls at his feet he drags her one way, then the other, by her streaming hair. His rage subsiding suddenly, he leaves the prostrate Mélisande with Arkel. "Is he drunk?" the old man asks. "No, no!" cries Mélisande, weeping. "If I were God," muses the white-bearded Arkel, "how I would pity the hearts of men!"

The orchestral interlude that follows, between scenes, is the most positive and emotional music of the score. If sufficiently intensified, its several climaxes can be made to sound almost Tchaikovskian. Here is open lament, rather than a further hint of "the great stream of human tears falling always through the shadows of the world." But did Debussy intend that this interlude should be so intensified? That is an issue for conductors and critics; the layman will need to know this opera far better than he will know it at a first, or a third or a fifth hearing to do much more than accept it as it comes to him, whether made bolder and in a sense "externalized," as some Debussy enthusiasts would have it, or purposely held within a narrow range of dynamics and accentuation, for the sake of mystery, as others demand for it.

Pelléas and Mélisande meet again at the fountain where she unwittingly tossed away her wedding ring. It is night; Golaud, she says, already is sleeping; in an hour the great gates of the castle will be closed; they must not linger. Pelléas tells her it is their farewell. Why must he go? "You know already," he says. "It is because I love you." In a low voice, she replies, simply, "I love you, too." Here is no great crash in the orchestra such as almost certainly would have been employed by one of the German writers of music-drama—no upward sweep of the voices to climactic notes as would have been the Italian opera composer's ordinary way of setting this avowal—instead, the orchestra is silent; the voices retain their conversational pitch and inflection. This is one of the most striking illustrations of Debussy's originality in his treatment of the dialogue. The effect is the more eloquent and sincere by reason of its quietness and its simplicity. The audience knows now what Golaud was never to know—that until that moment there had been no love-making between these two.

The scene at the fountain has moments in which the music again hovers close to sustained song, but never quite goes over into a singer's melody. Harsh sounds break in upon the little moment of tenderness. "They are closing the gates—we cannot return now." The lovers embrace. Mélisande, with her uncanny intuition, senses the presence of Golaud. He is behind a tree, she says. He has a sword. Pelléas has no weapon. In desperation, the lovers kiss. "The stars are falling," cries Pelléas as Golaud rushes on them and plunges his sword into the back of his half-brother. Mélisande flees, Golaud in pursuit.

The last act, in contrast with those preceding, has but a single scene. Mélisande is dying. Only slightly wounded by Golaud in his pursuit of her after he had killed Pelléas, she has since been delivered of her child, which is sleeping near her. A physician attends her. Arkel and Golaud are there, the latter a broken man, a prey to remorse and tortured because he still does not know whether Pelléas and Mélisande were guilty. "They kissed like little children," he laments; "I did it in spite of myself." Left alone with Mélisande, he makes one final desperate effort to learn from her the truth. When he asks her, she tells him simply that she loved Pelléas. Was it a guilty love? "No, no; we were not guilty," she replies; "Why do you ask me that?" The doctor and Arkel return, to find Golaud shivering and in despair.

The servants enter. "Why are they here?" asks Golaud. They drop to their knees at the sound of a distant bell. Mélisande is gone.

Arkel takes the baby. "It is the poor little one's turn," he says, as he carries the infant from the death chamber.

The music is grave and tender throughout the death scene. It has a muted, distant sound, with an other-worldliness in its closing moments. Save for Golaud's tortured inquiries at the bed of Mélisande, this is music of serenity and reticence, yet of an underlying sadness that needs no shrieks and no sobs, either in the pit or on the stage. Peculiarly delicate, exquisitely sensitive, it is as remote from the great threnodies of the Wagnerian orchestra as it is from the piercing outcries of the singers in corresponding scenes of Italian opera. It is a scene that has no parallel in its achievement of tragedy without anything to suggest an emotional outburst. Here is at once the most natural and the most unreal of operatic deaths; but that naturalness, that unreality, together characterize the entire progress of this music-drama. It conforms closer than perhaps any other (not to the exception of the later "Wozzeck" of Alban Berg) to the realism of the spoken drama; but, paradoxically, these realistic means are employed for the purpose of presenting a work that from the first is mysterious, dreamlike, shadowy, full of intimations of things beyond the realities of life; a work that leaves much to surmise and kindles the imagination at the same time that it tugs at the heart.

In the end, when there have been sufficient hearings of Debussy's music, the deep-lying humanity of "Pelléas et Mélisande" overshadows its fantasy; the dream becomes steadily less a dream, the dim is less dim, the obscure less obscure; not so much because the character of the story has changed with familiarity, but because the listener finds in the music much that the words and stage action cannot convey. It is the character of the listening that changes. The auditor no longer gropes for what he will not find. Instead, he is steeped in a familiar, consolatory glow. He realizes, at long last, that the intrusion of any obvious tune, or the development of sonorous orchestral pas-

NEW YORK PHILHARMONIC SYMPHONY ORCHESTRA—ARTURO TOSCANINI, CONDUCTOR

sages for their own sake, would break the spell. The strange quiet of the music is an essential of its appeal. Who—as one commentator has asked—relishes shouting and high laughter in the midst of reverie in a moonlit glade?

THE SYMPHONY

OF the ordinary qualities of musicality as distinguished from musicianship, only two are pre-requisite to a first enjoyment of a symphony. These are the ability to recognize melody and sensitiveness to musical sounds. Grasp of design will inevitably follow much hearing of music in its different forms. Unquestionably, appreciation and more particularly comprehension will be enlarged and the listener will derive a wider variety of pleasure from even a superficial acquaintance with the structural principles governing most symphonies. But this enlargement of his horizon need not be accomplished at one stroke. To repeat, all he needs at the outset is a feeling for musical sonority and an ear that knows and accepts melodic sequences as such. This problem of melody is the first and perhaps final one in all adaptability to music and musical experience. The difficulty with innumerable listeners at symphony concerts is that conceptions of melody are based on four-square hymn tunes or almost equally four-square popular songs and dance pieces, in which one melodic phrase or, perhaps, at the most, two or three are repeated immediately and with slight variations throughout the tune or refrain. The melody of much art-music is stated in the form of themes without this immediate repetition. If the basic phrase of much popular music should be stated only once at the outset and then wait some little time for repetition, it is more than likely that the untrained ear would see as little melody in this basic phrase as it sees in many melodic phrases of the symphony.

One of the fundamentals of musical enjoyment is the pleasure of recognition. In most instances recognition is derived through repetition. The most obvious form of music is that which brings immediate repetition and enables thereby the most ready recognition. But repetition which is not immediate and which, in bringing back a melodic idea after an interval in which other ideas have been set forth, presents that idea in a slightly varied or even materially altered form, is none the less melodic. If the ear can contrive to recognize a melodic phrase or fragment equivalent to the first phrase of any popular melody, after an interval, it can be said to have solved for itself the first problem in listening to symphonic music and, for that matter, to all music of an art character. Popular music or music of the obviously elementary character of the hymn tune and the dance tune, by piling repetition on repetition, makes a more immediate effect but quickly wears itself out by reason of the manner in which it fairly drums its one, two or three melodic sequences into the ear. The difference between a popular dance-tune and a symphonic movement based on some dance form may lie quite as much in the variety of phraseology of the symphonic movement, as against the poverty of phraseology in the one-idea popular dance, as in the quality of the phrases of either.

Let the listener, then, put away first of all the notion that a melody to be a melody must be a completed, rounded-out tune with a beginning and an ending that enable it to stand out separately as something that can be whistled, hummed or sung as a separate entity. With this obstacle cleared away, his listening will be more receptive to the melodic value of the fragments or group-ideas that are known as themes. Remembering that they have their own, inherent melodic charm quite as much when there is no immediate repetition as they would have if they were ground out, hand-organ fashion, with many such repetitions, the listener will find, with increased familiarity, that these themes are used as building blocks in the erection of a structure and as segments in the tracing of a design. His first pleasure will come from the themes themselves and their recurrence, a pleasure that will be partly that of melodic recognition and partly that of the human being's instinctive response to warm, rich and colorful sounds and combinations of sounds. The principle of repetition and recognition, which in its most rudimentary form explains the immediate appeal of popular music to the untutored or largely inexperienced ear, explains also the love of most enlightened and widely experienced listeners for the older and time-proven music in preference to the new and perhaps experimental. Just as a single hearing brings recognition through repetition of an obvious tune of the hand-organ variety, so repeated hearings bring recognition through repetition in an extended or complicated musical structure.

With new and unfamiliar music, even the most widely experienced and well-studied listener often misses the basic melodic substance at a first hearing and fancies that the new work is lacking in melody because of a failure to grasp the true quality of the thematic ideas through repetition or otherwise. With rehearings, music of a supposedly experimental character, which at first may have seemed barren of melodic ideas, frequently is discovered to have much the same appeal as the older music to which it may have been unfavorably compared. This is particularly true of works which by reason of some harmonic departure or irregularity of form sound strange and uncouth and unlike the music already known and loved. This necessity, for most listeners, of recognition through repetition, explains still further why much inferior music, music that is lacking in originality and personality, music that merely echoes what other men have written, and written better before them, often finds a ready response, the while music more starkly personal and distinctive fails of comprehension. The music which is largely borrowed from music already familiar, even though it be inferior to the sources of its borrowing, strikes a responsive chord of recognition. If it is slightly disguised and altered in its re-statement, differently colored or adapted to new ends, combined perhaps in such an assortment of borrowings that the originals are blurred and confused in the memory of all save a few, this medley of other men's music has in it the appeal of repetition, because the ear already has stored much of it away.

Power of reminiscence, therefore, often is on the side of feeble music. But time rights all such injustices. Lesser composers complain of the charge so often found in critical reviews that their music sounds like the music of Wagner, Brahms, Massenet, Puccini, Stravinsky, Debussy or Strauss, or perhaps all of these at one and the same time. While it is true that reminiscence in some degree is almost certain to be encountered in all music, it is worth remarking and remembering that when a Wagner, a Brahms, a Massenet, a Puccini, a Stravinsky, a Debussy or a Strauss comes along, he is not accused of writing like these lesser composers. The great storm-centers of music, the men of genius about whom there was controversy as to whether they were misunderstood, the Titans who afterwards became such universal favorites as to make ridiculous the critical and pedantic hostility with which their music was received when it was new, were never opposed primarily on the ground that *they* were writing other men's music. Rather, it was because in their daring and their powerful assertion of new ideas and new personalities they failed of the too-facile quality of reminiscence that they lacked comprehension at the outset.

Let us return to the thought that melodies or fragments of melodies in the form of the melodic phrases that we call themes, are the building blocks and the segments of design of a symphony. The listener will find in many symphonic movements, particularly the slow movements—adagio, andante, largo, and so forth; and notably the romanzas of some of the older works—songlike melodies in which the effect is as completely rounded as in any popular melody; the repetition may be as pronounced and as immediate, though the variety of expression, either through shifts of key or the harmonic treatment, will be much richer. The difficulty with such movements may be that the melodic phrases themselves will be much longer—in the case of Brahms, a single phrase may have the length of an entire refrain of some operetta song—but the grasp of such a phrase again is merely a matter of repetition. On first hearing, its length may cause it to elude an ear attuned primarily to short phrases; with two or three hearings, its melodic shape and appeal establish themselves. These song-like movements, with their more extended and easily recognized melody, are ordinarily the favorites of listeners who are attracted to melody more readily than to rhythmic vigor and vitality of motion. There are many others, however, who, even without a clear recognition of the thematic segments, respond more quickly to those movements of the symphony which build momentum through the alternation and super-position of small melodic phrases which are kept in a churning pulsation, often characteristic of the first and final movements of the symphonies, as distinguished from the song-like movements generally placed in the middle.

The symphony first movement in many instances is the one that sooner or later will bring the most un-learned listener to some comprehension of musical form. He will find, however, that form is not a straight-jacket and that the exceptions to any pre-scribed order or pattern are so numerous that, instead of rules of procedure, his listening will disclose only guides. He will hear much and read much, perhaps, of the sonata form, but it will be wise for him at the outset to regard the sonata form as something to be approximated, rather than succinctly demonstrated, by the symphonies as he hears them performed. This approximation as encountered in the first movement of many symphonies will bring to his attention a first theme and a second theme, two melodic statements that usually are of a contrasting character and in different keys; and he will eventually come to take delight in the repetitions, variations and transmutations to which these themes are subjected in what is styled their development. But he also will encounter in many works secondary themes and connecting passages so melodic in their character as to give them an interest of their own, and it is not to be recommended that he devote his listening to tagging these, mentally, as A, B, C, D, E, and so forth, after the fashion of an instructor bent on structural analysis.

There may even be some difficulty for the most experienced listener in separating first and second themes from their surroundings, particularly when, as is often the case, the former is preceded by an introduction which may be quite as melodic in character as the first theme. These labels are of little importance to one who listens for pleasure. They are chiefly of use when it becomes necessary to write or talk about musical composition; there must be some way, then, of identifying the different essential parts. A little experience in listening to symphonies, however, will disclose that introductions, however melodic their character, are not subsequently utilized for development and variation in contrast with other thematic material, as are the themes of the sonata form. Many symphonic movements will be found to have not only such an introduction preceding the

first statement of the themes which are subsequently
to be developed, but added material for a conclusion;
a coda which may be quite as melodic as either of
the principal themes.

All of this can be absorbed through repeated hearings and an additional pleasure derived through an
increased comprehension of an often intricate and
highly ingenious design. But it need not be a cause
for burning the midnight lamp and the cultivation
of headaches at the outset. A listener may be completely oblivious of any difference between a first
movement in sonata form and a second or third movement not in sonata form, and still find stimulus and
emotional beauty in the sonorities, the melodic material, the rhythmic life of music of the highest character.

The relation between the movements of the symphony will be found as variable as the details of musical form. Some unity of purpose, of key, of color,
of mood, of style or literary content inevitably binds
together the different movements, or the work fails
to hang together. But contrast is equally important
if monotony is not to be invited, and it is the rule,
rather than otherwise, for the several movements
to be different from one another in pace and even in
spirit. Occasionally, there is a community of themes,
as in the César Franck symphony, whereby the successive movements repeat something from the earlier
movements, but this does not preclude the contrast

of pace and spirit which is the composer's safeguard against monotony. There are symphonies of one movement only, with sections roughly corresponding to the three, four, five or more movements of other symphonies. There is the famous instance of the so-called "Unfinished" Symphony of Schubert, in which two movements of probably four projected (a third was completely sketched but only a few bars orchestrated in full) are self-sufficient when played without thought of further contrast or extension. There are works called symphonies which present in their successive sections the material and character of several individual compositions and only through painstaking study can be shown to possess in any section a tangible adherence to the sonata form. They are all for the ear, all for the enjoyment of listeners who may never have acquired any knowledge of musical notation or musical structure. Their form in many instances is to be regarded even by the scholar as primarily the scaffolding which serves the composer in the erection of his structure and, like the scaffolding of buildings made of steel and bricks and mortar, it is no longer for the eye once the structure is completed.

The pleasure that is apparent in the recognition of musical sound will expand with experience in identifying through successive hearings the individual qualities of the instruments of the orchestra and the special qualities which result from their use in varying combinations. The listener who begins with no more knowledge than that of the existence of a string choir or section composed of violins, violas, 'cellos and double basses; of a woodwind choir or section of flutes, oboes, clarinets, bassoons, English horn, French horn and an occasional less orthodox instrument, used for some special effect; a brass choir or section of trumpets, trombones and tubas, with others of their kin; and of a percussion section, in which the timpani and other drums may be supplemented by all manner of tinkling, chiming, rattling or booming devices from the triangle and the castanet to bells and gongs (plus, too, the piano), will not long rest content with so generalized a basis for the identification of instrumental color. As he hears phrases repeated by different groups and combinations of instruments as well as by solo voices, he will acquire some knowledge of their special properties. It may be superficial and elementary and subject to all manner of confusion and error, but he has only to continue hearing symphonic music to acquire a considerable store of knowledge about the orchestra, as compared to that of the layman who has heard no symphonic music.

Pleasurable listening to the symphonies, then, depends first upon ability to grasp and enjoy the melodic material which serves as the thematic basis of each work, in conjunction with a response to musical richness and color in combinations of sound. Out of this for most listeners should grow naturally a comprehension of musical design which, though never that of an expert or of the classroom, will be a source of increased pleasure. Intricacies of structure and harmonic individuality may be sensed without the ear seizing upon them in specific detail and by a process of isolation identifying them in musical terminology. With the hearing of many symphonies, many times, feeling for both design and harmonic structure may be developed without the listener having acquired any technical knowledge of counterpoint or the most simple chords. If, prompted by a desire to know more about what he has heard, he should decide to seek instruction or to instruct himself in the elements of music, it is never too late. No doubt, a multitude of persons could increase the pleasure derived from the music they hear if they could deal with many details of this music in its own terms. Certainly, they will be wise to consult program annotations and historical, critical or biographical material which will tend to supply a background for what they hear, even though false notions of the emotional or literary purpose of the composer not infrequently are engendered by a too-ready acceptance of legends and anecdotes more interesting than authentic.

THE ORCHESTRA

THE symphony orchestra, the most complete, the most sumptuous and most versatile of all mediums of musical expression, has come to its present virtuosity by slow degrees and is as much the product of evolution as any other manifestation of the tonal art. Although it may undergo many changes in the future, the orchestra of today is a definitely and carefully arranged ensemble comprising the most congenial representatives of the four great instrumental families (strings, woodwinds, brass and percussion) arranged in sections; first, according to the family to which they belong, and second, according to their pitch-range within the family, in the manner of a choir of human voices.

The strings are the hardest-working and hence the backbone of the orchestra. This is so because the stringed instruments, as a group, have a technical agility and fluency, a power of diverse expressiveness, and a breadth of pitch-range thus far not equalled by either the woodwinds or the brass. It is only natural, therefore, that so adaptable a family should be called upon to bear the major burden in any music for orchestra. The violins are the first and second sopranos, who are placed at the front of the orchestra, either facing each other at the left and right of the conductor, respectively, or massed together at the conductor's left. The violas, slightly larger than the violins and therefore of deeper tone, are the altos and generally are placed in front and a little to the right of the conductor. The 'cellos (properly violoncellos), held between the knees of the player, since they are much too large to go under the chin, represent the tenor voice and ordinarily are in front of the conductor, but slightly to the left; sometimes they are at the right. The double basses, of course, constitute the bass voice of the string choir and they usually are ranged around the very back of the orchestra. Since the basses are of such large proportions, the players must stand, or sit upon high stools, to manipulate them. Time was when other string instruments besides those named found a place in the orchestra, but with the coming of the great instrument makers the only string instruments retained were those played with bows, the harp excepted.

Among the woodwinds, the flute, which is of ancient lineage and vies with the drum for recognition as the very first musical instrument, is the soprano voice. The piccolo is a small flute which extends the upward range of its parent. The oboe, supplemented in the lower ranges by the English horn, and the clarinet (similarly extended by the bass clarinet) also have soprano characteristics. The bassoon commonly occupies a position quite like that of the 'cello. The deepest bass is the contra-bassoon. Composers have recognized that, as a whole, the woodwind family must be used sparingly and with much discretion for the reasons that each instrument has very definite types of music it plays either well or badly, that woodwind tone-quality tires the listener's ear quickly, and that the physical exigencies of breathing and blowing on the part of the player, combined with certain difficulties of execution presented by the structure of some of the instruments, render prolonged and arduous playing virtually impossible. The woodwinds are at their best in characteristic and colorful solo passages of reasonable length, in harmonic combinations of short duration among themselves, or in combination solo passages with an instrument of the string group.

The brass instruments constitute the "heavy artillery" of the orchestra, and while they figure as occasional soloists in passages generally intended to convey nobility or solitary grandeur, they serve chiefly to reinforce the impressive and thunderous climaxes of massed tone which strings and woodwinds could never achieve by themselves. The trumpets are the coloraturas and are possessed of considerable agility,

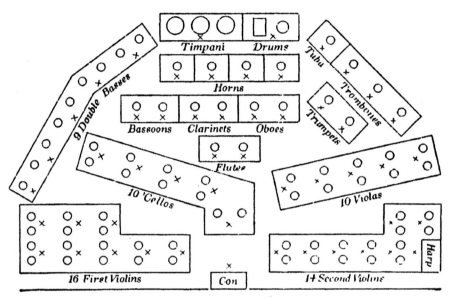

GENERAL SEATING PLAN FOR AN ORCHESTRA OF EIGHTY PIECES

due to tricks of tonguing to which they are amenable and to a well developed system of valve-fingering. The trombones are slower, more ponderous, and very majestic in their tenor, baritone and bass domain. The tuba co-operates with the double bass in giving a solid foundation to the harmonic structure.

And now must be mentioned a group of the most important color and harmony instruments in the entire ensemble—the French horns, horns in F, or simply horns, as they commonly are known. These luscious (and very temperamental) singers are hybrids in that they really are brass instruments in texture and mechanical construction, but their tone quality places them more properly with the woodwinds. They are descendants of the straight 18-foot Alpine horns but have been curled up like thread on a spool so that they may be held completely in the hands of the players and have acquired valves like the trumpet so that all tones of the scale are possible of production.

The percussion section, concerned mainly with accentuating and pointing up rhythms, is headed by the timpani, a set of two drums shaped like huge kettles, which can be tuned to definite pitches. Other familiar members of the family are the small drum, the bass drum, cymbals, triangle, orchestra bells, tam-tam, gong, chimes and innumerable other "traps" which contribute much of the "spice" of orchestral music.

There are no hard and fast rules as to the number of each species to be included in the orchestral body, but certain ratios have been discovered over the years which make for a satisfying acoustical balance, and which are generally observed by symphony orchestras. Thus the ensemble of the New York Philharmonic Society, which may be regarded as representative, embraces 36 violins (evenly divided as firsts and seconds), 14 violas, 12 violoncellos, 10 double basses, 4 flutes (one interchangeable with piccolo), 4 oboes (one interchangeable with English horn), 4 clarinets (one interchangeable with bass clarinet and another with E Flat clarinet), 4 bassoons (one interchangeable with contra-bassoon), 6 horns, 4 trumpets, 3 trombones, 1 tuba, 2 harps, timpani and other percussion devices as needed.

It was Monteverdi who first organized the orchestra along the lines by which we know it today. He realized the necessity of having a preponderance of strings, and it was not long after that the present well-balanced quartet of string choirs came into being. Probably because of their mechanical crudity and unwieldiness, the virtues of the wind instruments were not realized fully until long after Monteverdi's day, and they were used chiefly to double the string parts. Mozart was the first composer to make extensive use of the clarinet. Neither Bach nor Handel wrote for it. The English horn first appeared in Gluck's opera, "Alceste," in 1767. The tuba, the true and voluminous bass of which the orchestra was long in need, did not appear until comparatively recent times and therefore is heard only in the music of more modern composers. Schumann brought about very significant changes in orchestration by introducing valved trumpets and horns; Beethoven did much to individualize the orchestral voices. Weber, Wagner and Berlioz experimented widely and, for their time, recklessly, with the dramatic and emotional possibilities of the wind family, placing many new colors upon the orchestral palette. Wagner was particularly partial to the horns and used unprecedented numbers of them in some of his scores. The tenor tuba was one of his special requirements. With the desire rampant to draw ever more striking effects and richer hues from the ensemble, composers who followed Wagner, including Strauss, Debussy, Bruckner, Mahler, Ravel, Rimsky-Korsakoff, Stravinsky and others, have discovered still further resources, and so the search probably will go on so long as concerted instrumental music is acceptable to the public ear.

HAYDN'S SYMPHONIES

To see Franz Joseph Haydn and his work as a symphonic composer in the proper perspective, one must turn back in Austrian history to a day in the 18th century when the countryside was dotted with petty principalities, each presided over by a nobleman whose leisure and wealth had given him opportunity to acquire considerable culture. If he were living today, he probably would be classed as a "country gentleman." It so happened that music was the most widely cultivated of the arts among this gentry, so that often the prince was not only an amateur musician himself, but, as a rule, also had at his beck and call a company of musicians, headed by a Kapellmeister, whose business it was to furnish music for the castle on any and all occasions. These artists, living "under the protection" of the prince, were as much a part of his household as the servants and occupied only a slightly higher social position.

Haydn was one of these musicians. He spent the greater part of his long life (1732–1809) at the court

of the Counts Esterhazy at Eisenstadt, as Kapellmeister. Among other things, it devolved upon the
Kapellmeister personally to compose a large part of
the music which his musicians played, and since
functions for which music was required were frequent and not often of a nature to inspire the creative mind it is natural that Kapellmeisters, by and
large, brought forth great quantities of inconsequential music, much of which never was heard subsequently to the occasion for which it was written.
Thus even today, when there is the desire to characterize a composition of talented mediocrity, it is
styled "Kapellmeister music."

Haydn stands as the greatest composer of this
genus, and in his own day was widely celebrated. He
began his symphonic writing under the patronage of
Count Morzin in 1759. And, while many of his
fellow Kapellmeisters were satisfied to grind out the
daily round of composition with just enough artistic
quality and finesse to satisfy their masters, Haydn
was devoted to the art itself and was forever finding
ways of expanding, refining and improving the musical mediums in which he worked. So it was that
he turned the current of his genius into the symphony and brought about changes therein which have
remained in force to the present day.

That Haydn was the originator of the symphony
as an art form is a popular misconception which be-
clouds the composer's true service to the evolution

of music. He did not originate the symphonic form. There probably is no one person in music history to whom this extraordinary honor could be assigned. The symphony is the product of a long course of development begun, probably, when instrumental music first was permitted to be heard alone, independently of vocal or choral music for which it previously had been merely the accompaniment. Indeed those brief instrumental interludes between sections of a vocal work were at one time known as symphonies. John Christian Bach, Wagenseil, Abel, Stamitz and other "Mannheim symphonists" wrote the first symphonies recognizable to us as such. And Haydn profited much by his intensive study of the achievements of these men, particularly J. C. Bach. They had already gone a long way toward an improved standard of form and orchestration. Haydn took up their work and carried it forward to the high point of perfection it had reached at the close of the classic era and the advent of Beethoven.

Among the first impressions the listener gains on hearing a symphony by Haydn is one that the work is small (almost miniature) in proportions; another that it is gay or humorous—with some notable exceptions; and that it seems to be the apotheosis of grace, refinement and delicacy, with here and there a bit of peasant muscularity. These impressions tell virtually the whole story of Haydn's artistic philosophy and methods; the exigencies of the conditions under which he composed and the purposes to which the works were to be put make the reasons for this clear enough. Perhaps the particular symphony in hand was written for a birthday or a reception. We must see it in the light of its own time and against its original background.

At least a hundred and twenty-five symphonies are credited to this extraordinarily prolific composer. When one considers that Beethoven wrote nine symphonies and Brahms only four, such productivity seems almost incredible. But it must be remembered that a symphony by Brahms or Beethoven is a vastly different thing from a symphony by Haydn. Not only were the works of the later masters plotted out on a much larger and grander scale, but they were invested with considerably more spiritual substance, more complexity of thought and utterance, and more subtlety of import. To the listener, Haydn's symphonies may not seem diminutive in point of the actual amount of time consumed in performing them. But when they are shorn of all extraneous material (such as the note-for-note repetitions of whole sections which Haydn frequently employed, as did the other writers of his day) and really scraped to the bone for the bare essentials of their construction, one quickly discovers that they have been fabricated of relatively simple stuffs and on the whole quite economically.

Of these hundred and twenty-five symphonies,

certainly a good third (perhaps many more) are eminently playable and are still heard more or less regularly in modern orchestral programs. This represents a high endurance average, indeed, especially since the edification of posterity was probably one of the least of the considerations entering into Haydn's work-a-day business of composition. One is inclined to think of them collectively rather than individually because they seem so intimately bound up with each other and present such strong family resemblances. This is not to say, however, that there is any wearisome sameness about them, for Haydn was nothing if he was not musically fresh and resourceful. It is merely that we, in the twentieth century, are so far removed from the Haydn era that we have a very generalized idea of its topography and see the whole much more clearly than any of its parts. This homogeneous conception may also be ascribed to the circumstance that the symphonies are so similar in purpose and so completely abstract in artistic content that differentiation is difficult except in the actual hearing of the works themselves.

Among the most interesting, perhaps, are the twelve which Haydn wrote especially for the concerts given in London by Johann Peter Salomon. The latter was an orchestral leader, a violinist and a concert manager who contracted with Haydn for a series of symphonies to be given at performances under his sponsorship and with the composer conducting from the harpsichord. Haydn made a journey to England to fulfill this contract and met with a high degree of success. His creative talents must have been spurred by the venture, for some of his best symphonic works are to be found among those which he composed at the behest of the kindly and perspicacious London manager. Here might be mentioned S. No. 7 in D; S. No. 9 in B Flat, a work of uncommon humor and gaiety which has been described as "one of the greatest comedies in classical instrumental music"; and S. No. 11 in D, known as "The Clock" since the Andante movement is an unmistakable rhythmic imitation of the regular, mechanical "tick-tock" of a clock—especially one of grandfather dimensions.

T HE life of Wolfgang Amadeus Mozart was that
of a typical storybook musician. Success, failure,
pathos and humor succeeded each other in his brief
life-span of thirty-five years with almost fictional
regularity and invariability. Manifesting musical
genius virtually in babyhood, he quickly was recognized as a prodigy, not only as a pianist but as a composer, and he was dragged hither and yon over much
of Europe by an enterprising father to work his
wonders before crowned heads and people of influence who might assure him of an opulent future. He
was marvelled at, but his youthful triumphs were
over before he attained to manhood. When death
made its premature appearance, the brilliant, incom-
parable Mozart was thrust into a pauper's grave.

During his few feverish, debt-ridden years, Mozart
had found time to compose a prodigious number of
musical works that are anointed with immortality.
Sonatas, concertos, ensemble music of all kinds, operas and symphonies were among his output. And

in all these forms he attained a kind of ultimate perfection, as if he had reached his final goal, everywhere save in the symphony. There is reason to believe that Mozart would have lifted this form to still greater heights. He worked with unbelievable speed. It is recorded that one symphony was turned out complete in four days! The story persists that he composed everything mentally, even to details, before he set it down on paper, so that the actual writing of music to him was nothing more than the mechanical business of transcription. Whatever the truth of this, it remains that composition to Mozart was a miraculously spontaneous function, more so probably than was the case with any other composer on record with the possible exceptions of Haydn and Schubert, and that it is this very spontaneity, this impromptu freshness and prodigal exuberance, which give his works the intangible charm forever associated with his name.

Mozart was born after Haydn and died before him. Thus Mozart's creative career was completely surrounded by that of Haydn and the two men influenced and learned from each other to the mutual benefit of their respective creative productions. Moreover, their talents had a certain affinity; they had much the same aesthetic and philosophic attitudes toward their art, and since they both wrote music for the delectation and amusement of courts and social gatherings, they had much the same practical purposes in view. There is, however, a definite and important shade of difference in the character of their music which should not be over-looked. Haydn, as the older and more experienced servitor of the Austrian nobility, was somewhat more sophisticated and frankly entertaining in a practical way than Mozart; the music of the latter often takes on a poignancy and emotionalism of a deeper stratum. The difference in their social conditions sufficiently explains this shade of contrast. Mozart led a life of disappointments, frustrations, financial worries and uneven rhythms, whereas Haydn moved serenely through a well-ordered, placid and assured existence. And thus it is, since the world has come to lay greater store by musical works which show emotional and spiritual travail than by those reflecting lighter and sunnier moods, that Mozart is regarded by many to be essentially a greater composer than his contemporary. Except when considering their purely subjective connotations, it is very precarious criticism to place the symphonies of Mozart, as a whole, above those of Haydn.

Of the forty or more symphonies that came from the pen of Mozart, not over a half-dozen receive frequent performances today. This seeming neglect is explainable, for only this handful of works is really significant of the mature Mozartean genius, the remainder being, for the most part, youthful essays of small import. Works representing his highest artistic flights in this form were the three symphonies he wrote approximately three years before his death; upon this fact is based the surmise that had he lived longer he would have attained to new heights as a master of this form.

The three superlative works referred to are those in E Flat, G Minor, and C Major ("Jupiter"), composed within about six weeks of each other in 1788. It is a strange commentary that in this particular period he was in desperate straits, financial malaises were assailing him with more than usual rigor, and troubles of all kinds lay heavily upon him. These burdens seemed to stimulate rather than retard creative energy, and the result was that he surpassed himself in the production of beautiful music for orchestra. The first of the series, in E Flat, is particularly grateful melodically and has many of the Italian overtones found in his operas, notably "The Marriage of Figaro," "Don Giovanni" and "Così fan Tutte." Particularly in the Andante, the second movement, does he attain to a celestial beauty. It is a completely individual expression which sums up, in large measure, the particular genius that was Mozart.

The second, in G Minor (K. 550), is quite different in character from the first. Melancholy marks the opening, and there is less of abandon as the work progresses. The last of the trilogy, the "Jupiter," is one of the most widely celebrated of symphonies, not only for sheer beauty of musical content, but for the expertness with which it is constructed. Its large outlines are examples of the most chaste and finely wrought musical architecture of the period. Perfect cut and balance of parts, mathematically precise, yet fluent and intelligible polyphony, and, withal, artistic vitality, combine in making this final offering of Mozart to the treasury of the world's greatest symphonic music a crowning achievement for its composer. The Finale, comprising a fugal treatment of a four-note motive, stands as one of the noblest examples of counterpoint.

Brief mention may be made of a few earlier works which rise above the common run. One of these is the little symphony in C (K. 338) which was composed at Salzburg in 1780 and which is minus the traditional Minuet. The Finale dances along with the highest of high spirits. The Andante, longer than usual, is all poetry and fancy and affection garbed in the ingratiating vestments which Mozart knew so well how to design.

Then there are the two symphonies that appeared in the years 1782 and 1783. The first is in D (K. 385) and generally is known as the Haffner Symphony because of its association with Sigmund Haffner, burgomaster of Salzburg. Again it is the Andante movement which possesses the most winning qualities. This movement the young composer developed from the original Haffner Serenade written for a social affair at the burgomaster's home. The other sections were added when he conceived the idea of working the serenade into a symphony. This business of transplanting ideas and materials from one work to another, was a procedure very common in that musical era. Composers thought nothing of taking a melody or a general musical scheme from one of their earlier works (and even from works of other composers in some cases) and using it again in the composition with which they were at the moment engaged, if it seemed to be particularly suitable or if nothing better came to mind. A sort of candid and ingenuous plagiarism which, today, is frowned upon and even held illegal when it involves the pillaging of another composer's work. Thus it comes about that one overture has been known to serve for two quite different operas, and that a given composer has been extolled for a particular piece of fine musical invention which, upon investigation, has proved to be the product of someone else.

The second of these two symphonies, which generally are regarded as a pair, is the "Linz Symphony," in C (K. 425). This, too, is a small work, both in physical proportions and in style. It was written in four days while Mozart was en route from Salzburg to Vienna. Although it is scored for small orchestra and has much of the atmosphere of a chamber work, it demands great care in execution if its delicate and carefully calculated beauties are not to be shattered in performance.

The last of the symphonies of which we can take
fleeting notice here is that in D (K. 504) which
Mozart wrote with much care and into which he
poured an unusually large measure of his heady musical vintage. Since the symphony was to be played
during his visit to Prague (where his opera, "The Marriage of Figaro," was enjoying a great success after
its cool Vienna reception) Mozart was anxious to
give the best that was in him and set about the thing
with more than his wonted seriousness. Hence the
work takes on a character of greater profundity and
less blithesome spirit than some of the others. Deeper
emotions are evinced and something of a meditative
nature shows forth, although the work was written
with Mozart's customary magical dispatch.

LUDWIG VAN BEETHOVEN

LUDWIG VAN BEETHOVEN (born at Bonn, Germany, 1770; died at Vienna, 1827) probably will stand throughout time as the most significant, if not the greatest, symphonist who ever put pen to paper. His momentous rôle in the history of music was a dual one. On the one hand, he culminated the old classic school of symphonic composition which began approximately with John Christian Bach, proceeded through Stamitz and other Mannheimers, and came to fruition in the works of Haydn and Mozart. On the other, he played the part of a great beacon light illuminating the course of the music of the future, inaugurating the romantic era from which the Twentieth Century modernists have been trying to escape in their quest for novelty and unexplored paths.

Beethoven cannot be styled primarily an innovator inasmuch as he did not evolve nor establish any new compositional forms. Rather, he expanded, revivified, and gave a new import to forms already established. He poured the fresh wine of his tempestuous, unprecedented genius into the old bottles of tradition which might well have cracked and fallen into disuse after the passing of Haydn and Mozart had Beethoven never been born. Perhaps little remained to be said in the formal, felicitous, and elegantly engaging vocabulary of the conventional symphony of the day. Possibly, the répertoire had run out when Beethoven burst upon the scene to discourse with stentorian tones in a new and terrifying language which could only bewilder many of his contemporaries.

What precisely was Beethoven's contribution to symphonic music? To answer this question in full is beyond the province of this book. But a few of the more salient points of his bequest briefly may be noted. To begin with, Beethoven was strongly individualistic and, in a sense, harshly antisocial. He realized the stature of his own genius. In Nature only did he recognize his equal and for that reason he was a pantheist of the most ardent order. He was a person of strong emotional reactions, stormy temperament and philosophic depth. When such a genius sets himself to musical composition, he inevitably leaves the stamp of his peculiar nature upon anything that comes from his pen.

Personal considerations, then, formed the groundwork for Beethoven's enrichment of symphonic literature. He poured himself, his thoughts, and his feelings into music with a prodigality which had never been attempted before. Despair, exaltation, fear, love, humor—all emotional states found their way into tonal expression and externalization which was at times uncouth in its elemental straightforwardness. So intense and highly magnified were Beethoven's emotional responses, however, that, when translated into music, they seem to transcend the capacities of any one man and take on the grandeur of universality. The earth shakes with his laugher, Olympian deities share his exaltation, and all mankind laments with his despair.

Naturally the narrow symphonic dwelling of the classicists proved inadequate for the habitation of the leonine Beethoven, and he soon began pulling out walls, expanding rooms, and adding lofty corridors where his vast artistic ego might have space to move about and breathe. Without going into technical detail, it may be said that he immensely increased the physical proportions of the symphony as a whole by augmenting many of its parts, notably the development section in which the themes given out in the section of exposition are turned about, inverted, broken into fragments, tossed from key to key and manipulated generally after the manner of a juggler and his clubs. He replaced the minuet of the classic symphony with a scherzo (meaning "musical joke") which he treated with a brusque and sometimes peasant-like humor. Finally he stamped his foot impatiently for a new virtuosity among orchestral players. He drew much more heavily upon the resources and technical equipment of the executive musicians than was customary in his era, with the result that some of the latter pronounced their parts unplayable. Time and experience, however, taught them, as well as the public, the value and beauty of the new instrumental possibilities which this "mad man" threw open before them. Today they are commonplaces.

It must not be supposed that the master came to the battle fully armed and with the first stroke of his blade created a whole new world of symphonic art. Such was by no means the case. He approached his goal gradually and with slow and sometimes painful steps. In his early Vienna days he had gone to Haydn and Albrechtsberger for grounding in counterpoint and composition. Since Haydn and he lived in different worlds socially, temperamentally and artistically, Beethoven got on badly with him and later was moved to say, "Though I had some instruction from Haydn, I never learned anything from him." Yet his early symphonies, particularly the first, bear the unmistakable impress of Haydn, as is invariably the case where the old, experienced teacher and the young, inexperienced pupil are concerned. Beethoven had not yet found himself, and it was only natural that he should speak with the accents of his musical forefather. Mozart also influenced him greatly and for a considerable time. But Bach was his great love and artistic nutriment.

Details in the First Symphony (C Major) which identify the work as belonging strictly to Beethoven are the suggestions of the coming scherzo which he introduced into the minuet and trio, the characteristic trick of stating the opening measures in a tonality different from that of the work as a whole, and a few isolated instances where he made free with sober formality. The finale is one of the most plunging and spirited movements of its kind. The Second Symphony, which came about two years later, presented difficulties of architectural form; it is said that Beethoven rewrote the work three times. As one of the lesser known of the nine, the symphony is a transitional work with many reminiscences of the past and an almost equal number of prefigurations of the future. Its opening movement has several glimmers of Beethovenian fire, the Larghetto is dreamily songlike and limpid in character, and the Scherzo dances with an explosive, energetic humour. Berlioz considered the Finale a second scherzo.

With the Third Symphony in E Flat, known as the "Eroica," we come to one of the supreme masterpieces of symphonic literature, and one of the most opulent flowerings of mature genius. We see Beethoven for the first time, so far as orchestral music is concerned, in the full stride of his artistic wisdom and vision, with fetters sundered and recollections of his progenitors reduced to a minimum. Begun in

1803, finished in 1804, and given first to the public in 1805, this "Eroica" Symphony was Beethoven's favorite and it has become one of the favorites of the world. On the score Beethoven inscribed these words: "Composed to celebrate the memory of a great man." And thereby hang a number of possible but by no means proven tales.

The one which has obtained the widest currency and which seems most likely to be true is that the work originally was dedicated to Napoleon Bonaparte, whom the composer admired mightily as a republican and an emancipator. When news reached him that Napoleon had proclaimed himself Emperor, Beethoven was completely disillusioned in his idol, and enraged. "Then he, too, is only an ordinary human being!" he cried (Beethoven seems to have anticipated Nietzsche's *Ubermensch*). "Now we shall see him trample on the rights of men to gratify his own ambitions; he will exalt himself above everyone and become a tyrant!" Thereupon he tore the title page containing the dedication from the manuscript.

Details that have stirred up most interest and controversy in this Third Symphony (after the Napoleonic tempest in a tea cup) are the moods of the movements and the origins of some of the themes. Poetically and emotionally, the work divides into two quite distinct sections which the scholiasts have been unable to reconcile to their laboriously and often painfully preconceived notions of the music's import. The first two movements—Adagio, Allegro vivace; and Adagio—fit nicely into the heroic scheme, the first being of a noble, titanic magnificence, and the second, a funeral march. But in the third movement, the great Ludwig leaves his literary detectives on a limb by introducing a scherzo which seems to be entirely irrelevant to an epic concept. The Finale, a series of skilfully built variations, is jubilant in its sense of robustness, power and well-being. What became of the hero? Surely he must have gone to his grave with the funeral march of the second movement! Then what are these gay celebrations that follow upon his demise? It is all a very confusing problem in musical dialectic and it has enlisted the services of many wise men—including one who suggested that the order of the movements be changed to suit the story!

Of the themes, the first subject of the first movement is identical with one in Mozart's youthful opera, "Bastien and Bastienne." In the Finale, the variations are built on a melody that must have had a peculiar significance and fascination for Beethoven. Some think that it was a symbol to him of true greatness, of creative power, and of his own personal triumph over the vagaries and pitfalls of artistic conception. At any rate he used the theme three times,—once in the Contradanse in E Flat, again in the ballet, "The Creations of Prometheus," and finally in glorified and sublimated form in the "Eroica" Symphony.

The Fourth Symphony in B Flat is another even-numbered opus of the nine which does not fall in the category of works popular with the public. It is a curious fact that every odd-numbered symphony Beethoven wrote finds a place in the haven of public affection, while the intervening ones rate only polite acceptance. Thus symphonies number 1, 3, 5, 7 and 9 are favorites with conductors and public, while those numbered 2, 4, 6 and 8 are much less frequently performed. Number 6 has had periods of prosperity in which it might fairly claim exception to this rule, but not for long. Number 8 undoubtedly is growing in favor.

The composer left no clue to his literary intentions, if any, in his Fourth Symphony, but, needless to say, the program-trackers have pursued their business as conscientiously as ever and we have no end of interpretations to choose from. No less a personage than Sir George Grove, compiler of the distinguished musical encyclopedia bearing his name, has unearthed a moving and very charming romance in connection with the work. Says Sir George in his monumental treatise, "Beethoven and His Nine Symphonies": "In May of the year in which Beethoven was occupied over this symphony he became engaged to the Countess Thérèse, sister of his intimate friend, Franz von Brunswick; and the three famous and incoherent love-letters which were found in his desk after his death, and have been supposed to be addressed to the Countess Giulietta Guicciardi, were really written to that lady (Countess Thérèse). . . . Though he had often been involved in love affairs, none of them had yet been permanent; certainly he had never before gone so far as an engagement; and when writing the Symphony his heart must have been swelling with his new happiness. It is, in fact, the paean which he sings over his first conquest." All this is to be found with particular obviousness in the lovely Adagio, the highest aesthetic point of the symphony, according to Sir George. Others, notably Vincent d'Indy, disagree with this exegesis. But they return to the same point, M. d'Indy insisting that Giulietta Guicciardi was the lady in the case rather than Thérèse. The Fourth Symphony, it may be assumed, would loom larger if its immediate predecessor and successor were not such pre-eminent masterstrokes.

Like the "Eroica," Beethoven's fifth essay in symphonic form has been deluged with the elucidations of eager interpreters. Most of the contentions have revolved around the idea of man in combat with Fate. And for once there is a measure of substantiation from the creator himself for the connotation. Regarding the peremptory motive of four notes announced fortissimo without a bar of introduction in the first movement, Beethoven said, "So fate knocks at the door!" The work as a whole has a sense of portentous

mystery, anticipation and struggle which amply bears
out the interpretation put upon it, and it grips the
listener with its dramatic intensity.

The striking brevity and economy of the opening
theme just mentioned (it contains but four notes, and
three of them identical!) bring to mind the extraordinary amount of labor and painstaking craftsmanship which Beethoven expended upon his composition.
Music did not burst in its final and full-fledged
splendor from his creative mind at first draft as it
seems to have done with some composers. He did not
write spontaneously. He worked long and arduously
over even the most insignificant details until he had
molded and refined them precisely to his liking. His
famous sketch books, which have been an invaluable
key to the evolution of many of his works, reveal
that he jotted down ideas, fragmentary melodies and
harmonies, and all manner of odds and ends as a store-
house of material to be used at some time or other in
actual composition. These ideas he kept and nur-
tured like hot-house plants, and constantly worked
at them, mulled them over, transplanted them, clipped
them here, supplemented them there, and put them
through a process of controlled analysis and conscious
development which is unexampled in the annals of
any other creative musician. Often as not, when they
finally emerged in a finished work, they bore hardly
more than a family resemblance to their humble progenitors of the sketch books.

Because of this method of working, Beethoven, while he may often seem to be repetitious, is almost never redundant. Every phrase is pared to the bone of absolute essentials. And this gives a compact force and directness to his discourse which puts to shame the circuitous ramblings of many a more glib composer. Nowhere is this severe economy more apparent than in the Fifth Symphony. Not only did he cause the entire first movement to grow out of the celebrated Fate motive, but, by altering the intervals slightly, he made it do for the elaborate Finale as well.

"Pastoral" is the title Beethoven himself gave to his Symphony No. 6. Set in the soft, genial key of F Major, the work is concerned entirely with camera flashes of the outer world. The subjective rumblings and heart-burnings of the revolutionary philosopher for once are stilled and the simple peasant sits down to recount his pleasant experiences in the country. The symphony was composed in a suburb of Vienna during 1807–08 and is of no great historical importance aside from the circumstance that it contains five sections instead of the usual four and that each bears a definite descriptive title. The first is "Cheerful impressions awakened by arrival in the country"; the second, "Scene by the brook," in which bird-calls are introduced; third, "Merry gathering of country folk," wherein the performance of a rustic band is definitely mimicked; fourth, "Thunderstorm:

tempest," and fifth, "Shepherd's song; glad and grateful feelings after the storm."

Though we are little accustomed to Beethoven in the rôle of landscape painter, we recognize in this symphony his natural affinity to the things of the earth and the people of homely simplicity. He does not idealize nature or its phenomena nor dress it in symbolic robes. Instead, he transcribes literally the mood, the atmosphere, and the various events in a realistic way in which they cannot fail of instant recognition. (A similar procedure is followed in one of his violin and piano sonatas, that in G Major, opus 96.)

Symphonies Number 7 in A and Number 8 in F appeared during the same twelvemonth, 1812, following an interval of four years during which there was no symphonic activity on the composer's part. The Eighth, one of the shortest of classical symphonies, is of ruddy good humor, engaging melody, some of it Viennese in suggestion, with one movement, the second, suggesting a satirical fling at the Italians.

The Seventh, however, is another of the apices upon which the full powers of Beethoven's genius converged with epic result. Perhaps the most popular of all the symphonies, this one must be regarded as among the fullest and richest expressions of Beethoven's artistic personality. Wagner, in his enthusiasm, saw in it the "apotheosis of the dance," but d'Indy, from his later vantage point, pronounced it another pastoral symphony. "The Symphony in A," says d'Indy, "is a pastoral symphony pure and simple. In the rhythm of the first movement there is certainly nothing dance-like" (wherewith he dismisses the Wagner theory), "it seems rather as if inspired by the song of a bird. The Trio in the Scherzo reproduces, it is said, the melody of a pilgrim's chant heard at Teplitz in 1812; and the Finale is a village festival aptly characterized."

There are other even more divergent notions as to what the literary kernel of this work may be. These need not detain us, for the symphony is eminently capable of standing upon its own merits as "pure music" and is sufficiently provocative to inspire each listener individually with his own imaginings. The famous Allegretto is fraught with a special dramatic intensity and melodic appeal.

Although Beethoven himself said that he had "sketches" for a tenth symphony, and there are those who believe they have discovered these sketches in his note books, the peroration of this grand symphonic cycle is the Ninth in D Minor, frequently called the "Choral Symphony." Beethoven had worked on this colossal score intermittently for several years. It was not finished until the end of 1823 or the beginning of 1824. It seemed to come as the consummation of a lifelong ambition to write a symphonic composition with a choral climax. In his youth, Schiller's "Ode to Joy" inspired him with the thought of some such undertaking but it was long in coming to pass. He carried the intention in his mind throughout life, and had a trial flight with it in his Fantasy for orchestra, piano and chorus in 1808. At long last, after the extended rumination which was his wont, he managed to bring the concept to full and glorious fruition in the symphony which came into being just three years before his death.

Schiller's Ode still held sway as his inspirational basis and the composer took verses from the poem to put into the mouths of the singers. Three purely instrumental movements designed on a scale of great size and magnificence precede the choral portion, with a connecting link of instrumental and vocal recitative and some enigmatic repetitions of phrases from the purely instrumental movements.

THE SYMPHONIES OF BRAHMS

IF as recently as, let us say, 1900, when Johannes Brahms had been dead for three years, the statement had been made that the four Brahms symphonies were in danger of being over-played, or that they stood next to Beethoven's nine in popularity, there would have been a raising of eyebrows. Tchaikovsky was then at his zenith; staid Boston Symphony audiences wept over the lamentations of the "Pathétique." The music of Brahms, the songs excepted, was exclusively for the "high-brows"; it was abstruse and difficult; there were those who understood and those who pretended to understand, as there were those who didn't understand and made no pretense at understanding— the last-named comforted and, in a sense, encouraged by otherwise discerning critics like the late Henry T. Finck, long of the New York *Evening Post;* and by a famous conductor, afterward something of a Brahms specialist, Felix Weingartner. Nothing could be more unfair to the Felix Weingartner of later days than to go on quoting the depreciation mixed with

the praise in his book of more than thirty years ago;
it is enough to recall the singular fact that for the
Weingartner of that day, already established as one
of the world's eminent interpreters of symphony and
as a leader of great orchestras, the music of Brahms
was "scientific music, composed of sonorous forms
and phrases" and "not the music of humanity, mysterious but still infinitely expressive and comprehensible"; it was "not the language which the great masters knew how to speak, and did; the language, in
fact, which moves and stirs us to the depths of our
being, because we recognize in it our own joys and
sorrows, our struggles and our victories." For this
representative musician of his age, "the music of our
great masters is artistic; that of Brahms is artificial"
—and more that would be beside the point if re-stated
here, since this same conductor long since made hand-
some amends to Brahms, not only by what he wrote
and said, but by the character of the performances
of Brahms's music given under his eloquent baton.

There is but one way to account for the frequent
performance of the Brahms symphonies today wher-
ever there is a first-rate orchestra and a public thoroughly conversant with symphonic music. These
symphonies, quite as much as Beethoven's nine and
the two that are about all the world hears of Schubert's equally extended series, are precisely that "music of humanity, mysterious but still infinitely expressive and comprehensible" that the worthy conductor

THE USES OF BATON—WALTER DAMROSCH CONDUCTING

said they were not. While the Tchaikovsky symphonies and the once universally popular "From the New World" of Dvorak were gradually sating the public that formerly adored them (which is not to be construed as a denial either of their inspiration or their splendid workmanship) the Brahms symphonies were building a more lasting affection, slowly but certainly. They did not build this affection as "scientific music"; they built it because of a human appeal that today may fairly challenge that of the Beethoven symphonies.

Today we recognize in any comparison of the symphonic masterpieces of Brahms and Beethoven fully as many points of difference and separation as of similarity and kinship. The old extravagance by which the Brahms first Symphony, that in C minor, was called "The Tenth," as if it were another product from the brain of the Beethoven of the Nine, means little or nothing now, according to how it is construed. In the interim between the Beethoven Ninth and the Brahms First had appeared Schubert's C Major Symphony, which may challenge in greatness any work of either master, in the opinion of many a lover of symphony. Nor are the Schubert "Unfinished" and the four symphonies of Schumann, all of which antedated the Brahms First, to be brushed aside, weightier though the Brahms First undoubtedly is. What symphony is greatest among the great is of small concern to us here; that issue may easily resolve itself into one of personal predilections and, beyond that, of a variety of hair-splitting that we will be wise to ignore entirely. What we do not want to ignore is the significant fact that these symphonies, once considered abstruse and difficult, are fast becoming the property of every individual who comprehends the symphonies of other composers, and, thus accepted, are taking their place among the most loved.

What has brought about this change of attitude on the part of those who listen primarily to enjoy? There is one very simple answer. The melodies that escaped the ears of multitudes of listeners when these symphonies were relatively young are now readily grasped and eagerly awaited. For those who know these symphonies even casually (in the sense that the knowledge which comes from hearing occasional or even frequent performances is a casual knowledge) the Brahms four are among the most melodious of symphonies. Indeed, the charge has been heard in certain quarters that Brahms permitted himself to be led astray by the German Lied; that because his symphonies are *too songful* they are not symphonies! To grasp the Brahms melodies is to open the door to other qualities of these symphonies, their harmonic richness, their rhythmic variety, their still somewhat peculiar instrumental coloring, and their structural strength and cohesiveness. But the grasp of the melody must come first.

The controversy that raged about the Brahms symphonies when they were new made much of his right to succeed to the mantle of Beethoven. In referring to the Brahms First Symphony as "The Tenth," thereby associating it with the Beethoven Nine, the conductor and piano virtuoso, Hans von Bülow, brought down on the head of the composer the wrath of many a worshiper of Beethoven. Today, the *mot* about "The Tenth" has no such particular concern for us, in spite of the somewhat obvious resemblance between the principal melody of the last movement of Beethoven's Ninth and the melody which occupies a similar position in the Brahms First. Brahms's right to stand with Beethoven as a symphonist is based on quite other considerations than a likeness of theme or of treatment here and there. It rests, rather, on the strength and the nobility that his music possesses in common with that of his titanic predecessor, and is confirmed in the differences quite as much as in the resemblances between the two giants. Brahms, as has been well observed, has a prevailing strain of lyricism in his symphonies and is seldom dramatic; whereas Beethoven is more often dramatic than lyric. Beethoven's emotion is the more volcanic, the more eruptive, the more violent; Brahms is the apostle of resignation, Beethoven of protest. Unquestionably there is more of flame in Beethoven. His workshop was a forge where refractory material was hammered into shape, often after many trials. Brahms, in his study, took a delight in surmounting technical difficulties, but without any such travail as there is reason to believe Beethoven went through in achieving his ends. The singing of Brahms betrays more of conscientious application than of struggle. Be that as it may, he *sings*—and it is because he sings so divinely well that the old charge of mere intellectualism has little life in it today.

Among the characteristics of the Brahms symphonies which distinguish them from their antecessors, is the use of motto themes which can be regarded as distant relatives of the *leit-motif* of the Wagner music-dramas. These motto themes are not always easy to find and identify; they serve a structural and unifying purpose, rather than a dramatic or programmatic one. The Brahms symphonies have no stories to tell, no programs to embody; there is nothing of Berlioz's "idée fixe" in these mottoes, so far as has ever been disclosed (see Berlioz: Program Music, page 194); the motto is less an idea than a building block; or better, a recurring thread in the fabric of the sound. In the later D Minor symphony of César Franck, full-fledged melodic ideas are transferred from one movement to another in the full light of day for a purpose of unifying the three movements —establishing what is called a community of theme. Brahms does not do this; his mottoes are more fragmentary and no such stress is placed upon them, no such salience given them. The listener need not consider himself a musical numskull if, after many hearings of the Brahms symphonies, and the cultivation of much love for them, he finds himself still unable to put his finger on one of these mottoes; though he may have come to notice—even without being able to name them—the frequent use of thirds and sixths, the syncopations and the cross-rhythms (it is the effects that matter, not the names of things) that contribute similarly to the music's essentially Brahmsian character.

Brahms was North German—Low German. His art bears the stamp of his native heath, softened a little, no doubt, by his later life in Austria and his vacations in Italy. The North German is a dweller under grayer skies and in a harsher climate than the South German or the Austrian. It is not strange if the music of the North German is graver, and hence "grayer" than that of his southerly neighbor. But it is not necessarily any the less tender because its hues are not the brighter ones of the South. In Brahms was a melancholy, dreamy quality that was a heritage of the North. This was not a quality to call for "brilliant" instrumentation. Today, there is reason to doubt that the quality of Brahms's orchestration, once widely attacked as "thick" and "muddy," could be altered without taking from the symphonies something essential to their musical personality and upsetting the consonance between subject matter and treatment that invariably is a badge of genius. The sure thing is that Brahms scored his symphonies as he

wanted them scored. He knew what he was aiming
at, and that was not brilliance or high color in the
sense of Wagner or Strauss; he was not striving for
their glowing tapestry, their purple patches of tone,
any more than for the 18th century directness and
transparency of Haydn or Mozart. He has been described as the last of the classical symphonists (a
designation that could be argued all around Robin
Hood's barn) but this can be construed as having
more to do with form than with instrumentation.

If there is a grayness in the Brahms scoring it is
not a dull gray, but one that is continually alight with
an inner glow as warming as it is pervasive. It may be
doubted, indeed, whether the old color analogy retains
its meaning for present-day audiences; whether
depths of brown are not more nearly the parallel for
this music than gray, in the thought of many who find
an autumnal richness in the Brahms scoring, rather
than any wintry severity. Examination of the scores
tends to dispute at once the aspersion of "thickness."
To the contrary, there is much open mesh in the orchestral writing of Brahms and, considering that this
is music from the land of Wagner and Strauss, the
design running through this mesh is in many instances
slight and subtle rather than ponderous and broad.
Blank bars and pauses are numerous; the huge upbuildings of compact, dense masses of tone that are
to be found among the masters of orchestration who
succeeded Brahms, will be sought in vain; the writing

is open and broadly spaced as compared to much of
Wagner; the so-called thickness resolves itself largely
into questions of instrumental coloring and the effect
of contrapuntal strands crossing and re-crossing each
other, as distinct from the erection of great chord
structures and the quest of blocklike edifices of tone.

But if density is not characteristic of Brahms's
scoring, it also is to be noted that he does not cater
to the solo propensities of individual instruments,
preferring to let them sing in sections or choirs.
Those who have devoted much study to the pecu-
liarities of his instrumentation have found that he
uses sparingly the upper registers of the violins,
though he does not abjure them to the extent that
they are abjured in the darker-hued symphonies of
Sibelius. The more sombre violas are prominent and
often divided in two parts. The basses are deep. The
scintillance of divided violins that is so characteristic
a detail with Strauss apparently has little appeal for
Brahms. He courts richness, but sobriety. The woodwinds, too, are singers. It is to them that Brahms
turns, over and again, in voicing the thirds and sixths
that have sometimes the suggestion of Italian opera,
but of Italian opera as passed through the alembic of
the piano music of Chopin and his heirs. There also
is much of wide-spacing among the woodwinds. They
play an important part in the tracing of those subtle
designs that often disclose themselves to the listener
only after many hearings of the symphonies. The

markings of the scores show how careful he was of his balances, as between groups of instruments. The care that he took to prevent that very muddiness of which he formerly was accused is obvious, page upon page, as woodwinds are marked louder or softer than the strings. The beautiful use that Brahms makes of horns and trombones, the while he displays a certain reticence in the employment of the trumpets, is indicative of his will to richness rather than brilliance. The special coloristic effects of a Rimsky-Korsakoff are not to be sought in this orchestration, though there are some instances—such as the woodwind coda of the first movement of the second symphony—in which Brahms is momentarily kaleidoscopic and enchantingly so.

If, in the larger aspects of form, Brahms was a classicist rather than an innovator, his symphonies disclose enlargements and extensions of the models on which he built. The development or middle sections of those movements which preserve the sonata form tend to brevity, whereas the recapitulations take on a fresh importance with something particularly lovely saved for the end of the movements. On occasion it may even seem that Brahms is a little too fond of pretty endings; that he labors a little obviously to bring about a tender and appealing close; but in the course of these perorations there are delightful surprises, momentary digressions and fresh starts that readily offset, by reason of their special piquancy, this sense of conscious seeking for effective final bars, whether in the melodic curve of phrase or the sweetness of the chords. The general pattern of the four Brahms symphonies places the architectural weight and also the emotional tension in the first and final movements. Those intervening are given over to brooding reverie, in some complex extension of the Germanic Lied, or to a brisk liberation of the playful spirit that was as deep-seated in Brahms as his melancholy; a liberation that could be graceful on one occasion, peasant-like on another, and more than a little daemonic on a third.

Brahms wrote his first symphony when he was forty, Beethoven when he was thirty. Mozart and Schubert died in their thirties, closing for them the book of the symphony with unguessed masterpieces still ahead for them if they had lived. Had Brahms been cut off as they were, before middle age, the four great symphonic masterpieces forever associated with his genius not only never would have been, but much that is characteristic of them would have remained lost to music. Of all symphonies these are among the most individual, the most burdened with personal utterance, the most distinctive in their workmanship. Music may have their equal; that is opinion. But it has not their like; if they were gone, nothing else would duplicate them. If they had never been, would the course of music have been changed? One wonders. Brahms has had many imitators, almost as many as Wagner. They do not count. But has Brahms had a successor, in the sense that Brahms may be regarded as the successor of Beethoven? Was he the last of a great chain; or an intermediate link such as Schubert or Schumann, or Mozart before them?

Brahms's symphony Number 1, in C Minor, opus 68 (1887) has been styled his "Pathetic" symphony. The first movement, particularly, is that of struggle. Over throbbing drums is built a gigantic opening, an exordium that seems to sweep the heights and sound the depths with a relentless momentum. Thereafter is travail, upheaval, a succession of crests that rise only to be broken, yet all moving forward with the force and weight of the inevitable, until finally, with a reminiscence, softer now, of the opening, the movement closes in a sort of triumphant glow.

The second movement, the first of those brooding reveries that are so notably characteristic of the symphonies (though preceded by similar movements in Brahms's music in other forms), retains in the relatively placid flow of its Andante sostenuto an undercurrent of agitation, along with its exaltation and its thoughtfulness. Great as is the contrast between this slow movement and the Allegro that preceded it, to attempt to exchange for it the slow movement of any other of the Brahms symphonies is to be made conscious at once of the unity that binds this one to its companion movements of the C Minor.

The third movement, a departure from the scherzo form of Beethoven, as the Beethoven scherzo was a departure from the minuet of Haydn, is an allegretto of vernal charm, a little wistful rather than sportive, though gay in its externals. When it was newly written, it seemed disproportionately slight, in view of the weight of the movements surrounding it. That no longer disturbs us. There is plenty of bigness in what is to follow. This allegretto is a moment of feminine charm before the listener is swept away again on great tides of combative masculinity.

The last movement is no mere echo of the first. It soars more and seethes less. After another momentous introduction, comes a horn call as from mountain tops. A chorale that sounds a note of profoundest faith is intoned by the trombones. A broad, exultant theme, often likened to that which sweeps through the Finale of Beethoven's ninth symphony, carries in its great impetus the swelling note of victory. Here is melody for any ear—melody that "crashes through the clouds into the still abode of stars."

As the first symphony has been called Brahms's "Pathetic," so the second has been termed his "Pastoral." Undoubtedly the feeling for Nature strongly permeates this symphony; perhaps it is to be felt in the others with almost equal force. This Symphony No. 2, in D Major, opus 73 (1878), following within a year of the first symphony that was many years in maturing, is largely free of the agitation of its predecessor. Three of its four movements are flooded with sunlight; one is nocturnal in its dreaming.

The first movement begins with a brave singing, and it sings throughout. There is a profusion of melody. For Brahms, steeped as he was in the German Lied, bridge passages that sang came as naturally as basic themes that sang. In his melodic utterance he is not far from the world of his universally loved "Cradle Song," but he uses his material as a symphonist, with colossal mastery and resource. The coda of this movement, introducing a sudden play of woodwinds only to be likened to some of the writing in Wagner's "Meistersinger" Overture, is one of the most magical any writer of symphonies has devised.

The Adagio which follows this opening Allegro is perhaps the most profound slow movement composed by Brahms. It is largely free of the unrest that lies below the surface of its companion movement of the first symphony, the while it ponders what lies beyond the province of words to say. What does such music mean? There can be no answer that would not give rise to endless contradiction. Brahms expresses himself with the fullness of his genius for all who will understand. Why try to translate his musical speech into more concrete ideas? If ever music transcended word symbols it is here, in this grave and poetic revelation of eternal things, sensed by all human kind, but felt rather than defined.

The third movement is as delicate and as feminine as its companion of the first symphony. An Allegretto grazioso, with the grace the designation implies, it is the most smiling of all the Brahms symphonic movements. The smile is that of the open air. There is a touch of the pastoral in the melody. It is something of a world youthful, fresh and green.

The closing Allegro con spirito, if it has no such weight as the Finale of the first symphony, is a movement of Brahmsian bigness. The melodies are bold ones, the rhythms are rugged. In the energy of the entire movement has been seen a determination to shake off the idyllic reverie of the movements preceding it. Throughout the symphony are sombre moments and something of quiet tragedy provides an undercurrent for its surface cheerfulness.

The Third symphony, F Major, opus 90 (1884) has been styled Brahms's "Eroica" in kinship to Beethoven's symphony of the same number but not the same key. In its conflict is a note of heroic resignation that is much more characteristic of Brahms than of Beethoven. The first Allegro con brio is one of the composer's most spirited and highly energized. There is a furious impact in the opening subject. Characteristic of this symphony is its breadth of theme, with working-out sections correspondingly brief. Much has been said of a motto theme that Brahms uses in this symphony and extensively elsewhere—the notes F-A-F to represent "Frei aber froh" ("free but glad" or "free but cheerful"), but the structural uses to which this is put will scarcely interest the layman bent primarily on grasping the melodic content and the drama of this symphony. Drama there is, most of it packed into the final movement. The second, Andante, and the third, Poco allegretto, are filled with brooding, with a touch of intimacy that relates them to the composer's chamber music style. In this music is much of personal revelation, much to bring the listener close to the heart of Nature. The Andante has a song character; the Allegretto, something of the nostalgia associated with the music of Mozart. The Finale towers above these middle movements and brings on the dramatic dénouement. It begins in passionate agitation; there are unruly outcries and a sense of open conflict, with reminders of the first movement, both in spirit and the musical material. There is an ebb and flow as of waters. The last pages bring tranquility.

If at one time there was a tendency to regard all of the Brahms symphonies as "cerebral," rather than emotional or lyrical, the world has largely outgrown this attitude, save perhaps in respect to the Fourth Symphony, opus 98, in E Minor (1886). This is perhaps the most introspective of the series and has been construed as a philosopher's commentary on the tragedy of waning life. The Fourth is filled with longing and is autumnal in its coloring. The opening Allegro non troppo, and indeed the entire symphony, borders upon song, but song that is spun into arabesques and traceries of Brahms's most subtle workmanship. The second movement, Andante moderato, has an archaic and ballad suggestion, with more than a touch of mystery in a mood prevailingly elegiac. Horns and clarinets play an important part in the creation of an aura as of veiled, half-forgotten lands. The third movement, Allegro giocoso, has a rough, almost forced joviality with something of daemonic excitement. But it is by the final movement, Allegro energico e passionato, that the symphony is most commonly identified. Though in Germany it is often referred to as the "Elegiac" symphony, the world at large knows it as "the symphony with the passacaglia." An eight-measure theme serves as the basis for one of Brahms's most towering sets of variations. There are thirty-two of these variations, capped with a coda, in a movement of great power, with the theme maintained as a basso ostinato* throughout. Heard at the outset over a heavy chord given out by wind instruments, this theme has a somewhat archaic stateliness and pomp. Out of it is created a succession of new musical incidents, in which the theme is sometimes so wrapped up in counter-melodies that only the most expert and patient of investigators can put his finger on it and analyze the scheme. The move-

* See page 330.

ment is closely related in spirit to the first and has a deeply serious, thoughtful character, remote from any mere exercise of mastery in the building of a complicated structure such as this passacaglia (some will say chaconne) represents.

AN INDEX OF FIFTY SYMPHONIES

J. C. BACH (1735-1782)

Symphony in B Flat

Composed 1770. Three movements: I, Allegro assai; II, Andante; III, Presto. A considerably Latinized German, Johann Christian Bach (son of Johann Sebastian) undoubtedly was best known during his lifetime as an opera writer. Since the symphony is at least partly an outgrowth of the opera overture, it is not surprising that this early example of Bach's is conceived in the form of the Italian Overture, that is: two lively movements and one grave movement between, to be played without pause. The opening Allegro foreshadows the later classic sonata-allegro form; the Andante suggests that suave grace of the coming Mozart; and the closing Rondo presages the busy chatter of Haydn.

JOSEF HAYDN (1732-1809)

Symphony in D Major ("With the Horn Call"), B. & H. No. 31

Composed 1765. Four movements: I, Allegro; II, Adagio; III, Menuet; IV, Finale—Molto moderato, Presto. The title "Horn Call" is apropos to this work

not only because it embodies the joy and spirit of
the chase, but because it is believed to be the first
instance in which the score of a symphony called for
so many as four horns. The final movement is in variation form, the strings announcing a quiet theme
which is elaborated and refashioned seven times by
other instrumental combinations.

Symphony in D Major (Salomon No. 7)

Composed 1795. Four movements: I, Adagio; Allegro; II, Andante; III, Menuetto; IV, Allegro spirit-
oso. Of the prodigious number of symphonies by
Haydn, this famous example, for want of better designation, is known as the seventh of the Salomon
series, written for the concerts presented in London by Johann Peter Salomon, enterprising violinist,
leader, and manager, the composer presiding at the
harpsichord. In Haydn's own words, however, the
symphony is "the twelfth which I have composed in
England." Beginning with a slow, stately introduction in the manner of the "French Overture," as was
Haydn's wont, the symphony proceeds with an abundance of characteristic and felicitous melody.

*Symphony in D Major (Salomon No. 11) "The
Clock"*

Composed 1794. Four movements: I, Adagio;
Presto; II, Andante; III, Minuet and Trio; IV, Finale
—Vivace. Another of the symphonies written for
the Salomon concerts in London. It has been dubbed
"The Clock Symphony" because the second movement, in rondo form, is conceived in a 2/4 rhythm
of mechanical regularity and insistency to suggest
the tick-tock of a time-piece. The first movement
is in dance rhythm resembling a tarantella.

WOLFGANG AMADEUS MOZART
(1756–1791)

Symphony in D Major ("Haffner") K. No. 385.

Composed 1782. Four movements: I, Allegro con spirito; II, Andante; III, Menuetto; IV, Finale: Presto. The composer was asked by his father to write music for some special occasion at the home of Sigmund Haffner, a wealthy merchant and the burgomaster of Salzburg, who was much interested in the young Mozart. He accomplished the task in about ten days. The symphony at first was a sort of serenade with a march introduction, two minuets, and no parts for flutes or clarinets. Mozart later eliminated the march and one minuet and added to the scoring.

Symphony No. 41, in C Major, ("Jupiter") (K. 551)

Composed 1788. Four movements: I, Allegro vivace; II, Andante cantabile; III, Menuetto; Allegretto; IV, Finale: Allegro Molto. The first movement makes use of an air Mozart had written for an operatic singer. To the godlike serenity of the Andante and the other-worldliness of the delicate minuet has been attributed the appellation of "Jupiter," though its origin is disputed. The Finale, constructed fugally on a four-note theme used elsewhere by Mozart, is one of the noblest examples of his polyphonic writing. Scored for the usual instruments of Mozart's time.

Symphony in G Minor (K. 550)

Composed 1788. Four movements: I, Allegro molto; II, Andante; III, Menuetto: Allegro; IV, Finale: Allegro assai. It is a curious fact that the three most enduring Mozart symphonies—the E Flat, the present G Minor, and the C Major (Jupiter)—were all written within a few weeks of each other, the first being dated June 26, the second July 25, and the third August 10. These were unhappy days for the composer, who was in dire straits, financially. Some of the troubled melancholy of this state of affairs is reflected in the G Minor Symphony.

Symphony in E Flat (K 543)

Composed 1788. Four movements: I, Adagio, Allegro; II, Andante; III, Menuetto and Trio; IV, Finale: Allegro. This is the first of the surpassing trilogy of symphonies which Mozart wrote in quick succession during the spring and summer of 1788. Though the composer was passing through some of the most trying episodes of his life at this time, the E Flat Symphony discloses none of his troubles, unless an occasional fleecy cloud in the Andante could be said to cast an introspective shadow.

LUDWIG BEETHOVEN (1770–1827)

Symphony No. 1 in C Major

Composed 1799 or 1800. Four movements: I, Adagio molto; Allegro con brio; II, Andante cantabile con moto; III, Menuetto: Allegro molto e vivace; Trio; IV, Finale: Adagio; Allegro molto e vivace. Although Beethoven adhered rather closely to the stylistic traditions of Mozart and Haydn in this first flight into the symphonic sphere, there is much that foretells the more personal works that were to come. The third movement is most prophetic of this change, for, while it follows the general structure and meter of the old Minuet with Trio, it over-steps the spirit, hurries the pace, unbuttons formality, and prophesies the metamorphosis of an antiquated dance form into the Beethovenian Scherzo.

Symphony No. 2 in D Major

Composed 1802. Four movements: I, Adagio molto; Allegro con brio; II, Larghetto; III, Scherzo; IV, Finale: Allegro molto. Here Beethoven reveals himself in the dual role of culminator of the classic era in composition and herald of the new introspective school. He has not yet shaken off the last fetter that binds him to the past, nor has he fallen into the stride of his ripe genius as proclaimed by his next symphony, the "Eroica." The Second Symphony is a transitional work. It is in every sense pure music of a kind to which "programs" are not easily attached. And it shows further development along lines deplored by critics of the First Symphony, particularly in the Scherzo with its full-blown humor and sportive gaiety. The Larghetto is of a song-like character, and Berlioz described the Finale as a second scherzo.

Symphony No. 3 in E Flat Major ("Eroica")

Composed 1803–04. Four movements: I, Allegro con brio; II, Funeral March: Adagio assai; III, Scherzo: Allegro Vivace; Trio; IV, Finale: Allegro molto. Out of the maze of romantic and literary interpretations that have been assigned to this work at various times, the fact emerges that the symphony is Beethoven's impression of the life and character of some heroic personage. The Eroica was the first symphonic work in which Beethoven broke with the past and trusted entirely to his own musical concepts.

Symphony No. 4 in B Flat Major

Composed 1806. Four movements: I, Adagio; Allegro vivace; II, Adagio; III, Allegro vivace; IV,

Finale: Allegro ma non troppo. Berlioz held the Adagio to be the craft of the Archangel Michael rather than mere man, so enamoring is its song.

Symphony No. 5 in C Minor

Composed (finished) 1808. Four movements: I, Allegro con brio; II, Andante con moto; III, Scherzo; IV, Finale. Perhaps no work in symphonic form has attained wider popularity than this epic utterance. Innumerable literary interpretations have been put upon it, but the most pertinent seems to be that the symphony somehow represents the struggle between man and Fate. The portentous, summoning motive of four notes (three of which are identical) opens the first movement and establishes the deeply philosophic character of Beethoven's thesis. Weighty thoughts preoccupy the composer until he reaches the Scherzo. There he relaxes in a sort of clumsy, gargantuan dance, which gives new importance to the double basses. The Finale, entered without pause, is a splendid and heroic affirmation of conquering power. It contains a brief return to the Scherzo.

Symphony No. 6 in F. Major ("Pastoral"), Op. 68.

Composed 1807–08. Five movements: I, Cheerful impressions awakened by arrival in the country; II, Scene by the brook; III, Merry gathering of country-folk; IV, Thunderstorm: tempest; V, Shepherds' Song; glad and grateful feelings after the storm. "Pastoral Symphony, or a recollection of a country life. More an expression of a feeling than a painting." —Thus the composer characterized the most unique and frankly programmatic of his works in symphonic form. It contains imitative bird calls.

[172]

Symphony No. 7 in A Major, Op. 92

Composed 1812. Four movements: I, Poco sostenuto; Vivace; II, Allegretto; III, Presto; Assai meno
presto; IV, Finale: Allegro con brio. One of the sublime peaks of Beethoven's orchestral genius. The
famed Allegretto, with its mystic and sombre individuality, has defied the classification of more than a
century of program-hunters.

Symphony No. 8 in F Major, Op. 93

Composed 1812. Four movements: I, Allegro vivace e con brio; II, Allegretto scherzando; III, Tempo
di menuetto; IV, Allegro vivace. One of the shortest
of classic symphonies. Its spirit is that of rough humor and high vitality.

Symphony No. 9 in D Minor (Choral), Op. 125

Composed 1824. Four movements: I, Allegro, ma
non troppo, un poco maestoso; II, Molto vivace;
Presto; III, Adagio molto e cantabile; IV, Presto, etc.
The last of the Beethoven symphonies. The final
movement includes a vocal setting for chorus, quartet and soloists of Schiller's "Ode to Joy." The second movement (unconventionally) is a scherzo, and
the third is a strange but strikingly beautiful combination of two entirely dissimilar themes, both slow,
one Adagio, the other Andante.

FRANZ SCHUBERT (1797-1828)

Symphony No. 7 in C Major

Composed 1828. Four movements: I, Andante—
Allegro ma non troppo; II, Andante con moto; III,

Scherzo; IV, Finale. Scored for the usual orchestra. Although generally known as No. 7, it also is listed as No. 10 and sometimes No. 8. This is the symphony "of the heavenly lengths," so-styled because of the "heavenly" qualities of its melodies and the generosity with which Schubert spun them out. A horn call, as from another sphere, evokes at the outset a train of visions, culminating in the cosmic churning of the Finale. Written shortly before the composer's death, it stands as one of the most melodious of all symphonies.

Symphony No. 8 in B Minor ("Unfinished")

Composed 1822. Two movements: I, Allegro; II, Andante. A popular misconception must be dispelled regarding this most lyric of symphonies: it was not left incomplete through the untimely death of the composer, as Schubert died some six years after he had ceased to work on it. There are in existence sketches for a third movement, a scherzo, of which only nine measures were orchestrated. The symphony lay unperformed until 1865, when it was given at a concert of the Gesellschaft der Musikfreunde in Vienna.

FELIX MENDELSSOHN (1809–1847)

Symphony in D Major, Op. 107 ("Reformation")

Composed 1830. Three movements: I, Andante; Allegro con fuoco; II, Allegro vivace; III, Andante; Andante con moto (Chorale: "Ein' feste Burg ist unser Gott"); Allegro vivace; Allegro maestoso. Noteworthy is the use in the first movement of the "Dresden Amen," which later was to become the Grail motive in Wagner's "Parsifal", and the incorporation of Luther's hymn, "A Mighty Fortress Is Our God," in the third movement, which can be regarded as a telescoping of two movements. Scored for the usual orchestra. Mendelssohn, born to the Jewish faith, became a Protestant Christian while a boy.

Symphony No. 5 in A Minor ("Scotch")

Composed 1842. Four movements: I, Andante con moto; Allegro un poco agitato; II, Vivace non troppo; III, Adagio; IV, Allegro vivacissimo; Allegro maestoso. Although Mendelssohn visited Scotland in 1829 it was not until thirteen years later that he found the time and inclination to set down his Scottish impressions in a symphony. The work is a series of moods and landscape pictures, and is properly played without pause between movements.

Symphony in A Major ("Italian"), Op. 90

Composed 1833. Four movements: I, Allegro vivace; II, Andante con moto; III, Con moto moderato; IV, Saltarello: Presto. Just as the Scotch Symphony is a synthesis of impressions gleaned by the composer during his visit to the British Isles, so this work represents salient memorabilia of his sojourn in Italy during 1830–31. The final Saltarello, an ancient Roman dance similar to the Tarantella, undoubtedly was inspired by the Roman Carnival which Mendelssohn attended and in which he took keen delight.

ROBERT SCHUMANN (1810–1856)

Symphony No. 1 in B Flat Major, Op. 38 ("Spring")

Composed 1841. Four movements: I, Andante un poco maestoso; Allegro molto vivace; II, Larghetto;

III, Scherzo: Molto vivace; Trio I: Molto piu vivace; Trio II; IV, Allegro animato e grazioso. This first step by Schumann was inspired by a poem of Adolph Böttger. The symphony has no program in the proper sense of the word, but in its suggestions of the coming of Spring and the flowering of Nature, it has come to be known as the Spring Symphony. Schumann himself at first considered giving literary titles to the movements suggestive of the season.

Symphony No. 3 in E Flat, Op. 97 ("Rhenish")

Composed 1850. Five movements: I, Lebhaft; II, Scherzo: Sehr mässig; III, Nicht schnell; IV, Feierlich; V, Lebhaft. The appellation, "Rhenish," as applied to this symphony, was authorized by Schumann, who said that the work was inspired by his first sight of the cathedral at Cologne and that he wished to impart some of the spiritual atmosphere of the Rhine. The installation ceremony for the Archbishop of Cologne was the specific incentive for the fourth movement, which the composer indicated to be played "in the character of an accompaniment to a solemn ceremony." The Scherzo movement has what is said to be an old German drinking song as its theme.

Symphony No. 4 in D Minor, Op. 120

Composed 1841. Four movements: I, Ziemlich langsam; Lebhaft; II, Romanze: Ziemlich langsam; III, Scherzo: Lebhaft; Trio; IV, Finale: Langsam; Lebhaft. Published as the Fourth, this symphony in reality is the second in order of composition. In the opinion of one noted commentator the work represents Schumann's nuptial hymn and takes on the character of a symphonic poem through its unity of thematic material and continuity of mood. The movements are intended to be played without pause.

HECTOR BERLIOZ (1803–1869)

Symphony, No. 1, in C Major, Op. 14a ("Fantastic")

Composed 1830. This symphony is the first part of a work entitled "Episode in the Life of an Artist," of which the second part is a lyric monodrama, "Lelio; or, The Return to Life." Its elaborate "program," portrayed in five sections, concerns a young musician who poisons himself with opium in a fit of amorous despair and subsequently dreams of his loved one, who appears to him as a melody. Part I depicts his passion; Part II is a brilliant fête at which the loved one is present; Part III is a scene in the fields; Part IV discloses that he has killed the woman and is on his way to the scaffold, and Part V shows him in the orgies of the Witches' Sabbath. It contains a motto device or theme styled the "Idée fixe." (See page 194.)

JOHANNES BRAHMS (1833–1897)

Symphony No. 1 in C Minor, Op. 68

Composed 1876. Four movements: I, Un poco sostenuto; Allegro; II, Andante sostenuto; III, Un poco allegretto e grazioso; IV, Adagio; Piu Andante; Allegro non troppo ma con brio. Sublime is the epithet most frequently heard when this first Brahms symphony is under discussion. The majesty of the opening movement, the meditative lyricism and emotion of the second, and the delicate beauties of the third stamp the symphony as a work of superlative genius. But the full revelation of Brahms's capacities is reserved for the resplendent finale.

[177]

Symphony No. 2 in D Major, Op. 73

Composed 1877. Four movements: I, Allegro non troppo; II, Adagio non troppo; III, Allegretto grazioso, quasi andantino; IV, Allegro con spirito. Vying with the C Minor for first place in order of popularity among the Brahms symphonies, this one in D Major possesses merits of equally high order, but it departs considerably in character from its predecessor. As Hanslick pointed out, it represents a return to "the earth that laughs and blossoms in the vernal months." Indeed, in Central Europe it frequently is styled Brahms's "Pastoral" Symphony. The slow movement, however, is as deeply meditative as anything Brahms or any other composer has conceived.

Symphony No. 3 in F Major, Op. 90

Composed 1883. Four movements: I, Allegro con brio; II, Andante; III, Poco allegretto; IV, Allegro. The least performed of the Brahms symphonies, the Third does not lend itself particularly well to descriptive classification, and there is much divergence of opinion as to the composer's intentions. Richter and Hanslick dubbed it a second "Eroica," Kalbeck thought the inspiration came from a statue of Germania near Rüdesheim on the Rhine, and Clara Schumann went so far as to make up a program for it as a "Forest Idyl." There is a sense of power and strength in the first and last movements; but nothing of war-like conflict enters in, nor is there any tragic dénouement.

Symphony No. 4 in E Minor, Op. 98

Composed 1884–85. Four movements: I, Allegro non troppo; II, Andante moderato; III, Allegro giocoso; IV, Allegro energico e passionato. The last work in symphonic form to be written by Brahms, this E Minor Symphony is more and more frequently heard with the passing of years. The melodious Andante with its lovely second subject for 'celli, contrasts strikingly with the brusquely humorous Scherzo (third movement) and the rugged Finale, which is a passacaglia consisting of thirty-two variations on an eight-measure subject. The mastery with which Brahms manipulates this theme and the truly majestic climax to which he brings it in the conclusion combine to make it a triumph of variation writing.

ANTONIN DVORAK (1841–1904)

Symphony No. 5, Op. 95 ("From the New World,")

Composed 1893. Four movements: I, Adagio; Allegro molto; II, Largo; III, Scherzo; IV, Finale: Allegro con fuoco. The Bohemian composer discloses in this symphony the impressions of America which he gathered during a short term of residence in the United States. His themes are not note for note transcriptions of Negro and Indian music, but represent rather a distillation of the inner mood and substance which stamps the material as characteristic. The second movement is probably the most widely popular of all symphonic excerpts.

PETER ILYICH TCHAIKOVSKY (1840–1893)

Symphony No. 4 in F Minor

Composed 1877–78. Four movements: I, Andante sostenuto; moderato con anima; II, Andantino; III,

[179]

Scherzo; IV, Allegro con fuoco. Like much of Tchaikovsky's music, this symphony is overcast with spiritual gloom and foreboding, and is a vehicle for very personal emotional expression. It is dedicated to the composer's wealthy patroness, Nadejda Filaretovna von Meck, to whom he penned a highly detailed analysis of its significance. The chief thought of the symphony, he explained, was the power of fate, announced in the opening theme, which hinders in the pursuit of happiness and to which one can only submit and vainly complain.

Symphony No. 5 in E Minor

Composed 1888. Four movements: I, Andante; Allegro con anima; II, Andante cantabile; III, Valse: Allegro moderato; IV, Finale: Andante maestoso; Allegro vivace. This symphony is one of the most popular works of its kind with the public, although Tchaikovsky was cool toward it and complained of a dearth of ideas during the writing of it. Perhaps the best known portion is the Andante cantabile with its poignant and dramatic melody voiced with moving effect by the horn.

Symphony No. 6 in B Minor, Op. 74 ("Pathetic")

Composed 1889. Four movements: I, Adagio; Allegro non troppo; II, Allegro con grazia; III, Allegro molto vivace; IV, Finale: Adagio lamentoso. Perhaps in anticipation of his own death, which was to come to pass shortly, or perhaps as a paean of universal dread concerning the mortality of all earthly things, Tchaikovsky gave to the world in this symphony a tonal depiction of anguish, fear, bitter-sweet nostalgia and longing not duplicated in the entire sphere of music.

ALEXANDER BORODIN (1833–1887)

Symphony No. 2 in B Minor, Op. 5

Composed 1877. Four movements: I, Allegro moderato; II, Molto vivo; III, Andante; IV, Allegro. Professor at the Russian Academy of Medicine and Surgery and busily engaged in lecture and laboratory work, Dr. Borodin could indulge his genius for musical composition only at intervals. He was six years finishing this Second Symphony, a work nationalistic in the Glinka tradition. In the words of his friend, Stasov, the composer "was haunted when he wrote this symphony by the picture of feudal Russia, and tried to paint it in this music."

ANTON BRUCKNER (1824–1896)

Symphony No. 5 in B Flat Major

Composed 1877. Four movements: I, Adagio; Allegro; II, Adagio; III, Scherzo: Molto vivace; Trio; Allegretto; IV, Adagio; Allegro. One of the most representative examples of exalted aspiration and individual style, this symphony exhibits an abundance of the contrapuntal dexterity for which the composer was noted, and demonstrates the community of themes device which later was used to such good effect by Franck and others. The instrumentation is conventional except in the Finale and the Coda where auxiliary woodwind, brass and percussion instruments are added.

GUSTAV MAHLER (1860–1911)

Symphony No. 2 in C Minor ("Resurrection")

Composed 1894. Five movements: I, Allegro maestoso. "With serious and solemn expression throughout"; II, Andante moderato. "Very leisurely"; III, "With quietly flowing movement"; IV, "Primal Light, very solemn but in a simple manner; like a choral"; V, Finale. Though Mahler decried programs for his music, this colossal work follows a definite literary outline concerning the death of a hero who has fallen in his pursuit of knowledge of life and death. The first movement, purely orchestral, represents lamentation and turmoil. The second is a dance intermezzo and the third, a scherzo, delineates the hero's disgust with the stupidity and vulgarity of the world, interpreted in terms of St. Anthony of Padua's sermon to the fishes. A contralto solo, "Primal Light," composes the fourth movement. In the Finale, orchestra, chorus and soloists join in proclaiming the Day of Resurrection. The text comprises excerpts from Klopstock's ode, "Resurrection," passages from "Des Knaben Wunderhorn," and original verses by the composer. The last three movements are given without pause.

CÉSAR FRANCK (1822–1890)

Symphony in D Minor

Composed 1888. Three movements: I, Lento; Allegro non troppo; II, Allegretto; III, Allegro non troppo. The greatest symphony to have been written in France (Franck was Belgian by birth) was not highly regarded by contemporaries. Only the passing of time impressed upon the world the beauties of the symphony's close-knit melodies, the skill of its construction (which follows the cyclic form, in carrying over thematic material from movement to movement, culminating in a grand fusion of all salient elements in the finale) and the religious nobility of its conception.

FRANZ SCHUBERT

VINCENT D'INDY (1851–1931)

Symphony, "Summer Day on the Mountain"

Published 1906. Three movements: I, Aurore:
Très modéré; II, Jour—(Après-midi, sous les Pins:
Très modéré; III, Soir: Très animé et joyeux). A definitely programmed work, this symphony was spoken
of by d'Indy as a series of "symphonic pictures." In
the score are printed selections from Roger de Pampe-
lonne's "Les Heures de la Montagne: (Poèmes en
Prose)" from which the music obviously derives its
inspiration. D'Indy was a true Pantheist in the
Beethoven manner, and in this earnestly contrived
delineation and glorification of his natural deity he
accomplished a pastoral masterpiece which probably
will stand as his greatest work. The first movement
depicts dawn in the mountains; the second, day and
afternoon under the pines, and the third, joyous,
mysterious night.

SIR EDWARD ELGAR (1857–1934)

Symphony No. 1, in A Flat, Op. 55

Composed 1908. Four movements: I, Andante
nobilmente e semplice; Allegro; II, Allegro molto;
III, Adagio; IV, Lento; Allegro. Matters of great
moment obviously were contemplated by Elgar in
this work, though no program was given to the world.
Some have seen in it the eternal struggle of man
against his omnipresent and unyielding environment.
Others tried to put upon it the more personal label
of an exposition of the life and death of General
Gordon, but this brought a quick denial. The symphony is generally regarded as one of the best examples of Elgar's work in serious and noble vein.

JEAN SIBELIUS (1865–   )

Symphony No. 1 in E Minor, Op. 39

Composed 1899. Four movements: I, Andante ma
non troppo; Allegro energico; II, Andante ma non
troppo lento; III, Allegro; IV, Finale (Quasi una
Fantasia): Andante; Allegro molto. The greatest
exponent of Finnish nationalism in music, Sibelius
stands out as one of the most independent composers
living today. His first symphony, with the turbu-
lence of its opening movement, the gentle pathos of
the second, the fantastic folk humor of the Scherzo,
and the tragic restlessness of the Finale, is prepara-
tory for bolder ventures to come.

Symphony No. 2 in D Major, Op. 43

Composed 1901–02. Four movements: I, Allegretto; II, Tempo andante ma rubato; III, Vivacissimo; Lento e suave; IV, Finale: Allegro moderato.
Sometimes known as Sibelius's "Pastoral" Symphony,
this work marks a departure from the first, a striking out upon new and original paths. According to
one authority the composer's intention was to depict
in the first movement the quiet, pastoral life of the
Finns undisturbed by oppression; the second reveals
mingled patriotic feeling and timidity of soul; the
third discloses the awakening of the national spirit;
the Finale symbolizes hope and comfort in the anticipated coming of a deliverer.

Symphony No. 4 in A Minor, Op. 63

Composed 1911. Four movements: I, Tempo molto
moderato quasi adagio; II, Allegro molto vivace; III,
Il tempo largo; IV, Allegro. Here Sibelius departed
from his naturalistic, patriotic thesis to write pure
music in the strictest sense, and to experiment along

personal lines of symphonic construction. Written with rigid economy and strict exclusion of literary allusions, the work is a compact exposition and development of musical ideas that bear the stamp of an original thinker in musical form.

Symphony No. 7, Op. 105

Published 1925. In one movement. Here Sibelius departed, not only from his own accustomed manner, but from the beaten track of the symphony as an art form, to deliver himself of a musical abstraction in one long movement with no indication of fundamental tonality nor description of inspirational intent other than joy in the manipulation of musical materials. A brass motive in fanfare style, introduced by solo trombone, dominates a work of much intricacy of design.

IGOR STRAVINSKY (1882–   )

Symphony of Psalms

Composed 1930. Three movements: I, Psalm XXXVIII (Verses 13 and 14); II, Psalm XXXIX (Verses 2, 3 and 4); III, Psalm CL (Entire). This work is a setting of verses chosen from three of the Psalms (in the Vulgate) for orchestra and chorus. Stravinsky has indicated that the movements are to be played without pause and that either children's or women's voices should compose the chorus, the former preferred. One of the most interesting physical characteristics of the work is its instrumentation. Violins and violas are dispensed with; the woodwind contains no clarinets, but five flutes, piccolo, four oboes, English horn, three bassoons, and a double-bassoon are called for. The symphony was written for the fiftieth anniversary of the Boston Symphony Orchestra and is dedicated to "The glory of God."

SERGEI RACHMANINOFF (1873–   )

Symphony No. 2 in E Minor, Op. 27

Composed 1906–07. Four movements: I, Largo; Allegro moderato; II, Allegro molto; III, Adagio; IV, Allegro vivace. Although he gratefully acknowledges assistance and advice from Tchaikovsky, Rachmaninoff disclaims any direct creative affinity with him. Certain Tchaikovskian implications, however, are to be found in this E Minor Symphony, with its darkling hues and sombre discourses, though there is no suggestion of the hysteria which beset the composer of the "Pathétique."

DMITRI SHOSTAKOVICH (1906–   )

Symphony, Op. 10

Composed 1925. Four movements: I, Allegretto; Allegro non troppo; II, Allegro; III, Lento; IV, Allegro molto. Shostakovich, one of the youngest of contemporary Russian composers, is also considered one of the most successful. He is in sympathy with the use of music for propaganda purposes. "I am a Soviet composer," he has said, "and I see our epoch as something heroic, spirited, and joyous."

VAUGHAN WILLIAMS (1872–   )

A London Symphony

Composed 1912–13. Four movements and epilogue: I, Lento; Allegro risoluto; II, Lento; III, Scherzo (Nocturne); Allegro vivace; IV, Andante con moto; Maestoso alla marcia; Epilogue: Andante sostenuto.

[186]

Although a vivid and detailed program was written in explanation of the symphony by one of its first conductors, Albert Coates, who found in the work a definite series of London mood-pictures, ranging from the Thames to the Strand and from Bloomsbury to the restless streets pounded by the feet of "Hunger Marchers," Mr. Vaughan Williams does not seem to share his literary conception. The latter has been quoted as saying that "The title might run 'A Symphony by a Londoner,' that is to say, various sights and sounds of London may have influenced the composer, but it would not be helpful to describe these." And again, ". . . if the hearers recognize a few suggestions of such things as the Westminster chimes, or the lavender cry, these must be treated as accidents and not essentials of the music."

PROGRAM–MUSIC

PROGRAM music requires of the listener less of any special musical preparation than a knowledge of the composer's intention in designing his music to present some literary idea, a narrative, a mood-picture, a bit of characterization or a definite emotional state associated with particular sights, sounds, thought or experiences. This does not mean, however, that program music of any high quality is lacking in musical interest if left unexplained as to this extra-musical content. It is primarily music and only incidentally what its program implies. Indeed, the test of the value of most program music may be said to be its power to establish itself as music entirely independent of the story or other non-musical message it seeks to convey.

For the listener, most music is, in a sense, program music, since it relates itself to life and the experiences or the emotional states of life; and, by prompting in the listener thoughts and images that are concerned with life, rather than with musical sound and musical

design, it creates momentary programs corresponding, if only for the one individual, to the avowed programs in the music known as program music. That
much music without an avowed program had, in the
mind of the composer, a background of thought or
experience which, if he had chosen to make it known,
would have constituted a program, is beyond question. This only tends to emphasize the more that what
is important is the music inspired by the program,
rather than the program itself. But since there is a
tendency on the part of many listeners to create for
themselves some sort of program for music that
comes to their ears without any explanation of the
composer's special purposes in fashioning it, the
avowed program may serve an important end in
placing composer and listener in agreement as to
these purposes.

If there are as many conceptions of the meaning of
a given piece of music as there are listeners, obviously
the composer's intentions are being misconstrued, and
if he has some particular set of circumstances or
mood-pictures to convey, he is not accomplishing his
purpose. If only the musical effect of the work is important, these widely diverging conceptions of what
the music means or represents can do him no harm.
But if the effectiveness of the music lies largely in
the association, a literary association or one in some
manner related to tangible human experience, his
failure to indicate the association may easily result in

other associations less fortunate for his music. It be-
hooves the listener, therefore, to know what there is
to know about music which has an avowed programmatic basis. Through program annotations or other
printed synopses of the composer's intentions, he is
placed in a position to sense and respond to these associations. Certainly, the listener who ignores the
explanation placed before him in the program books
of most symphony concerts is inviting the misunder-
standing that could be avoided with a very little effort on his part and, in doing this, risking the loss of
an added pleasure that is experienced by others, if not
by him. Among musicians, there will continue probably for all time difference of opinion as to whether
avowed programs ever are necessary for the best music. The belief is held by many purists that music of
the highest type speaks a language so entirely its own
that it needs no anchor in tangible considerations and
is only impeded by non-musical connotations. For
them, melodic and harmonic interest, the interest of
design and workmanship, determine entirely the effectiveness of a composition; and story-telling music,
consequently, is an inferior product. But there is no
escaping the ordinary lessons of human experience,
and one of these is that association does heighten
pleasure for multitudes of listeners. In its most elementary form, there has always been in music a sort
of imitation which even primitive people have found
a source of delight. This imitation may very well

have begun with the reproduction of the sounds in Nature to which music is most closely akin—sounds such as the calls of birds, the murmuring of brooks and the sighing of wind in the trees. Even in a highly developed state, similar imitation has found place in works by great masters of composition. It would be difficult to deny, because of its clear echo of the sounds of Nature, the place which Beethoven's "Pastoral" Symphony holds in the affections of those acquainted with the standard symphonic répertoire. For the listener not to recognize the scenes of the countryside which this symphony suggests is to lose something of the charm of the work. Yet, as program music, the "Pastoral" Symphony presents no such necessity of consulting an analysis as works by Liszt, Berlioz and Strauss, in which particular incidents are presented, sometimes in a manner of detailed description. Program music may be music that is continuously pictorial and anecdotal, like Richard Strauss's tone-poem, "Don Quixote," or it may be an atmospheric mood-picture with little more than the title to explain the contents, as Debussy's "Afternoon of a Faun." It may be the composer's emotional reaction to a literary passage, such as inspired Liszt's "Les Préludes." It may be filled with swirling, almost moving-picture action, like the same composer's "Mazeppa." It may serve as a prelude for a drama, by forecasting action or painting background, as do some of the overtures of Beethoven. But, in each instance, there is an association for the listener that goes beyond purely musical consideration and is largely the same for all listeners, because of the association having been pre-determined through the avowed program. Knowledge of the purposes of such works is to be looked upon as a cultural aspect for any listener. In most cases, the time and effort required of him to know what he needs to know are negligible; but to attempt to read program annotations while the music is being performed must remain one of the cardinal sins against the art. It is better to be completely ignorant of everything except the effect of the music as music, than to miss this effect for the sake of all the background that can be acquired.

As typical examples of program music may be named the following:

J. S. Bach—Capriccio on the Departure of a Loved Brother (for piano).
Beethoven—"Pastoral" Symphony, No. 6; "Leonore" Overture, No. 3.
Berlioz—"Fantastic" Symphony; "Harold in Italy" Symphony.
Schumann—"Rhenish" Symphony.
Liszt—Symphonic Poems, "Les Préludes," "Mazeppa"; "Dante" Symphony.
Wagner—A "Faust" Overture.
Borodin—"On the Steppes of Central Asia."
Moussorgsky—"Night on the Bald Mountain"; "Pictures from an Exposition."
Tchaikovsky—"Francesca da Rimini."
Rachmaninoff—"The Isle of the Dead."

Rimsky-Korsakoff—"Scheherezade."
Smetana—"My Fatherland," six symphonic poems.
Dvorák—"From the New World" Symphony.
Strauss—Tone-Poems, "Don Juan," "Macbeth," "Heldenleben," "Death and Transfiguration," "Also Sprach Zarathustra," "Till Eulenspiegel," "Don Quixote"; "Domestic" Symphony; "Alpine" Symphony.
Debussy—"Afternoon of a Faun"; "Iberia"; "La Mer."
D'Indy—"Istar" Variations; "Mountain" Symphony.
Sibelius—"Finlandia"; "En Saga"; "Tapiola"; "The Swan of Tuonela."
Mahler—"Resurrection" Symphony.
Dukas—"The Apprentice Sorcerer."
Ravel—"Mother Goose" Suite; "Daphnis and Chloë" (two suites): "La Valse."
Stravinsky—"The Fire Bird" and other ballet suites.
Honegger—"Pacific 231."

The list could be extended to many times this length. Contained, however, are examples of virtually every form of program music, from works that are so classified by reason *of their titles only* to those that have elaborate programs as detailed as a motion picture scenario.

Three examples will suffice to illustrate the manner in which the literary program has been used as the scaffolding for program music. The first is Berlioz's "Fantastic" Symphony; the second, Strauss's "Don Quixote"; the third, Debussy's "Afternoon of a Faun."

When Berlioz published the score of the "Fantastic" he prefaced it with an elaborate statement of its

[193]

expressional scheme. As translated by Harry Brett for the Breitkopf and Härtel edition of the full score, this reads as follows:

PROGRAMME

OF THE SYMPHONY

A young musician of unhealthily sensitive nature and endowed with vivid imagination has poisoned himself with opium in a paroxysm of lovesick despair. The narcotic dose he had taken was too weak to cause death, but it has thrown him into a long sleep accompanied by the most extraordinary visions. In this condition his sensations, his feelings, and his memories find utterance in his sick brain in the form of musical imagery. Even the Beloved One takes the form of a melody in his mind, like a fixed idea which is ever returning and which he hears everywhere. [This recurring melody, or *idée fixe*, which typifies the Beloved One, is first heard in the *Allegro*, in C major.]

FIRST MOVEMENT

DREAMS, PASSIONS

(*Largo*, C minor, 4–4; *Allegro agitato e appassionato assai*, C major, 4–4)

At first he thinks of the uneasy and nervous condition of his mind, of sombre longings, of depression and joyous elation without any recognizable cause, which he experienced before the Beloved One had appeared to him. Then he remembers the ardent love with which she suddenly inspired him; he thinks of his almost insane anxiety of mind, of his raging jealousy, of his reawakening love, of his religious consolation.

[194]

SECOND MOVEMENT

A BALL

(*Allegro non troppo*, A major, 3–8)

In a ballroom, amidst the confusion of a brilliant festival, he finds the Beloved One again.

THIRD MOVEMENT

SCENE IN THE FIELDS

(*Adagio*, F major, 6–8)

It is a summer evening. He is in the country, musing, when he hears two shepherd lads who play, in alternation, the *ranz des vaches* (the tune used by the Swiss shepherds to call their flocks). This pastoral duet, the quiet scene, the soft whisperings of the trees stirred by the zephyr-wind, some prospects of hope recently made known to him, all these sensations unite to impart a long-unknown repose to his heart and to lend a smiling color to his imagination. And then She appears once more. His heart stops beating, painful forebodings fill his soul. "Should she prove false to him!" One of the shepherds resumes the melody, but the other answers him no more. . . . Sunset . . . distant rolling of thunder . . . loneliness . . . silence. . . .

FOURTH MOVEMENT

MARCH TO THE SCAFFOLD

(*Allegretto non troppo*, G minor and B-flat major, 4–4)

He dreams that he has murdered his Beloved, that he has been condemned to death and is being led to execution. A march that is alternately sombre and wild, brilliant and solemn, accompanies the procession. . . . The tumultuous outbursts are followed without modulation by measured steps. At last the fixed idea returns, for a moment a last thought of love is revived—which is cut short by the death-blow.

WITCHES' SABBATH

(*Larghetto,* C major, 4–4; and *Allegro,* E-flat major,
C minor, and C major, 6–8)

He dreams that he is present at a witches' revel, surrounded by horrible spirits, amidst sorcerers and monsters
in many fearful forms, who have come together for his
funeral. Strange sounds, groans, shrill laughter, distant
yells, which other cries seem to answer. The Beloved Melody is heard again, but it has lost its shy and noble character; it has become a vulgar, trivial, grotesque dance
tune. She it is who comes to attend the witches' meeting.
Riotous howls and shouts greet her arrival. . . . She joins
the infernal orgy . . . bells toll for the dead . . . a
burlesque parody of the *Dies iræ* . . . the Witches' round
dance. . . . The dance and the *Dies iræ* are heard together.

Though Strauss did not similarly preface the orchestral score of his "Don Quixote" with a detailed
explanation, an arrangement for two pianos is even
more generously annotated. A solo 'cello represents
Don Quixote. Sancho Panza is first personified by the
bass clarinet and tenor tuba, afterward by a solo
viola. The work takes the form of an introduction,
theme, ten variations and finale. Each of the variations represents an adventure, and the entire work
may be indexed as follows:

Introduction—Don Quixote goes mad.
Theme—Don Quixote and Sancho Panza.
Variation I—The Adventure with the Windmills.
Variation II—The Battle with the Sheep.
Variation III—Colloquies of Knight and Squire.

Variation IV—The Adventure with the Pilgrims.
Variation V—The Knight's Vigil.
Variation VI—The False Dulcinea.
Variation VII—The Ride through the Air.
Variation VIII—The Voyage in the Enchanted Boat.
Variation IX—The Combat with the Two Magicians.
Variation X—The Defeat of Don Quixote.
Finale—Don Quixote's Death.

Each of these divisions has been subjected to much more detailed explanation. There is, for instance, the theme of the "Ideal Woman," heard in the introduction in the voice of the oboe, accompanied by harp and muted strings. In the fifth variation, descriptive of the knight's vigil beside his arms while Sancho Panza sleeps, a horn melody in the bass brings back this theme to represent the knight's dream of Dulcinea. In the next variation, the sixth, when the crack-brained gallant is deceived into thinking that a round-visaged and flat-nosed peasant girl is Dulcinea, transformed by some wicked enchanter, there is a parody on the "Ideal Woman" theme, played by oboes and tambourine. As another instance, the introduction presents some strangely unrelated chords that are associated with the idea of the knight's addled wits. At the end, when Don Quixote's reason is restored, these chords are heard again but have become orderly and coherent.

Debussy's "Afternoon of a Faun" is described as a Prelude to Mallarmé's poem of that title. A digest of that poem, prepared by Edmund Gosse, the English writer, is commonly accepted as presenting in words of understandable prose what Debussy has shadowed forth in his music, though no attempt should be made to find parallels for the verbal phrases or to discover specific incidents in the music. Mr. Gosse's digest, which is to be looked upon as a clue to the musical content rather than as a specific program for the prelude, follows:

"A faun—a simple, sensuous, passionate being—wakens in the forest at daybreak and tries to recall his experience of the previous afternoon. Was he the fortunate recipient of an actual visit from nymphs, white and golden goddesses, divinely tender and indulgent? Or is the memory he seems to retain nothing but the shadow of a vision, no more substantial than the 'arid rain' of notes from his own flute? He cannot tell. Yet surely there was, surely there is, an animal whiteness among the brown reeds of the lake that shines yonder. Were they, are they, swans? No! But Naiads plunging? Perhaps! Vaguer and vaguer grows the impression of this delicious experience. He would resign his woodland godship to retain it. A garden of lilies, golden-headed, white-stalked, behind the trellis of red roses? Ah! the effort is too great for his poor brain. Perhaps if he selects one lily from the garth of lilies, one benign and beneficent yielder of her cup to thirsty lips, the memory, the ever-receding memory, may be forced back. So when he has glutted upon a bunch of grapes,

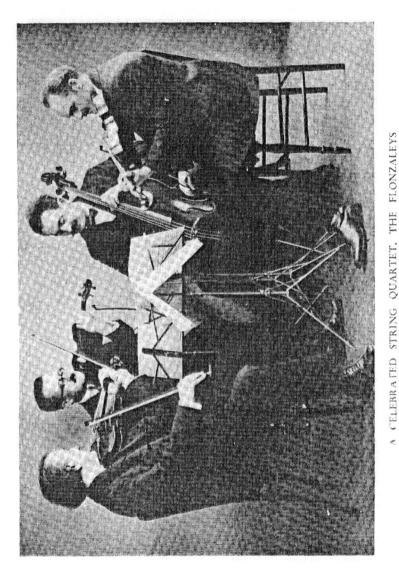

A CELEBRATED STRING QUARTET. THE FLONZALEYS

he is wont to toss the empty skins into the air and blow them out in a visionary greediness. But no, the delicious hour grows vaguer; experience or dream, he will never know which it was. The sun is warm, the grasses yielding; and he curls himself up again, after worshipping the efficacious star of wine, that he may pursue the dubious ecstasy into the more hopeful boscages of sleep."

It will be borne in mind, of course, that Debussy did not set Mr. Gosse's English digest of Mallarmé's French poem; nor did he set the poem, itself. But from that poem was derived the inspiration for the Prelude and it is impossible to hear Debussy's music without believing that he had in mind—if not the detail—the parallel for the atmosphere and the feeling of the poem; to a degree that a Prelude written only as music with no thought of a program would never have suggested, though from the same hand.

PIANO MUSIC

The piano probably owes its distinction as the most universally used of all musical instruments to the circumstance that, with the single exception of the organ, whose adaptability to music of varying character is more restricted, it alone of all instruments is complete in itself; that is to say, capable of presenting all parts of a complicated musical structure without the assistance of any other instrument. In this respect the piano and the organ are approached only by the violin in such special cases as some of Bach's unaccompanied works for that instrument. In its retention of the same kind of tone throughout its entire range, subject only to modifications incident to nuancing and the illusory differences in timbre suggested by difference of pitch, lies the advantage it possesses of being able to achieve a tonal unity and a homogeneity of musical effect not possible to any combination of solo instruments of what may be termed the single-line type.

This basic uniformity of color is both a strength and a limitation, but the highly developed art of

[200]

using the piano has converted its very limitations into assets. The most obvious of its limitations is, of course, its inability to approximate either the human voice or instruments of the string, the wood-wind or the brass families in the statement of a singing melody, but this is amply atoned for by the development of an accompanying succession of harmonic progressions that add color and a sense of completeness denied to the human voice and all other solo instruments. This is approached in a measure by the violin through feats of virtuosity, but in imitative fashion only. Its uniformity of color makes possible to the piano a unified tonal effect of distinctive value in contrapuntal music, in which two or more voices carry on independent melodic lines at the same time.

In supplying a melody in one part, with a complete accompaniment by means of purely pianistic devices of harmonic treatment, as in Chopin, the piano achieves much the same effect as the accompanied aria sung by the human voice, but with the greater advantage of an interdependence of melody and accompanying figures. The tone of the piano, it is true, begins to die out immediately after it is produced, but, although that may be a weakness in legato passages, the vanishing tone in itself provides opportunity for special effects of atmosphere and mood on the piano, difficult to duplicate in the same degree with the human voice or any other instrument.

[201]

The piano has the great advantage of having a far more extended compass than any other instrument or the human voice, and lends itself to the publishment of every kind of mood, lyrical or dramatic. It can be shimmeringly suggestive of reflections in the water or realistically descriptive of mechanical life. It is equally suitable for delicate polyphonic tracery and for massive edifices of harmonic chord formations. In fact, inasmuch as there is no restriction (excepting that imposed by the physical limitations of hands and fingers) to the number of notes that may be played at one time, it occupies a position altogether unique as a medium for harmonic richness and variety.

The first thing that the listener to piano music must realize is, that he is not to expect the kind of melodic singing possible to the voice or the violin, and this irrespective of the innovations of Chopin, innovations whose field of application must necessarily be limited. He also must be alert to distinguish between the different styles of music that he may hear, so as not to expect richly colorful harmonic music in works of the more chaste polyphonic style; or brilliant bravura effects in the half-mists and tremulous shadows of works of the Impressionistic school. And since the piano répertoire reaches back into the pre-piano period of the harpsichord it is important to understand the basic differences between the two types of instrument.

Early Keyboard Instruments

The keyboard instruments that followed the harp and the lute and were the immediate predecessors of the piano fall into two general classifications, the harpsichord and the clavichord, and their characteristic tonal possibilities naturally influenced or determined the kind of music written for them. These earlier instruments were much smaller than the piano, with much more limited sonority, range and color of tone. The action was fundamentally different in the harpsichord and the clavichord and that of the piano is different again.

In the harpsichord family, which included the spinet and the virginal, the tone was produced by a plucking of the strings. When the key was depressed it raised a little wooden "jack" with a quill claw on the end of it and this claw plucked the string, thus producing a tone that could not be sustained, so that a smooth, singing melodic line was out of the question. As a result, the composers for these instruments resorted to all kinds of embellishments in slower movements in order to cover up this deficiency and create the semblance of a sustained effect. Moreover, there was practically no possibility of varying the quantity of the tone by the touch, that being provided for in many of the harpsichords by means of two banks of keys, one bank producing a louder tone than the other.

In the clavichord, on the other hand, the tone, instead of being plucked, was produced by a pressing or gentle striking of the string by a metal tangent so delicately adjusted that by varying the pressure of the fingers on the keys the tone could be made to "breathe" or vibrate very sensitively, with varying degrees of tone, and could be sustained a certain length of time. The tone was very small but sweet, and Bach preferred this instrument to the harpsichord as being more intimate and more responsive and in that way more like the organ. Most of the other composers of his time, especially outside of Germany, wrote almost exclusively for the harpsichord, outstanding among them being Couperin in France and Scarlatti in Italy. The Italian Concerto is one of the more important works Bach wrote for the harpsichord. As this instrument does not admit of a sustained tone, it is essentially a medium for light, sparkling, running figures, such as dance movements, and we find composers of that day fond of writing suites of such movements.

In 1711 an Italian named Cristofori brought out the first piano, calling it a fortepiano or pianoforte because it could produce both loud and soft tones and shadings between. Instead of the string being plucked, as in the harpsichord, or pressed, as in the clavichord, it was struck by a hammer, following the principle involved in playing the dulcimer. While the first pianos sounded much more sonorous than the harpsichord or the clavichord, their tone was, of course, thin and shallow as compared with that of our instruments of today. For some reason they did not appeal strongly to composers at once and it was not until about 1770 that they began to take the place of the older instruments; and even then the harpsichord retained a lingering hold upon the affections of musicians for some time, so that we find compositions designated as for either harpsichord or pianoforte.

BACH, COUPERIN AND SCARLATTI

Up to the time of Johann Sebastian Bach, almost all music had been polyphonic, but gradually a sentiment had been growing in favor of getting away from the heavier and more churchly music of the renowned Buxtehude and the pre-Bachian organ composers in Germany and turning to the more light-hearted dance music of the folk. Bach, born in Germany in 1685, Scarlatti, born in Italy in the same year (some say 1683), and Couperin, born in France in 1668, form a sort of triple starting-point for the study of the modern piano repertory. Couperin wrote exclusively for the clavecin, the French harpsichord, his compositions consisting of many suites of short dance movements and also many short pieces that he called "Portraits," supposedly depicting various persons or types, mostly feminine, that he knew, while still other pieces were named for outdoor objects, such as windmills. His use of the dance rhythms of his time had a definite influence upon Bach, as shown by the latter's similar procedure in his various suites of dance forms; while his "Portraits" served as a new departure for composers and constituted the seed of the multifarious short forms to be developed later, such as the "Moment Musical," the nocturne, the "Song Without Words," the Chopin prelude, and so on. Couperin was court musician to Louis XIV and there is a certain inherent aristocratic refinement and elegance in his music. His pieces are for the most part miniatures of delicate charm, with an almost precieux tinge, and are bespangled with all kinds of embellishments, partly the result of the virtual impossibility of sustaining the tone of the instrument he wrote for, and in part a reflection of the highly ornate court life of his time. Someone has said that "in Chopin's music alone the spirits of music again whispered so softly together."

Domenico Scarlatti, son of a distinguished musician, was the most brilliant virtuoso of his time on the harpsichord, or the clavicembalo or gravicembalo, as it was called in Italy. As he extended his technical capacities as a performer he incorporated his new technical fluency in his compositions and in so doing definitely broke down the last barriers limiting harpsichord music to the more compact polyphonic style of the organ. Among the features that Scarlatti introduced were widely spread passages of arpeggio figures, the crossing of the hands, passages of double notes and rapid repetitions of the same note. He has been called the Liszt of his period and the father of modern piano playing. Like Couperin, he used dance forms for many of his hundreds of compositions, but many others are simply called sonatas, the term signifying for him a one-movement composition mainly concerned with one musical idea.

Whereas the music of Couperin and Scarlatti, being essentially harpsichord music, needs to be treated as such, hence, kept within a small framework of tone, when played on the modern piano, to avoid breaking the butterfly on the wheel, that of Bach, breathing for the most part his strong feeling for organ style, is enhanced when given the benefit of the greater sonorities of the modern instruments. The added problems involved for the player in transferring a contrapuntal composition from a two-manual (double keyboard) instrument for which it was intended to the single keyboard of the piano is illustrated by the "Goldberg Variations," which Bach wrote for a pupil of his as something with which to while away the sleepless hours of his ducal patron. The problem of preserving contrapuntal clarity is more complicated in using one keyboard.

With his special love for the clavichord, Bach wrote for that instrument the majority of his compositions that we now hear on the piano, notably the collection of Forty-eight Preludes and Fugues known as the Well-Tempered Clavichord; so-called because of the approximately equalized system of tuning keyboard instruments that he devised, which made it possible for the first time to play in all the twelve keys of the octave with equally satisfactory effect. In this collection, he goes the rounds of the twenty-four major and minor tonalities twice, each fugue being prefaced with a prelude in the same key, in some cases bearing a definite spiritual affinity to the fugue and so, in a sense, preparing for it, but in many others having no relationship except that of tonality. On the infrequent occasions when Bach wrote specifically for the harpsichord, as in the case of the Italian Concerto, a solo work despite its name, he adopted a less compact style than he used with the clavichord and composed in a more vivacious spirit. He became acquainted with the early piano but he was evidently not attracted to it, as he wrote nothing expressly for it.

Bach was not interested in creating new forms, but was content to take the forms he found at hand as vehicles for his musical ideas. So the fugue, a form in which one subject keeps recurring in different "voices," became at his hands one of the finest flowerings of polyphonic writing. He gave it a new vitality, and through his wealth of harmonic resources and his great sense of architectural symmetry he converted it into a plastic and richly expressive medium for the many shades of his all-embracing

[208]

range of lofty emotion. The emotion of Bach, it should be realized, is not the emotion we find later in Chopin's music, for instance. Bach's was what might be called universal emotion. Chopin's emotion, on the other hand, was intensely personal, introspective, and more readily communicable, perhaps because more recognizably human.

Bach perfected not only the fugue but also the suite. As first developed, the suite consisted of four dance forms, slow and fast alternating, the original skeleton being the moderately paced Allemande, the sprightly Courant, the slow and stately Sarabande and the vivacious Gigue. It became customary to introduce other dances also and even to begin the suite with an introductory movement such as a prelude. Bach brought the form to its highest estate in his French Suites, his so-called English Suites, and the Partitas, or German suites. It may be noted that he definitely regularized, if he did not actually introduce, the use of the thumb in the playing of the scales.

DEVELOPMENT OF THE SONATA

In the meantime the sonata had been taking shape in Italy, and as first cousin to the suite, rather than its direct offspring, as popularly believed, it was becoming a more and more crystallized form in Germany. It belongs to the domain of homophonic music, that is, music in which definite melodic lines, instead of being placed against other melodic lines as in polyphonic music, are provided with a background of harmony in the other parts. At first a one-movement piece, called a sonata because it "sounded" on an instrument, or group of instruments, instead of being sung, it was gradually extended to two and then three movements and ultimately attained four. Bach's son, Carl Philip Emanuel Bach, undertook to establish it as a form and did so much towards that end that he earned the title, Father of the Sonata. Although he prescribed three movements, of contrasting character, he did not alter the prevailing custom of treating of but one principal theme in the first movement. It remained for Josef Haydn (1732–1809) to introduce a second principal theme, and from that time on the first movement was to concern itself with two main ideas, or subjects, of somewhat contrasting character, and the first-movement form became crystallized as what is rather confusingly known as sonata form. Thanks to the way Haydn enlarged its possibilities, the sonata became the most popular form of piano music, and from then on composers for the keyboard instruments were to devote themselves almost exclusively to homophonic music, a culmination also hastened by the new interest they were beginning to take in the folksongs sung by the people.

The development of the sonata more or less paralleled that of the symphony, which was an outgrowth of the music assigned to the orchestra in operas, while from the symphony sprang the concerto, at first intended to be played by a small group of instruments (designated as the "concertino") alternating with a larger group, but soon molded into an extended composition for one solo instrument and orchestra. As such it steadily grew in popularity. It is, in reality, a sonata for the solo instrument and a group of other instruments; just as a symphony is a sonata for the orchestra proper.

MOZART

Haydn's young contemporary, Mozart (1756–1791) began in childhood to use the sonata for the expression of his fertile musical imagination. His genius revealed itself in his earliest years, so that by the time he was fifteen years old he had composed eighty works, including several symphonies. His was an inexhaustible fountain of melody and he let it bubble over in a great number of sonatas and concertos, as well as shorter pieces such as rondos and fantasies, the latter pieces of irregular form.

During his career the piano began definitely to supersede the harpsichord, and so we find some of his compositions designated for "harpsichord or piano." His sonatas are by no means of uniform merit. Many of them, like many of Haydn's, were undoubtedly written for the use of pupils, but they are all marked by melodic spontaneity. In one of the favorites, the one in A major ending with the thrice-familiar

[211]

"Turkish Rondo," he replaced the accepted first-movement form with a set of variations on a theme, an example followed by Beethoven later.

Like Haydn, he is quite emancipated from the contrapuntal style of Bach, which would have fettered his exuberantly lyric spirit. There is inimitable grace in the flow of his melodies, and in its profusion of ornament, trills and turns and filigree work generally, his music shows the unmistakable influence of the florid style of Italian opera music of the time. He wrote operatically for the piano. Though most of his mature years were overcast with sorrow, disappointment and financial distress, his piano music, with all its sincerity of feeling and, above all, its wistfulness in the slow movements, never took on the tragic import that was later to inform Beethoven's. It was prevailingly objective, whereas that of Beethoven, after he had really found himself, was prevailingly subjective. Mozart was absorbed in the musical idea of itself; to Beethoven the significance of a musical idea often lay in its being the embodiment of a poetic or philosophic concept.

BEETHOVEN

With the advent of Ludwig van Beethoven (1770–1827) a new element was infused into music. Like Bach, who took the existing form of the fugue and glorified it as a means of dignified emotional expression, he used the form he found in vogue, the sonata, and broadened its capacities as a vehicle for conveying profound human meaning in a manner never dreamt of by his predecessors. Mozart in using this form had been pre-occupied primarily with expressing beauty, while conforming to certain standards of design. Beethoven, the natural depth of whose nature was intensified by the great suffering that was his lot—the defect of hearing that was to be his crowning affliction beginning before he was thirty years old and becoming progressively worse until he was stone deaf—at first accepted the general principles laid down for the form but gradually expanded its architectural proportions, and at the same time made of it an infinitely more elastic medium than it had been. He introduced a sportive, often brusque movement that he called a Scherzo, with which he frequently replaced the Minuet (Haydn's innovation); and he kept adding new harmonic devices and progressions and exploring the fertile field of modulation, so that, while his keen sense of form almost invariably enabled him to preserve a perfect balance, he immeasurably enriched the possibilities not only of the sonata but of music generally. He was quick to appreciate the new range of opportunities offered by the pianoforte for greater sonority and variety of tonal effects, while the pedal alone opened up to him a new vista of expressive possibilities. Hence, with his impelling vision of greater harmonic richness and of structural expansion tempered by artistic symmetry, and with now a suitable instrument at hand with which to realize it, he gave ever fuller scope to his forceful and dramatic ideas and the consuming fervor of his creative spirit.

His earliest sonatas still show unmistakably the influence of Haydn and Mozart in a style that seems tenuous as compared with that of his later development, but his was a nature too ruggedly independent to be content with any degree of imitation of others whatsoever, and it was not long before he was interweaving a far larger and deeper emotional significance in his musical materials. Gradually he showed less and less hesitation in modifying the prescribed barriers of the sonata, as we see in the so-called "Moonlight" Sonata; and by the time he reaches his last four works his form has practically ceased to bear any semblance to the early sonata, so far afield have his poetic flights, his philosophic visions and his mysticism carried him, breaking down all formal obstacles to their adequate expression on the way. He retains a varying number of movements—his last, and in some respects greatest sonata, opus 111, has but two—but he has travelled far from the original principles in dealing with them, so much more involved has his musical thinking become.

It is customary to divide Beethoven's creative work approximately into three periods, according to which his second period in his piano work begins with the "Waldstein" Sonata, opus 53, and embraces the towering "Appassionata" Sonata, opus 57, a music-drama of intensified emotional conflict; while his third period covers the A Major Sonata, opus 101, and the remaining four highly sublimated works.

Beethoven also wrote five concertos for piano, of which the third, in C minor, opus 37, belongs to his first period, and the fourth, in G major, opus 58, and fifth in E flat, opus 73, commonly called the "Emperor," fall in his middle period. To his late middle period belongs also his "Les Adieux" Sonata, opus 81a, with its three movements specifically styled "les adieux, l'absence et le retour"; regarded by many as one of the finest examples of program music. Beethoven has been quoted as saying that he never worked without a picture in his mind, but, whatever he may have meant by a "picture," he always resented it violently if anyone else undertook to affix a pictorial title to his music.

THE ROMANTIC SCHOOL AND SCHUBERT

In adapting the form to his musical ideas and in giving expression so freely and powerfully to the inner emotions that swayed him, Beethoven unconsciously prepared the way for the Romantic movement in music, which paralleled the similar movement in literature at the beginning of the nineteenth century. He was the bridge between the Classic and Romantic Schools. The Classicists were concerned primarily with beauty of idea and design,

[215]

fitting their ideas to definite forms; the Romanticists were absorbed in their individual feelings and moods and to the extent that these came to govern and determine the form. The Classicists' appeal is primarily to our aesthetic sensibilities; the Romanticists stimulate our imagination and enlist our participation in their personal joys and sorrows. The former were more objective in their approach to music; the latter were intensely subjective. This differentiation may seem to ignore Bach, but his was the fundamental universal emotion of a great soul rather than the introspective dreamings and self-revelations of a man among men, and he was necessarily governed by his large sense of architectural unity. Beethoven was a being of heroic stature but struggling in the same way as the multitudes of little men among whom he moved.

The Romanticists often had little feeling for large architectural design and worked in comparatively small forms, such as songs without words, nocturnes, romances, impromptus, ballads, rhapsodies, and so on. Franz Schubert (1797–1828) is sometimes called "the little Beethoven" because of a spiritual kinship in the character of many of their musical ideas. His record of composing 1100 works, 650 of which were songs, in his short life of thirty-two years has never been equalled by another composer. His best work for the piano was in such small forms as the Impromptu and the "Moment Musical."

CHOPIN

The two greatest figures of the Romantic movement in piano literature following Beethoven were
Chopin and Schumann, men of essentially different
nature, pointing to different lines of evolution.
Frederic Chopin (1810–1849), a native of Poland,
who spent most of his life in Paris, was perhaps the
Arch-Romanticist. He was a man of passionate
patriotism, suffering deeply under the subjugation
of his countrymen, and it is in his work that we find
the dawn of nationalism in music. With a Slavic
strain of melancholy in his nature, he was hyper-
sensitive and almost savagely intense in his feelings,
and, above all, he was a poet, with a new vision of
poetic expression in music. No other composer has
ever communed quite so intimately with his instrument. He once wrote to a friend: "How often I tell
my piano all the things I long to say to you." It is
perhaps because of the new possibilities he revealed of
expressing and communicating through the piano the
most subtle shadings of intimate personal feeling
that he has been called "the pianist's composer." And
if at times his introspectiveness seems to be sicklied
o'er with the pale cast of morbidity there are many
other times when he is in an essentially healthy and
even virile mood. He was fundamentally much
healthier than many pianists would have us believe.

Chopin brought a new sensuousness and new possibilities of tone-color in infinitesimal shadings into

music by his lavish use of semitones, which gave rainbow tints to his profuse embellishments. His chromaticism, as the employment of semitones is called, provided him with an added plasticity in harmonic devices and a richer resourcefulness in modulation, as well as a new subtlety of the melodic line. As Mozart was influenced in his instrumental work by the ornate vocal style of Italian opera of his era, the music of Chopin became a sort of re-distillation of Italian opera as represented by Bellini, his contemporary for a time in Paris. The difference in his use of ornaments and that of his predecessors lies in the fact that with him ornamentation is never something extraneous to the melodic line but, rather, an essential and eloquent part of his poetic conception. He makes the piano sing as no one else has done, and his melodies insinuate themselves into the inner human consciousness so effectually that the sensitive listener often finds his own most intimate moods expressed. There is infallible grace and elegance in his style and the most subtle delicacy of nuance. And while there is a very fluid quality in his dreamier and more introspective moments there is a marked lilt in his mazurkas and waltzes and a strong, dominating compactness of rhythm in his polonaises. It is in the mazurka and the polonaise, both Polish dance forms, that his nationalism manifests itself most concretely.

As a gesture to the traditions of his predecessors, Chopin essayed a few works in the larger forms, among them two sonatas, so warmly Romantic in spirit as to obscure their free formal treatment, and also two concertos, which are handicapped by inept instrumentation of the orchestral parts, but which contain much beautiful music for the piano, especially in the case of the concerto in E minor. In the main, he confined himself to smaller forms, such as the nocturne, prelude, etude, and impromptu. The scherzo he expanded into a battle-ground for dramatic emotions. The ballade was his own design for a suitable canvas in the painting of romantic and emotional adventure. The tarantelle, the barcarolle, the berceuse, and the fantasie, were other Chopin forms.

LISZT

The iridescent, gossamer-like tracery that was characteristic of Chopin's melodic line, was to be greatly elaborated upon and externalized, and invested with vivid coloring and dramatic fire by the Hungarian, Franz Liszt (1811–1886). He had a marked poetic side, but he believed in making music an exciting physical experience. Inspired by Paganini's extraordinary feats on the violin, he developed and expanded the technic of piano playing beyond the wildest dreams of his predecessors and his rivals, who soon ceased to be his rivals, and he astounded the whole musical world with his colossal prowess. His success was sensational. He was the first to give a one-man piano recital, which took place in 1839.

He may be regarded as the first traveling virtuoso to achieve world fame as a pianist, as Paganini did as a violinist. Later in life he became a great teacher, the class of those grouped about him at his home in Weimar serving as the nursery for many of the outstanding pianists who followed him.

With his unprecedented and amazing technical equipment as an executant, it was but natural that in composing for his instrument Liszt should be tempted to write many things that are little more than virtuoso show-pieces. Much of his music falls into that category. He makes more exhaustive use of all the registers of the piano than had anyone before him and revels in elaborately wrought bravura cadenzas, long trills, far-flung arpeggios, rapid scale passages for both single and double notes, tremolos for broken octaves and glissandos not only for single fingers but in octaves and other double-note combinations as well, and demands not only temperamental dash and fire from the player but such orchestral effects of sonority and color from the instrument as result in great masses of tone. The listener's reaction to much of it necessarily is on the physical plane, but this style exerted a far-reaching influence upon subsequent writing for the piano in expanding its expressive powers for other music not necessarily or inherently of virtuoso character.

When Liszt gives his poetic side more scope, as in such things as the D flat Etude, the "Liebesträume" and the "Waldersrauschen," in which he employs his pyrotechnics with either an atmospheric or a dramatic effect, we see how much he owes to Chopin in lyrical expression and the creation of mood. His deeper and more reflective nature found its most eloquent utterance in his one serious essay in the sonata framework, his Sonata in B minor, a loose-jointed, one-movement work that resembles the sonata proper far less even than do Chopin's.

In Liszt's case, we find nationalism in his fifteen Hungarian rhapsodies and his Hungarian Fantasy for piano and orchestra, which are collections of idealized versions of folk-dances of his native Hungary grouped together with due contrast of character and used as pegs on which to hang all kinds of scintillating adornment and even tawdry trappings from the virtuoso's bag of tricks, always culminating in climaxes of imposing virtuoso brilliance. His two concertos, likewise essentially Hungarian in spirit, have more personal musical inspiration but are written in much the same style. Most of his concert etudes are little more than tours de force and belong to the same manner of writing. He was also fond of writing descriptive music and labelling it with concrete titles, as in his sets of pieces called "Years of Pilgrimage in Italy and Switzerland." He made effectively elaborate transcriptions for piano of many of Bach's organ preludes and fugues and some of Paganini's violin etudes and did similar service for many of the songs of Schubert and others. In his day a hybrid form of fantasia on the airs of operas had acquired something of a vogue, destined, however, to be short-lived; Liszt is credited with upwards of a hundred such fantasia. Only his legitimately conceived transcriptions of excerpts from Wagner's music dramas retain their vitality in this department of his activity.

SCHUMANN

While Chopin was introducing a new sensuousness into music, which Liszt was to carry to the point of a veritable apotheosis of the physical, Robert Schumann (1810–1856) was ushering in a more literary strain. An omnivorous reader from his early childhood, when he eagerly devoured all the poets and contemporary prose writers he could find on the shelves of his father's bookstore and became steeped in the spirit of the Romantic movement in letters, he carried over into his music the sublimated visualizations of his wide-reaching and richly stored imagination. As a boy, instead of drawing pictures of his schoolfellows with pencil and paper, he composed portraits of them in piano pieces of characteristic style, a conceit that he was to develop later as a definite artistic device, notably in his "Carnaval." His ambition to become a pianist being balked at an early point in his career through a disastrous attempt he made to force his progress by having the weak fourth finger of his right hand held up by an attachment from the ceiling while he was practising with the other fingers, he thenceforward confined his attention to composing and editing a magazine devoted to expounding the ideals of the new Romantic movement in music and to encouraging new talent.

Like Chopin, he was intensely poetic, but he was not tortured by patriotic suffering, and, while he was essentially human and had profound "Innigkeit," or "inwardness" of feeling, he was blessed with a healthier nature and was more intellectual, with a leaning towards the mystical. If Chopin's poetry was the poetry of emotion, Schumann's was rather the poetry of the intellect, of an imagination more literary, more romantic in the broad sense of the word. He had a fine melodic gift but it does not so generally stand on its own feet as does that of either Schubert or Chopin; more frequently than not it is linked with some literary suggestion. Unlike Chopin, he uses comparatively little elaborate figuration or passage work; he thinks chordally rather than horizontally. He employs little ornamentation. He is fond of syncopation, and he developed an individual way of placing the melody in the middle of the harmonic scheme and building up around it. He likes massive tonal effects, and his fondness for the damper pedal, which he liked to hold down while playing all the notes of the scale at once, is reflected in his writing.

With Bach as his idol and his model, he applied

himself diligently to the problems of counterpoint but he never acquired great facility in that branch of the composer's technic. Melody and harmony were the elements of paramount importance to him. He once said, "Music is like chess. Melody, the queen, has the greater power, but it is harmony, the king, that turns the scale." His sense of structure often was weak when he tried to hold a large form together. He succeeded when his ideas were so spontaneous as to carry him along and more or less automatically take formal shape, as in his G minor Sonata, but in other cases, such as the F sharp minor Sonata, there are many places where the carpenter work whereby he bridged his way over the chasms between his inspirational moments is all too obvious. Chopin, too, resorted to padding in places but less frequently than Schumann, and less clumsily, for Chopin was a more skilful craftsman. Schumann's beautiful Concerto in A minor for piano and orchestra, the only work he wrote in this form, is one of the more compactly written of his longer compositions, while the big Fantasy in C, although loosely knit, contains some of his loftiest and most inspired music.

From the standpoint of form he was really only thoroughly at home in the smaller framework of various designs, some of them, as the novelette and the intermezzo, of his own devising, and many of his more extended works, such as the "Carnaval," the "Kreisleriana," the "Davidsbündlertänze" and the

[224]

Humoreske, are merely collections of short pieces, the "Faschingsschwank aus Wien," too, being a "Vienna Carnival Scene" in five different aspects.

Schumann was the first to make a practice of using concrete titles. Beethoven, in addition to giving programmatic names to the movements of his "Les Adieux" Sonata, had affixed the title, "Rage over the Lost Penny," to a rondo and even Bach had written a highly descriptive "Caprice on the Departure of a Beloved Brother." But Schumann drew freely upon pictorial names for his shorter pieces, such as we find in the "Scenes from Childhood," the "Carnaval," the Fantasie Pieces, opus 12, the "Album for the Young" and the "Forest Scenes," though he insisted that his titles were always added after the pieces were composed.

In his Symphonic Etudes, a set of elaborate but vividly conceived variations on a theme of his own, we have perhaps his most consistently sustained high level of writing for the piano. The master composers developed two distinctive methods of treating the variation form. Composers of the Haydn-Mozart school regarded the melodic line of the theme as of prime importance and contented themselves with embroidering it in various elaborate ways. A more subtle approach was to concentrate upon the inner thought of the theme, and, incidentally, its harmonic essence, and to seek as varied ways as possible of expressing its inherent shades of meaning, more or less independently of the melodic contour of the tune proper. This plan offers a much wider scope for ingenuity and imagination and it was emphatically Schumann's guiding principle, eloquently exemplified in the Symphonic Etudes, as it was to be that of Brahms a little later.

BRAHMS

As Bach was Schumann's ideal, so Beethoven was the great inspiration of Johannes Brahms (1833–1897). And as the one trend of the Romantic movement, that of the sensuous appeal of music, unwittingly initiated by Chopin, reached its culmination in Liszt, so the divergent trend towards something approaching asceticism achieved its logical development in Brahms. Schumann, after examining the manuscripts brought to him by the twenty-year-old composer, enthusiastically pronounced Brahms the successor of Beethoven, and a strong personal friendship soon afterwards sprang up between the two men. It was to be cut short by Schumann's mental eclipse and early death but was to prove the starting point for a lifelong friendship between Brahms and Clara Schumann, Robert's wife, of indubitable artistic advantage to both.

Brahms was a man of great intellect and profound feeling, a classicist in his instinctive insistence upon purity of form and symmetry, a romanticist in the significance of his musical thought and its largeness of utterance, which demanded an individual approach. He was so uncompromisingly sincere in his idealistic attitude towards music that all external effect-seeking was repugnant to him. More rugged by nature and with a more brusque exterior than Schumann, yet just as capable of tenderness of feeling, which in his earlier years of composing he seemed to try deliberately to minimize, perhaps because in early manhood he was handicapped by an almost feminine delicacy of appearance completely at variance with his true nature, he has frequently been accused of being austere and even impersonal in his music. His piano works disclose a parallel evolution in his character and in his attitude towards the instrument. In his earlier compositions he thought orchestrally and they are for the most part more noteworthy for their spacious, heroic scale of conception than for qualities of winsome charm such as we find in the piano works of Schumann; but in his later compositions, when he came back to the piano after expressing himself through other mediums, he developed an intimacy of contact with the instrument and an approach as personal as Chopin's, though his individual vocabulary was not so readily understandable to others. Many of these later short pieces are of ineffable tenderness.

Brahms was not content with the merely harmonically accompanied melodic line. To him the combination of polyphonic writing, varied harmonic resources and new conceptions of rhythmic treatment offered vastly richer possibilities for investing a melody with significance. He early attained to a mastery of polyphonic writing, and as he had a keen architectural sense and the classicist's feeling for proportion as well as the romanticist's sensitiveness to harmonic coloring, he brought boldness and vigor to his piano canvases. In his earlier music he made the most taxing demands upon the player's hands with extended chord positions in building up towering edifices of sound, but in his later years he took cognizance of the limitations of the physical tools for playing. One of the devices he especially favored was that of placing the melody in a middle voice, as Schumann did, and, like Schumann again, he used very little or no passage work. He spaced his accompaniment figures widely and he was fond of drawing upon the high and low registers of the piano at the same time, leaving empty sound-hollows between. He indulged in unusual and unexpected rhythmic patterns, while his elasticity of metrical design, tempered, though it invariably was, by justness of balance, still disturbs the conventionally four-square mind.

Like Bach and Beethoven before him, he made use of the forms at hand without trying to devise new ones. His rhapsodies, it is true, as compared with Liszt's compositions similarly named, seem almost like a distinctive form, having a marked affiliation with the ballade family. Besides the rhapsodies he wrote three sonatas, two concertos, which unfold themselves unwillingly to any but the most persistently serious treasure-seekers; intermezzi, capriccios, variations, ballades, romances and waltzes. Two of his most noteworthy works for the piano are elaborate sets of variations, one on a theme by Handel, the other on a less consequential theme of Paganini's. The former contains the richer kernels of musical thought, while the Paganini set discloses an unprecedented resourcefulness in multifarious technical devices of colossal difficulty to the performer but embodying the concepts of an amazingly fertile musical imagination. The Paganini-Brahms Variations are generally conceded to be the most difficult work ever written for the piano. Brahms also arranged for two pianos his orchestral Variations on a Theme of Haydn.

Debussy

Towards the end of the nineteenth century the new French movements of Symbolism in poetry and Impressionism in painting found their counterpart in music with the advent of Claude Debussy (1862–1918). And just as the Romanticists had refused to be fettered by accepted formalism in expressing their own individual feelings, so Debussy and his followers turned away from the intense and over-emotional in music and, like their fellow Impressionists in painting, undertook to depict objects, scenes, incidents, not as these would appear to the photographic eye but as

[229]

they would be perceived through a mental screen of subjective reaction of the individual's senses, and subject to physical conditions of atmospheric haze. It might even be something ever so intangible or evanescent—Debussy used a Baudelaire quotation, "Les sons et les parfums tournent dans l'air du soir," as the title for one of his piano preludes. Acutely sensitive as he was to beauty in its most subtle manifestations, Debussy naturally reflected the spirit of the Symbolist poets with whom he associated, Mallarmé and Verlaine and their fellows; and just as that school of poets "suggested" certain sensations or thought-pictures by means of word sounds, so he "suggested" similar things with the tones of music. Perhaps the supreme example is the tone poem for orchestra, "L'après-midi d'un faune," in which his atmospheric and suggestive music reflects Mallarmé's symbolistic imagery.

Debussy, a spirit in revolt against all traditional restrictions, rules and regulations in creative work from the time of his early student days at the Paris Conservatoire, gave his conservative elders and colleagues shock after shock after his return from his sojourn in Rome, to which his winning of the coveted Prix de Rome had entitled him. The Romanticists' broodings of the spirit were not for him, but he avidly seized upon the sensuous beauty he found ready to hand in music and proceeded to expand its possibilities by developing a new technic in writing that was to open up unimagined vistas of seductive color and "atmosphere." The Impressionists in painting based their technic for reproducing their impressions of a scene or object as affected by light and atmospheric conditions on certain scientific laws concerning light rays.

Debussy achieved his effects of atmospherically blurred outlines in music by isolating overtones hitherto only sensed but never consciously employed and making positive use of them in note combinations, and so creating shimmering chords of unresolved dissonance, while other combinations, too, that had been considered so dissonant as to require prompt resolution had such a poignant beauty for him that he would place one after another of them in long rows without the slightest pretense of resolving them. He found that a plentiful use of the damper pedal also aids in producing the effect he so desired. Another device he liked to resort to was the use of the whole-tone scale, the scale consisting, for instance, of C, D, E, F sharp, G sharp and A sharp, as the harmonic basis for a piece, or part of a piece, instead of the conventional major or minor; for the mere fact of its having no semitones and, therefore, no leading-tone (the seventh degree of a major or minor scale *leading* by a half-step into the home tone, or tonic) deprives it of any sense of definite tonality, and that in itself makes for the floating, unanchored effect he loved in his harmonies. He may first have become interested in this scale on a trip to Russia as a youth, but in any case the exotic music he heard at the Paris Exposition in 1889 exerted a powerful influence upon him and undoubtedly stimulated his interest both in it and in the pentatonic, or five-tone, scale, such as is obtained by playing five black keys on the piano in succession, beginning with F sharp.

There are many instances of this use of the whole-tone scale and one prelude in the first book of Preludes, entitled "Voiles," is written entirely in this scale with the exception of a passage in the pentatonic scale. The latter is to be observed in "Reflets dans l'eau," "Pagodes" and "The Maid with the Flaxen Hair." In "Pagodes" the use of the pentatonic scale incidentally feeds his love for local color, evidenced elsewhere in such pieces as the "Soirée dans Grenade" and "La Puerta del Vino," with their Spanish habanera movement; the "Collines d'Anacapri," with its use of an Italian song tune; "Golliwog's Cakewalk" and "General Lavine," with their American cakewalk idiom, and "Minstrels," an "impression" of a music-hall turn in which even the Broadway of thirty years ago is conjured up with a snatch of an American popular song.

Debussy, probably under the influence of the Gregorian chant, as he heard it in Rome, explored the earlier phases of ecclesiastical music, making a note of some of the early church modes and even ninth century Organum, as a primitive polyphony in a succession of intervals of fourths and fifths was called. We find such early modes or scales as the Dorian and Phrygian in his works, while his use of Organum is one of the most effective elements in his "Submerged Cathedral."

One of the most-discussed influences upon Debussy was that exercised by Moussorgsky from the time Debussy read the score of "Boris Godounoff." The Russian composer's independence of convention and passion for freedom in style fanned the flame of the young French musician's liberty-loving ardor. For a time he was under Wagner's spell, but he early began to agitate against the Teutonic influence upon French music and to urge a return to a more Gallic simplicity of style and continence of expression, as found in Couperin and his colleagues of the clavecin period. From time to time he tried to recreate the style of that period, in such forms as the passepied, the sarabande, the minuet and even the sonata. This ideal naturally was conducive to cultivating a pronounced economy of means.

Debussy followed Liszt's example in that his harmonic figurations, unlike Chopin's, are rarely an integral part of the melodic line, and the technical influence of Liszt is especially apparent in such works as "Fireworks" and "Reflections in the Water," but his background of veil-like mistiness is the antipodes of the forthright brilliance of Liszt. Upon the new possibilities of color and sensuous subtlety that Chopin had brought into music with his chromaticism Debussy superimposed the blending of overtones that seems to lift music's feet definitely off the ground.

Debussy's piano compositions comprise two books of twelve preludes each, bearing such titles as "Delphic Dancers," "Wind across the Plain," "Puck's Dance," "Ondine" and "Fairies Are Exquisite Dancers"; the "Children's Corner," a set of six pieces, including "The Snow Is Dancing"; two arabesques, a ballade, etudes, "Goldfish," "Bells through the Leaves," "Gardens in the Rain" and "L'Île joyeuse."

Debussy's most outstanding follower, but one whose strong individuality early asserted itself, is Maurice Ravel, born in 1875 and still living. His technic has much in common with that of Debussy but his music is conceived on broader structural lines and is developed more in accordance with traditional principles. Like Debussy, he is fond of atmospheric effects, but he uses stronger lights and more definite outlines and his music is more scintillating, stemming more directly from Lisztian brilliance. His "Jeux d'Eau" ("The Fountain") is the most popular of his piano pieces.

A Russian to be radically influenced by Debussy was Alexander Scriabin (1871-1915), a composer of strongly individual potentialities, who had begun his career by writing in the Chopinesque manner but had early betrayed independent tendencies. When he became acquainted with French Impressionism he yielded so completely to its spell that he not only adopted its technic as it stood but went even further in exploiting the use of overtones that Debussy had initiated. He introduced a new basis of composing. Instead of following traditional lines in using fundamental chords consisting of intervals of thirds, as, for instance, C to E, E to G, and so on, Scriabin would take intervals of fourths and group them in a chord to serve as the harmonic basis of a composition. His so-called "mystic chord," as an example, is made up of C, F sharp, B flat, E, A and D, this combination providing him with the harmonic foundation for several of his compositions. Dissonance, indefinite tonality and rhythmic complexities characterize his more representative music. A theosophist and mystical visionary, he tried to make music the spokesman of his metaphysical and philosophical theories. He wrote prolifically for the piano and his evolution may be traced through his ten piano sonatas.

A fellow-student of Scriabin at the Moscow Conservatory, Sergei Rachmaninoff has chosen to pursue the path of more-or-less traditional Romanticism and to adhere to the orchestral style of writing for the piano developed by Liszt. While there are suggestions of the Chopin influence in the chromaticism of such pieces as the Prelude in E flat, his Lisztian ancestry is clearly revealed in the brilliant figurations of his compositions and his manner of exploiting the color possibilities of the piano; as well as in the melodic character of his earlier pieces. He has written many other preludes besides the one in C sharp minor that first brought him world fame, and numerous other short pieces, in addition to concertos, transcriptions and sets of variations.

Post-War Piano Music

After the Great War a reaction against Impressionism set in and since then the so-called ultra-modern school has shot off at various tangents. One of the outstanding developments has been the cultivation of polytonality, the writing of a composition in more than one key at the same time—in a piano piece, one key for the right hand part and an entirely different tonality for the left. A group of young composers in Paris once known as "the Six" but no longer in any way affiliated, and headed by Darius Milhaud and Arthur Honegger, first fostered it and the principle has since been employed by practically all modernistic composers from time to time. A set of "Saudades de Brazil" for piano by Milhaud, a collection of Brazilian dance forms, provides good illustrations of polytonality.

Of almost equal importance is atonality, the elimination of all key signatures and all definite tonality whatever, which is the special child of the Central European modernists, headed by Arnold Schönberg.

In his desire to rid music of all cluttering conventions, Schönberg, moreover, has reduced matters of form to the most fragmentary scraps of figures, carrying the housecleaning of non-essentials to extreme lengths. His few piano pieces remain all but undecipherable to the uninitiated.

With the doors opened to excessive dissonance by the admitting of polytonality and atonality into the modern scheme, and with modern composers indulging at the same time an atavistic desire to write contrapuntally rather than harmonically—in other words, to think their music in horizontal lines rather than vertically in its harmonic relationships—what is called a "new counterpoint," usually rather ineptly termed "linear counterpoint," has sprung into being, in which the most dissonant combinations are freely recognized, as against the restrictions of the counterpoint of the classical composers. And this, in its turn, naturally makes for greater simplicity of design in writing. The German, Paul Hindemith, has been regarded as especially adept in this art.

Many of the more recent compositions for the piano come under the heading of the rather vague term "neo-classicism," applied to a tendency becoming more and more apparent on the part of the extremists to revert to the classical masters' principles of form. The extremists adjust those principles to the development of brief, sententious ideas or rhythmic patterns. Melody in the generally understood sense of the term has been anathema to many of these moderns. Rhythm is of much greater importance to them. And for that reason jazz has had a very far-reaching effect upon them, although jazz-inspired pieces for the piano have proved to possess only ephemeral interest for the public.

In their drastic reaction against the soft edges of Impressionism and all idealism in music, and in their craving to represent uncompromisingly the harsh mechanistic realism of life as they see it, some modern composers have tried to eliminate the human element from music and to make it merely the reflection of the mechanistic age. And to this end the piano is treated primarily as a percussive instrument and its percussive properties are duly exploited to the utmost.

In the past the art of the pianist has been directed toward overcoming the instrument's natural shortcomings. Consequently, good piano playing has involved the ability to produce a warm, sensitive singing tone in melodic passages, the possession of technical fluency adequate to cope easily with whatever problems may present themselves, a dependable command of beauty of tone and skill in tone-coloring, a strong fundamental sense of rhythm, a firm grasp of structural design, close attention to the expressive molding and polishing of a phrase and, back of all these things, understanding of the composer played and the ideals and spirit of the school he represents; a keen feeling, therefore, for the essential style of the composition in hand, a widely sweeping imagination and—temperament.

VIOLIN MUSIC

EVEN more than with the piano, the story of violin music is the story of the great virtuosi of the instrument. Scarcely a program is to be heard today that does not bear the name, as the composer of a work to be performed, of at least one of a long line of famous executants of the past. And this aside from many transcriptions by violinists of music originally written for some other medium. The piano, it is true, has had its composers like Chopin and Liszt, —and, in our own time, Rachmaninoff—who have been as notable keyboard artists as they were creative musicians. Scarlatti and Couperin were noted players of the harpsichord. Bach, Mozart and Beethoven had one foot on sea and one on shore, if we can use the Shakespearean expression to denote performance and composition. But they wrote other music of importance besides piano music, whereas many of the names associated with violin composition have virtually no other currency today.

The greatest of violin concertos—those of Brahms

and Beethoven, to which might as well be added that of Mendelssohn—were composed, it is true, by men who were pianists rather than violinists; and no concert violinist of today can afford to ignore the violin compositions of Bach, who, as has been told so many times, preferred the viola to the violin, because he liked best to be "in the middle of things," but whose greatest ability as an executant undoubtedly was as an organist. Plenty of other violin music has been written by non-violinists. The fact remains, however, that to hear many violin recitals is to become acquainted with the names of many of the masters of the bow who in former times occupied the place of our reigning virtuosi. There may be more of sympathy and understanding, therefore, in listening to violin music if a backward glance is cast over two centuries of ascendency for masters of the violin.

Arcangelo Corelli (1653–1713) was the first of those whose compositions linger today on violin programs to recall prowess as a violin executant. Though it cannot be said that he invented the early violin sonata, to him was due its enduring line and character. His were the days of the Sonata da Camera and Sonata da Chiesa—the one of the room, the other of the church. They consisted of several more or less loosely connected movements, usually three or four, all in the same key. The chamber or room sonata was of a worldly character, made up of light dance tunes and sometimes of arias and tunes derived from popular songs. The church sonata made use of more serious movements, some of them of the fugal character of the vocal music of the church.

Corelli composed in terms of his instrument. In enlarging and individualizing the Sonata da Camera and the Sonata da Chiesa, as he had inherited them from his predecessors, he conceived melodies of an essentially instrumental character, whether in the rapid figurations of his fast movements, or the noble and dignified melodies of his slow ones. The typical Corelli sonata began with a Grave (prelude), followed by a livelier movement, a Corrente or Allegro, then an Adagio or other slow movement, such as a Largo or Sarabande; and, for a lively conclusion, an Allegro, Gavotte or Giga. His famous "La Folia," the Corelli work most frequently played today, was not in this form, however, but that of a theme and variations.

Johann Sebastian Bach was a contemporary of Corelli. So was George Frederick Handel. Handel's own violin music, we read, was too difficult for Corelli to play, because it was in an alien style. If this was true of Handel and the most eminent virtuoso of the age, one wonders who there was that could play the far more difficult violin music of Bach. Today, violinists toss off the Handel sonatas as a minor undertaking. They approach the unaccompanied partitas and suites of Bach (one of which contains the gigantic Chaconne) in the spirit of do or die. There can be no questioning the enormous development of violin technique since Bach's time. Paganini and his successors of the last century added immeasurably to the resources at the command of every first-rank violinist. Yet Bach wrote music that is still difficult to play cleanly and correctly. Various theories have been advanced, one being that the curved bow of Bach's time enabled the simultaneous sounding of notes on several strings in a manner not feasible with the modern bow. This additional facility in chord passages, supposed to have been true of playing with the old bow, was attended by a loss of volume, vitality and quality of tone. The theory is by no means universally held. The mystery remains as to whether at Cöthen, where Bach wrote much of this music, or at Leipsig, where his later years were spent, any fiddler was to be found who could make a presentable showing in the performance of his music.

Bach made use of Corelli's outline and filled it with a genius Corelli did not possess. From the organ and the clavier he borrowed contrapuntal upbuildings that become violinistic only by grace of extraordinary technique. His addiction to the fugue led him to change the instrument from one of a "single line" to a fair imitation of an instrument of several voices. In doing this, he made endless trouble for violinists of future generations, but he contributed to their répertoire what may well prove to be the most enduring music they possess. As Chopin sought, with partial success, to overcome the limitations of the piano, inherently an instrument better adapted to harmony and counterpoint than to song, so Bach strove with a proportionate success, to convert the singing supremacy of the violin into contrapuntal self-sufficiency.

Giuseppe Tartini (1692–1770) carried further the perfection of the old sonata as represented by the music of Corelli. In his music, the basic themes gained in breadth, there was more variety in passage work, modulations were more free. He worked chiefly in the form of the church sonata, though he could be worldly in the choice of his material. No consistent patron of violin recitals is likely to go long without hearing Tartini's so-called "Devil's Trill" sonata—the trill of which is supposed to have been heard in a dream, played by the devil himself. His violin art was more famous in his own day than his composition. Violinists still credit him with the basic principles of their bowing. He was one of the first to delve expertly into problems of intonation. Moreover, he was a teacher of other famous violinists, among them Nardini, whose D major sonata is still much cherished, and Leclair, a French master, who brought lightness and elegance to compositions that reflected his own racial traits. Tartini was the last of the violin masters to preserve the spirit of the church in the Sonata di Chiesa. Violin playing and violin music became increasingly secular, and this, with the rise of the German school of composition, which tended toward the symphony and reacted inevitably on Italy, paved the way for the concerto.

Today's concerto, as we know it, is often bloodbrother to the symphony, whether a concerto for the violin or "against the violin," as the Brahms violin concerto was deprecatingly styled. Giuseppe Torelli is called the inventor of the violin concerto, although today we would classify his form merely as an expansion of the old sonata. What he did was to increase the importance of what may as well be termed the accompaniment of the old sonata, which boasted no such equality of parts as the modern sonata but left the violin in an unmistakable solo rôle. Torelli made use of accompanying instruments, either more strings or a lute or an organ, to enrich these compositions; a step which Antonio Vivaldi (1680–1743) carried still further. With Bach and Handel among the many other composers who fell into line, there was evolved the type of composition known as the concerto grosso—chamber music rather than music for the solo violin—which went its separate way into a separate répertoire, along with orchestral suites and other ensemble compositions. Beethoven, Brahms and Mendelssohn each wrote one concerto for the violin. Vivaldi wrote a hundred and fifty. Like Corelli and Tartini, he was a virtuoso of the first rank in his day.

Ten years after the death of Vivaldi was born

[245]

Giovanni Battista Viotta (1753–1824), who was destined to become the greatest player of the end of the
eighteenth century and the first quarter of the nineteenth. In his day lived Haydn, Mozart and Beethoven, the last of these surviving him. Haydn had developed the sonata form and established the symphony
in such a way as to give a new meaning to both.
Viotta turned to these for the basis of a new violin
concerto and wrote twenty-nine works in a form
much the same as the concertos that are favorites
today. He was the first really to wed the violin to
the full orchestra as others were to do with the piano;
the violin part remaining, however, a solo part. Viotta's music has a Mozartean simplicity, if something
less than Mozart's genius.

Of those who walked in Viotta's footsteps, Rode,
Kreutzer and Spohr are only names to us now, great
as were their reputations, both as violinists and composers of music for violinists to play. Beethoven's
"Kreutzer" sonata immortalizes Rudolph Kreutzer
in a way none of his own concertos do, though there
is nothing to show that he ever played the work
Beethoven dedicated to him. Spohr is for our time
one of those great names that live only in books—
few except antiquarians know a phrase of the music
that once was described as "like an autograph in the
book of time, a thing of his inmost self for future
generations to contemplate with reverence." Nor is
the once notable Molique likely to confront the con-

cert patron of today. But the sonatas of Mozart and Beethoven, in which the violin and the piano are of equal importance, and the mighty D Major Concerto of the latter—which some have preferred to style "a tenth symphony with violin obbligato"—are part of the blood, bone and sinew of the world's musical life. The Mozart violin concertos—seven of them—figure less consistently than the sonatas; indeed, it is possible to attend concerts for years without hearing a one of them; yet in places they touch heights as sublime as any of the other music of this protean genius.

As Liszt was the supreme international virtuoso of the piano, in the modern sense, so Niccolo Paganini (1782–1840) was the unparalleled showman of the violin. In his day something of an apparition, and in some quarters believed to be linked with the devil, largely because of his cadaverous appearance and peculiar behavior (now known to be due to tuberculosis of the throat, which made it all but impossible for him to take proper nourishment or to speak above a whisper) he contributed more to violin technique than any other individual, before or since. As with Liszt, he had need of music that he alone could play. Only a small fraction of the music that Paganini wrote to exploit his own art has been passed on to the fiddlers of subsequent generations in published works. Their musical value in most cases is secondary to their technical display. Other composers, Liszt and Brahms

among them, have made use of Paganini's ideas for
music likely to be longer-lived than his own. Still,
there is a personality as well as a brave show of fireworks in some of the caprices and the two concertos
that sometimes find a place in the modern concert
répertoire; the latter, it must be admitted, very
rarely. As a composer, Paganini is at least no such
completely dead letter as Rode or Kreutzer; he has
survived better than Spohr, who at one time might
have been regarded as much the more "serious" writer
of the two.

Until Johannes Brahms shall come upon the scene
to give it new life, the violin sonata languishes. The
concerto reigns. Among those contributing to its
importance in the first part of the last century must
be named Heinrich Wilhelm Ernst (1814–1865), a
brilliant Moravian whose playing was admired in
many lands. His Concerto in F Sharp Minor was
once widely popular and is still played, perhaps because it is studded with difficulties that would have
been worthy of Paganini. That it has paled for the
public would seem to mean merely that its musical
material is not that of the first order, something that
has to be confessed of most of the compositions
which violinists have written for themselves and for
other violinists. For a time works of this type hold
on as showpieces. Eventually they wear out their
welcome because they have so little of consequence,
other than the swagger of their bravura, to com-

municate to a later day. So it is with the music of
Charles de Bériot (1802–1870), who wrote no less
than ten concertos; his star pupil, Henri Vieuxtemps
(1820–1881), and the brilliant Pole, Henri Wieniawski (1835–1880)—three of the most gifted violinists the world has produced. They are waning
figures now as composers of violin music, where once
they were universally played. De Bériot had a touch
of fantasy, Vieuxtemps a glitter and Wieniawski a fire
that for a time could be mistaken for something of
genius. Their music still makes a brilliant effect when
sensationally played, but this is the success of the performer rather than the music.

Between Beethoven and Brahms there was, in fact,
but one important composer for the violin, technical
progress aside, and that was Felix Mendelssohn (1809–
1847). His violin concerto is the most played of all,
partly because its melodies are of the most popular
appeal, partly because its difficulties, if by no means
inconsiderable, do not restrict it to a few supreme
masters of the bow. It is a work of much warmth
and tenderness and flawlessly written. In the ninety-
one years that have elapsed since it was composed, it
has not lost its freshness or its charm, in spite of un-
dergoing about everything in the way of performances, good, bad and indifferent, that any really popular composition may have to endure. Like every
modern concerto, it needs the orchestra if it is to
be heard in its most glamorous estate, yet it fares very

well in the concert hall with piano accompaniment.

Greatest of all violin concertos is that of Johannes Brahms (1833–1897) though there were many who would have debated that position at the time it was written (1879). More than the Beethoven or Mendelssohn concertos it is essentially an orchestral composition—a "symphony" in much the same sense as the four Brahms works that bear this designation; save that there is a solo violin part that has no parallel in any one of these other works. To understand the Brahms symphonies is to understand this concerto, and vice versa. The same lofty and tender melodies, long of phrase and contemplative in spirit, characterize the one, as the other. There is the same intricacy of structure, the same rhythmic variety, the same personal quality in the orchestral scoring. Long regarded as a difficult work to grasp, this concerto has attained a remarkable popularity in the last two decades and is now more frequently performed at orchestral concerts than the G minor concerto of Max Bruch, which once rivalled Mendelssohn's in popularity, or the Tchaikovsky concerto, which so famous a master as the late Leopold Auer at first considered unplayable, though he lived to teach it to one after another of his sensational pupils.

What the Brahms concerto is to violin and orchestra, the Brahms sonatas in G, A and D minor are for violin and piano—there has been no music to rival them as staples of the répertoire since Brahms's death, though the A Major Sonata of César Franck, contemporaneous with those of Brahms, has had a like appeal. Among the last compositions of Debussy was a violin and piano sonata that has yet to find its definite place, either among his successes or his failures. Ravel, Szymanowski and others of our own time have written characteristic pieces for the violin and Stravinsky has contributed a concerto that has had a considerable number of performances in spite of widespread critical denigration. The Elgar and Sibelius concertos give more promise of survival.

More and more, violinists have resorted to transcriptions of music not originally for violin in their effort to vary programs of which Bach, Mozart, Beethoven, Mendelssohn and Brahms are the pillars. A frequent concession to popular taste is Lalo's "Symphonie Espagñole," a work which might as well be called a concerto and which, like the Mendelssohn concerto, has borne up surprisingly well under the assaults of students and amateurs of all degrees of proficiency or the lack of it.

As the violin is essentially a melodic instrument—the colossal experiments of Bach notwithstanding—it is not surprising that the post-war era of modernity, scornful of the singing type of melody, should have produced little music of consequence for it. Latter-day violinists have been content to produce mostly small pieces in attempting composition. Fritz Kreisler's morceaux are the best known of these.

Whether they will retain their charm, with its pre-vailing echo of the old Vienna that passed with the World War, is for the future to say. Some of the Spanish lilts of Pablo de Sarasate (1844–1908), the Kreisler of his day, are still heard in the concert hall, but with decreasing frequency. The world has vir-tually forgotten the violin music of the great Josef Joachim (1831–1907), for whom Brahms wrote his violin concerto and who in turn prepared the cadenza commonly played in performances of that work; as it has forgotten the compositions of Ole Bull, Eduard Remenyi and August Wilhelmj. Here and there a transcription, like that by Wilhelmj of the "Prize Song" from Wagner's "Die Meistersinger," provides violin teachers with teaching material for their young hopefuls, who, in turn, sometimes carry this music over into the concert room, faded as it is.

To understand violin music is easier than to under-stand piano or organ music. It is the nearest to vocal music in singing quality, if, indeed, it does not, at times, surpass vocal music in pure song. Moreover, it possesses spectacular elements that exert a more exciting appeal, perhaps, than can be contrived in any other solo music, save possibly that of the human voice. But it has its share of nobility. What Bach contributed to it alone would give it place beside music in the other forms. The genius that has gone into it from such composers as Mozart, Beethoven, Mendelssohn and Brahms—with Bruch, Elgar, Sibelius and others to be considered in any final estimate of whether violin music is rich or poor—should be sufficient to retain the love and interest of layman and musician alike.

THE SONG

THE one serious barrier that exists for most listeners at a song recital, whatever their knowledge or lack of knowledge of music in other forms, is that of language. The art-song is a mating of poetry and music. There is more of intimate detail and less of broad lines in this relationship of text and notes than in the dramatic music of the theatre. Emotions are less generalized, less elemental; there is more of introspection, particularly in the German Lied, than ordinarily enters into the opera aria. The song that is only a swinging tune, like an Arditi waltz, is likely to have only a very brief day. Yesterday's operettas abounded in such tunes. They may come back pleasantly enough in revivals in the theatre but they rarely serve any purpose on the concert platform. To be the right setting for a poem worthy of the name, a song must be something that grows out of the words to an extent rare, indeed, with a four-square tune. Not to comprehend the words, or to comprehend them in only a generalized way, so as to miss delicate inflections and shadings wherein the music mirrors the text, is an unquestioned handicap to the fullest enjoyment of many art-songs.

But is it to be expected that every intelligent music patron will be a linguist to the extent that he can understand a half dozen languages: French, German, Italian, Czech, Russian, plus any one of three or four others that may figure on the song programs he hears? The fact that must be faced is that in America, at least, the number to whom the words of song programs in several foreign languages are comprehensible is relatively small. What, then, is to be done about it, other than to recommend additional language study? —a course not likely to be followed by more than a very small fraction of those who stand in need of it. The reading of translations is the most obvious of substitutes for first-hand knowledge of the original texts. Unfortunately, translations are not always to be had. With only a title as a guide, and that title perhaps only in the foreign original, the song listener would seem to be in danger of complete mystification as to what a German, a French, a Russian or a Norwegian song is about. The listener who knew German or French as a second language would be no better off than the one who knew only English or Italian when the song was one in Russian or Norwegian. And his neighbor, who might know all of these languages and Spanish besides, would be equally at sea if the singer resorted to Czech, Rumanian,

Hungarian, Polish or Greek. That the greatest need is for a knowledge of German, French and Italian does not change the circumstance that listeners who have some comprehension of these tongues are occasionally placed in the same position as are those who know only English, when songs in still other languages are presented.

But the case should not be viewed too darkly. If a multitude of listeners fail to get out of the songs they hear what a few get out of them, they still do not find this so serious a loss as to prevent keen enjoyment of a well-sung program in several foreign tongues. The problem is particularly an American and, it may be assumed, also an English one. The German is largely content with his own songs. The same is true of the Frenchman and the Italian. The American song still occupies a secondary place on our programs. The use of translations is less prevalent with us than in many of the countries of Europe. Many of our most popular recitalists are foreign artists who confine themselves largely to the music of their own lands. What they do exceedingly well in German, French or Italian they would do clumsily in any other tongue, even if there were a readier acceptance of translations than there is. The issue of whether imperfect translations are to be preferred to texts that are only vaguely understood need not be argued here, as the aesthetic considerations that would enter into any such discussion would lead us far afield. The simple fact is that the common practice is to present German, French, Italian and Spanish songs in the original, with more frequent exceptions made for songs in other foreign languages. That audiences not made up exclusively or even largely of linguists derive pleasure and satisfaction from recitals at which this practice prevails would seem to be proof enough that here is a case of half a loaf being better than none.

Such, indeed, is the power of the greater art-songs that, when well delivered, they establish their mood, irrespective of verbal and poetic details that may be missed by a majority of those listening. That these details play a subtle part in the mood building, even when there is little or no recognition of them for their own sake, is obvious and supplies one of the tests of the superior song. The mood established, with or without a full comprehension of the text, the listener may find in the music a beauty and an expressiveness—the expressiveness that admittedly is a little more generalized for one listener than for his linguist neighbor, but none the less valid—that he would not have felt of the same music if it had been treated as instrumental music, without the color and sound of words. The human voice has the power to suggest by its inflections and its emphasis the meanings of words not specifically understood. And the very closeness of the music to the words, when it has, in fact, grown out of them, tends to make comprehensible much in a setting of an alien text that would be meaningless if considered alone. The full loaf is still denied. But the half loaf, once the mood of a song has been established, is a treasure no listener need forego, particularly since he belongs to the majority; the majority that has only a smattering, at best, of the foreign languages figuring in song programs of the day.

The composer, the singer and the accompanist conspire to achieve this establishment of the mood. If the listener can consult a translation and in some degree familiarize himself with the nature of the text, even though none of the phrases of the translation remain with him (it may be preferable in some instances that they should not) he will be just that much more receptive, ordinarily; just that much readier to recognize and respond to the mood. He may not hear a German song as a German hears it, or a French song as a Frenchman hears it, but if the song means something to him, by reason of the mood and the music, he not only is experiencing something worth while for himself, but he is paying the greatest possible compliment to the composer and the interpreter.

As what is probably the oldest branch of musical art, and that which, by reason of its ties to language, has remained the most national, the song reflects its racial origins strongly. Composers who would suggest national or local color turn, ordinarily, either to the folk-song or the folk-dance. And since many songs were danced and many dances were sung, there can be no clear dividing line between the two phases of primitive music that never have lost their power to influence and sustain the art of composition. There are those who contend that all subsequent song has its roots in the folk-song, much as the art-song may have been influenced by other mediums of musical expression. The music of the early church resulted in the upbuilding of important musical forms, secular as well as liturgical. The lyric drama and the oratorio also played an important part in shaping containers into which song material could be poured. But that material, it may be argued, was drawn from a reservoir older than the memories of men. Every melodic phrase written down by an art-composer had figured in the songs of the people; songs that seem to have sprung from the soil. That today's folk-song was yesterday's art-song, as today's art-song may have been yesterday's folk-song, is at least arguable. We know melodies of fairly recent origin which had a definite authorship but in some way got adrift; the song was remembered, the composer forgotten. Some folk-songs are centuries older than others, irrespective of the countries in which they are to be found. That the younger ones should be classed as of anonymous rather than of folk origin is obvious in many cases. The French Revolution, which produced in Rouget de Lisle's "La Marseillaise" a song of known authorship, evolved other songs that might be said to have sprung of the people like folk-songs, yet doubtless were as much the conception of some one individual as was "La Marseillaise." Going back only a little earlier in French history, there is dispute as to whether Lully was the composer of "Au claire de la lune." Folklorists maintain with what would seem to be a preponderant show of proof that the melody is much older. But the troubadours and trouvères of France in many instances were composers in as true a sense as Lully. Here and there a troubadour song is attributed to some individual by name. How many other traditional melodies in France might have been legitimately his, or the creations of singing contemporaries who were composers like him, is pure conjecture. The lay that is supposed to have sprung from the soil may have cost some trouvère or minnesinger his hour of labor in some tapestried hall with the only soil in sight that which came in with him on his bardic boots. Or the very air that is attributed to a particular troubadour in a particular instance may have been as clearly an adaptation on his part of an older tune as the folklorists say "Au claire de la lune" was in the case of Lully.

Leaving to specialists all further inquiry into this complicated subject, the layman who finds the folk-song agreeable because of its easily-followed melody will soon discover that in many instances the art-song has much the same lyrical attraction for him, irrespective of his comprehension of its poetic content.

He is then on the high road to an understanding and love of still other art-songs in which the melody is less readily grasped, because less regular, but which, once it is recognized, asserts the same kind of lyric appeal. As an example of a song that is as tuneful and regular as any folk-song, let us cite the Brahms "Wiegenlied." Here is a melody quite as easily taken in as, let us say, the traditional Christmas song, "Silent Night, Holy Night," which may be regarded as a folk-tune; yet it is the conscious art-product of one of the world's greatest composers. From this Brahms cradle song to the same composer's "Sapphische Ode," with its regular, repetitious melody, is only a step. But once that step is taken, one Brahms song after another comes naturally within the understanding of the listener; provided, of course, he have those ordinary responses to mood which, experience shows, are not confined to linguists who understand the poems. Musically, some of the Brahms songs seem remote from the folk-like regularity of the "Wiegenlied" or the "Sapphische Ode," when a direct comparison is made. But the connecting links, as presented by other songs that partake, at one and the same time, of both those that are simple and those that are complex, are so numerous and so graduated in character that the listener who has come to know any of the Brahms songs is unlikely to find difficulty in accepting and comprehending them all, if he perseveres in his listening.

What has been said of Brahms may be regarded as true of all German Lieder, and, by extension, of all vocal music likely to be encountered in the recital room. That the Lied, as represented by such composers as Beethoven, Schubert, Schumann, Franz, Brahms, Wolf and Richard Strauss, should be the backbone of song programs in a country drawing its musical material from all lands is to be explained partly by the musical genius possessed by a handful of composers who would have been giants among their fellows if they had never written one song. Wolf and Franz may be considered exceptions in that their careers were chiefly as song writers. It is only necessary to consider the multitude of lesser composers who wrote Lieder quite as industriously, and to little purpose, to realize that the German and Austrian approach to the song was not what has made Lieder so important; but the genius that has been poured into it. In Italy and France more genius has gone into opera than into song. With Wagner and Weber exceptions among those who wrote for the voice, the heyday of German Lieder found more of genius expended upon the song than the theatre. Of later composers, Richard Strauss has attained a fairly equal eminence in song, opera and symphonic music, succeeding in what Schubert, Schumann and Beethoven attempted. Only Beethoven of these masters gained a foothold on the stage. Wolf's "Corregidor" is an opera that deserves to be better known; but even if it were accorded the occasional performances it deserves, instead of being something to consult in the library and the class-room, Wolf would remain as essentially a song composer as Verdi or Bizet remains an opera composer.

The Lied, as it figures on song programs today, may be said to have begun with Haydn and Mozart, neither of whom has any such importance as a song composer as he has as a symphonist or a writer of chamber music; nor yet, in Mozart's case, a composer of operas. (Haydn, too, was an opera composer, but under circumstances that limited his development in this direction. It is by no means certain that our later world does him full justice for the stage works he prepared as entertainment for the provincial court of the Esterhazys.) Mozart's independent vocal music, it is true, partook of the aria; but some of his opera airs, it is equally true, partook of the Lied. Haydn lent a ready ear to folk-song, not only in his vocal music but in his symphonies and his quartets. Neither composer had that absorption in words that was to come in the next stage of Germanic song, though they were aware of how Gluck had preached for opera his doctrine that, on the stage, music must be the handmaiden of the poem. The finest of Mozart's Lieder, "Das Veilchen," is an indication of what he might have accomplished if he had devoted himself more seriously to song composition. "An Chloe" is an example of the manner in which Mozart turned to Italian forms as readily as to German; like various Haydn songs, it is in the style of the canzonet. "Unglueckliche Liebe," "Abendempfindung," "Trennung und Wiedervereinigung," "Zu meiner Zeit," and "Komm' lieber Mai" are other Mozart songs occasionally encountered on recital programs, but the listener is much more apt to be confronted with airs from the Mozart operas. These, certainly, are more representative of Mozart's genius and stand alone beautifully as art works of the highest finish. Two of Haydn's settings of English words, "She never told her love" and "My mother bids me bind my hair" are as representative as any.

Beethoven's earnestness is to be found quite as much in his vocal music as in his orchestra, chamber or piano compositions. He did not set trivial texts as Haydn and Mozart did. His most indifferent music was that which he wrote for social purposes, as Mozart did before him and Schubert in his time—music for the ballroom that could have little or no serious art purpose. His choral works aside, Beethoven composed for the voice sparingly. It can still be argued that he did not understand the voice, on the basis of what can be termed instrumental writing for the singers in his masses, parts of his opera, "Fidelio," the "Choral Fantasia" and the vocal parts of the Ninth Symphony. This, his songs tend to disprove, as does the independent Scena and Aria for Soprano, "Ah perfido," which many still mistakenly regard as an excerpt from "Fidelio." Beethoven was sometimes scornful of the traditional limitations of his orchestral instruments—he made the double basses cavort in a way that scandalized some musicians of his day—and he showed a similar disdain for what was "easy" or "comfortable" for singers, when to consider his vocalists would have been to hamper his inspiration. Time has proved that he wrote nothing that could not be sung. He merely compelled singers to be better musicians and better executants, as he compelled double-bass players to be. Songs such as "Adelaide" and "Ich liebe dich" are conventional enough; "An die Hoffnung" is no out-of-the-ordinary task. There is, indeed, almost every kind of voice-writing to be found in Beethoven's music, from that of the Italians who preceded Mozart to prefigurations of Wagner and Brahms. In the spirit of his vocal music, he anticipated the romanticism of Weber and Schumann, the while he preserved something of the classicism of Gluck and the Gothic spirit of Bach.

Beethoven's greatest single contribution to the development of the Lied is to be found in his song cycle, "An die ferne Geliebte." Of the Lieder composers who were to follow, Schubert and Schumann were to make much of the song cycle. At a much later time, Mahler was to give to it the dimensions of a symphonic composition for voice and orchestra. "An die ferne Geliebte," the setting of verses by an obscure young medical man, Al. Jeitteles, is notable

[265]

for the manner in which the songs follow one another, so bound together by the accompaniment that the piano part plays almost as important a rôle as the voice in the building of the poetic mood. If Beethoven was not the first to write the "composed-through" song, with each verse or stanza given its own music—as distinct from the strophic song in which an identical melody sufficed for successive stanzas—he did much to bring this conception to the ascendency it since has held. In "An die ferne Geliebte" he went much further and gave the world its first *composed-through cycle* of songs, each having a life of its own, but being part of a larger entity that embraced all.

The ill-fated Franz Schubert, whose career as a composer covered only about half as many years as that of Beethoven, wrote more than 600 songs, including more recognized masterpieces than can be credited to any other song composer, Brahms and Wolf not excepted. With Schubert, there was a new balance between melodic form and emotional meaning. Every phrase he wrote was singable, every song lyrical; yet not only were the poems of more importance to the success of the songs than with any previous Lieder composer, but the piano part continuously rivalled the voice as a means of mirroring and communicating the texts. A new feeling was given to vocal music by the restless changes of key into which the accompaniments led the voice. Schubert, for his day, and indeed for all time, was a master of modulation. He gave the Lied a new freedom, a new elasticity of form. Yet none of this was at the expense of melody. The Schubert songs, widely varied in character as they are, are as recognizably melodious as any corresponding number of opera airs. The folk quality abides in them, though Schubert cut his way free from the monotonous repetition of folk-forms. If Hugo Wolf was to go further in so shaping his melodies as to give the texts a maximum of expressiveness, he had ample precedent for each of his innovations or departures in Schubert's free modelling, whereby it was the poetic content that determined the shape of the musical container.

Of Schubert's 600 songs, as many as 150 were written in a single year; once, we are told, he composed eight in a day. If he was not always discriminating in the choice of his texts—some eighty-five poets being included among those whose verses he used—he was aware of the special virtues of Goethe and Schiller; more than seventy of his lyrics came from the one, between forty and fifty from the other. To choose between the Schubert songs, in any attempt to single out a few as representative, is difficult. Singers today, as yesterday and tomorrow, are prone to pattern their programs one upon another, and certain songs thus are endlessly repeated while others of equal genius are slighted. Occasionally a recitalist has the courage to make use of a relatively little-sung Lied by Schubert and the listener is astonished by its beauty.

Of those that are almost certain to be encountered, early or late, "Gretchen am Spinnrade," "Der Erlkönig," "Der Doppelgänger," "Am Meer," "Der Wanderer," "An die Musik," "Der Tod und das Mädchen," "Dem Unendlichen," and "Die Allmacht" are songs of power and depth, but of a wide variety of expressiveness. That variety is provided with still more obvious contrasts when songs like "Ständchen"—the household "Schubert's Serenade"—and "Die Forelle" are considered. Some of the most loved of the Schubert songs are to be found in the song cycles, "Die schöne Müllerin" and "Die Winterreise"—"Ungeduld," "Der Lindenbaum," "Frühlingstraum," "Die Post," "Der Wegweiser," among others equally celebrated—songs that can be regarded as on the very summit of the then newly-awakened German romanticism. The two cycles differ from Beethoven's "An die ferne Geliebte" in that the songs may be said to be bound together by a unity of spirit rather than a welding of the music. There is here such a surrender on the part of the musician to the poet as music had never known before; out of it came a glory of music and not a mere embellishment of words.

Born a year before Schubert, but destined to live on for more than forty years after Schubert's death, Karl Loewe (1796–1869) perfected parallel to the Lied the story-telling ballad, of which "Edward" and "Archibald Douglas" remain the best known. Loewe, too, wrote an "Erl King," and if it has not held place with Schubert's, it remains a striking example of his poetic feeling and power of musical expression. Ordinarily, his structure consisted of short, varied melodic sections, so contrived as to tell a story directly and vividly. The same treatment evolved some beautifully effective songs that can be classified under the Lied; "Die Uhr" for example, a composition that deserves to figure more often on song programs than it does. The larger ballads have a rich bardic savor; their effect is almost that of recitation; but it is recitation in music; they need to be sung and well sung. Like Schubert and Schumann, Loewe aspired to the theatre; but his five operas, only one of which—"Die drei Wünsche"—was ever performed, merely demonstrated what other Lieder composers had to learn, to their sorrow, that the dramatic song and the opera air inhabit two quite different worlds.

Mendelssohn, intervening between Schubert and his true successors, contributed charming melodies to the song répertoire, but scarcely in a manner to influence the development of the Lied. His songs possess fluency and grace rather than poetic depth. They break no paths; they are highly regular and conventional in form. A more positive influence, by reason of the Lied-character of airs in his operas, was Weber, but he does not figure as an important song composer. Liszt, in his internationalism, wrote songs of the most varied character. It is still possible, today, for a recitalist to devote a group, with or without "Die Lorelei," to the Liszt songs. The one that bears up best, perhaps, is "Mignon." But with Liszt, as with Chopin, who also wrote some charming songs, vocal music was secondary to other forms of composition. He was only on the fringes of the great development of the Lied.

Robert Schumann (1810–1856) was Schubert's direct successor as master of the Lied. He made the piano part still more important to the song, and depended still more on the accompaniment to establish the mood of the text. If he was not so great a melodist as Schubert, he was equally the poet and the romantic. Indeed, his choice of texts, if somewhat less wide as to range, indicates a more finely cultivated taste than that of his predecessor. What Goethe was to Schubert, Heine was to Schumann. His "Dichterliebe" and "Frauenliebe und-Leben" cycles represent a looser grouping of songs than Beethoven's "An die ferne Geliebte," with no such welding of the numbers, but they are remarkable for their cumulative effect. "Widmung," "Im Walde," "Stille Thränen," "Liebesbotschaft," "Der Nussbaum" and "Die Lotusblume" are but some of Schumann's many touching and essentially youthful songs, which combine a fluent lyricism with a distinctive treatment of the piano part. The cycles, like Schubert's, contain many of their creator's finest songs. These are more apt to be heard separately than in full performances of the cycles themselves, never frequent events in the concert halls. "The Two Grenadiers" we have with us always. "Ich grolle nicht" is another song seldom long absent from recital lists. The spirit of the German Volkslied is strong in Schumann's songs, even those which place the largest dependence on the piano. But, like Schubert, and like the later Hugo Wolf, he resisted the tendency of the folk-song to harness the same recurring musical strophe to successive stanzas of the words. If not to the same extent as Wolf, he was one of the composers who contrived for the Lied a new freedom of form. If, today, the Schumann songs do not rank as high as those of Schubert or Brahms, this may well be a question of relative musical inspiration. In one work at least, "Frauenliebe und-Leben," he surpassed all other song writers in a blend of psychology and feeling delineating the pure woman's soul. However much the world, and more particularly the musical world, may veer away from the romanticism which this group of songs so richly represents, the achievement remains one of the most remarkable in all song literature.

Robert Franz (1815–1892) was a song composer of a more limited range of expression than the other great Lieder writers, but one of a rare spirituality. He abjured the passionate and the dramatic; realism was repugnant to him. The serene and the idyllic in poetry had an especial appeal for his muse; something of the ethical entered into his choice of texts. Though he used the strophic form freely, his melodies were much less suggestive of folk-song than those of Brahms. Tenderness and gentle pathos were his most characteristic expression. Within his smaller compass, he treated words with rare sensibility and his music was of admirable workmanship and much polish. "Im Herbst," "In meinem Auge" and "Schlummerlied" are among the most characteristic of the Franz songs.

With Johannes Brahms, the art-song was brought to its most melodious expression and given its greatest perfection of formal musical structure. The richness and variety of his accompaniments surpassed that of either Schubert or Schumann. In depth of thought and poetry it is questionable whether any songs have transcended his, but as each of the great Lieder composers has had a differing and highly personal expression, comparisons between them necessarily resolve themselves largely into preferences that are equally individual. Brahms, and Richard Strauss after him, loved the landscape through which his song-characters moved. Nature could be said to have its own soul-state for him. "Die Mainacht," "Feldeinsamkeit," "An die Nachtigall," with their aura of external influences, were as characteristic of Brahms as "Death and the Maiden" or "Der Doppelgänger" was of Schubert. If "Auf dem Kirchhofe" suggests a Schubertian darkness of thought, it yet conveys the mood of resignation that was peculiarly Brahmsian, in contrast to the despair of Schubert. The jovial muscularity of "Der Schmied" would scarcely have emanated from any of the earlier Lieder composers; though conceivably Wagner or Strauss might have written such a work. "Botschaft" has been described as "the perfect love song." In spirit at least, if not in details of the writing, "Von ewiger Liebe" might conceivably have been an inspiration of Beethoven, if there had been no Brahms; but it is difficult to think of "Immer leiser wird mein Schlummer" as a song by any composer but Brahms. The "Four Serious Songs" of Brahms, his last published compositions, though among his loftiest compositions, are only rarely heard.

As there are about 200 of the Brahms Lieder, the fifteen to thirty that figure commonly in song lists represent only a fraction of those the world should know. In general, it may be said that Brahms, of all the great Lieder composers, was closest in spirit to the German folk-song. In spite of the elaboration of his accompaniments, he often retained the simplicity of folk melody and was less intent than Hugo Wolf upon varying either the melody or the form to give the most adroit inflection to the words. Brahms sometimes, in fact, used the same melody for successive stanzas of quite different meanings, leaving to the accompaniment and the singer the necessary changes of mood.

[273]

Brahms's great contemporary of the theatre, Richard Wagner, was not a song composer, though a handful of compositions in song form have been published. "Im Triebhaus," "Schmerzen" and "Träume," the songs that have been designated as studies for "Tristan und Isolde," sometimes take their place in Lieder recitals; their relation to "Tristan" is best recognized when they are heard with orchestra.

Hugo Wolf (1860–1903) significantly styled his vocal works "Songs for Voice and Piano." Often they seem built out of figurations in the accompaniments, though quite as often the effect is that of singer and pianist being relatively free of one another. Wolf is far more restless than Brahms, and in this he recalls Schubert. His melody often borders on declamation and it is in this contrast with the folklike singing of Brahms that a subject is found for much debate, as to whether the one transcends the other, or vice versa—a question of the approach and the end sought, quite as much as it is of creative gifts or technical address. That Wolf went beyond all other Lieder composers of the German-Austrian school in a mating of music and words is quite generally conceded. Whether his melodic substance has the richness and appeal of that of Schubert or Brahms is a question that each individual can best answer to his own satisfaction from actual hearing of the songs, independent of the opinions of critics.

The greatest single contribution of Wolf to song-writing, an essential factor in his setting of texts so as to give the feeling that words and music must have been created together by the same musical poet, is to be found in the increased freedom of his song-form. Of the great Lieder composers, he is the furthest removed from the folk spirit; as he is the most far-going in his adherence to the "composed-through" song. He boldly invaded those realms that Franz purposely avoided. Individual songs by Schubert and Beethoven may challenge him in this, but, by and large, he was the most dramatic of composers of the Lied. From among many, may be cited "Zur Ruh'," "Auch kleine Dinge," "Biterolf," "Verborgenheit" and "Gesang Weyläs" as examples of the finest flowerings of his gifts.

Richard Strauss, born 1864, is the most renowned of living song writers, as he is the most celebrated of living writers of music for the stage and for the orchestra. His recent songs have not been numerous or of the quality of his Lieder of thirty and forty years ago. Either humorous or sentimental in cast, about fifteen of these have attained widespread popularity among singers and listeners. They bespeak the tenderer side of Strauss's nature and often possess an individual charm of melody, brilliantly set off by picturesque accompaniments. A few are strained and labored; but for the most part these songs reflect keen insight into the value of the texts, drawn chiefly from modern German poets. "Traum durch

[275]

die Dämmerung," "Morgen," "Freundliche Vision," "Ruhe, meine Seele," "Heimliche Afforderung," "Cäcilie" and "Allerseelen" alone would represent a considerable contribution to the world's store of art if Strauss had written nothing else. Gustav Mahler and others of the Straussian era also composed effective songs, but with the composers already named a sufficient survey has been given of Germanic Lieder.

If the Lied is the backbone of the song répertoire it is far from being the sum total of it. In Moussorgsky, Russia has given the world a writer of songs as distinctive, if perhaps not of such universal appeal, as those of any of the German masters. The sardonic humor of such songs as "The Goat," "The Seminarist" and "The Flea" has scarcely a parallel, though foreshadowed by Berlioz. Peasants and children have their special spokesman in this composer, who contrives to speak their language as well as to characterize them with unique fidelity. No composer among the Germans or Austrians strove more earnestly to find the musical equivalent for the verbal phrase; Moussorgsky is possibly the most literal of all great song writers in this respect. His melodic substance is recognizably Russian, but rarely Oriental like that of Borodin or Rimsky-Korsakoff. His song cycles are perhaps less cycles than groupings of songs— seven in "The Nursery" set, six in "No Sunlight," four in the despairing "Death." His "Gopak" and "Hebrew Song" are two of the most familiar, but not the most characteristic, in that either might have been written by any one of a number of other Russian composers of his day. Tchaikovsky's few songs have among them works to suggest the German Lieder composers; Rubinstein followed much the same path. Glinka's "Midnight Review" is typical of a long line of story-telling songs, in which the music is less interesting for its own sake than for the uses to which it is put. Of many lesser Russian song writers there is no need to speak.

Grieg in Norway brought an individual touch, largely by reason of his harmonic personality and the melodic idioms he derived from the folk lays of his people, to songs that otherwise have many of the characteristics of German Lieder. "Ein Schwan," "Erstes Begegnen," "Im Kahne," "Die alte Mutter," and "Ich liebe dich" commonly have figured on our programs in German translations. "The Dream," to identify it by its English title, may be heard abroad in any one of as many as five languages.

Of French songs those of Claude Debussy are the most distinctive. Of necessity somewhat more positive of line than his most "impressionistic" piano music, many of them contrive to convey the same fugitive, illusive quality, the same passing impressions, the same sense of atmosphere rather than of definite emotions. Typical are "Mandoline," "Le Chevelure," "Green," "Beau Soir," "Recueillement," "Nuit d'Étoiles," "Le Balcon," "La Flute de Pan."

Franck's "La Procession" and "Marriage of the Roses,"
Duparc's "Phidylé" and "Invitation au Voyage"
Massenet's "Elegie," Gounod's "Le Soir" and Berlioz's
"La Captive" may be cited as representing various
types of French song, shading from the mystic and
the exalted to the worldly and the affectionate.
Gabriel Fauré's songs, if not often heard in this
country, hold a place of high esteem with his countrymen; as do those of Alfred Bruneau and Vincent
d'Indy.

Italy has contributed little and Spain less to what
may be termed the international song répertoire, with
due exception made for those seventeenth and eighteenth century Italian classics that so frequently supply all or part of the opening group at song recitals
—music of a certain severity of style and simplicity
of treatment that singers find useful for warming
up the voice; and teachers, for instruction purposes.
They require a dignity and aristocracy of style only
occasionally accorded them. What is not commonly
realized is that many of these are airs excerpted from
operas or cantatas, as are the Handel and Gluck
numbers frequently grouped with them on singers'
programs. Later opera airs betray their stage origin
somewhat obtrusively when brought into the recital
hall, but airs from the operas of the period before
Mozart seldom convey any real suggestion of the
stage. The Bach cantatas are drawn similarly upon,
with equal disregard for the original purpose of the

PEOPLES SYMPHONY ORCHESTRA OF BOSTON, FABIEN SEVITZKY, CONDUCTOR
WITH CHORUS IN AN ORATORIO PERFORMANCE

airs excerpted. The song program thus becomes a pageant of many nationalities and eras, with works in English by American or British composers having to compete with a preponderance of numbers by greater musical figures presented in foreign tongues.

CHAMBER MUSIC

TWO questions present themselves at once in any consideration of chamber music. Why do many musicians limit their enthusiasms and affections to this form of music, with only a grudging acknowledgment here and there of musical worth in some other form? Why, in contradistinction to this, do most laymen expect boredom, if forced by circumstances to attend a program of chamber music, even though they may have acquired some understanding of symphonic music, recital music and the music of the theater? The answer to each of these questions is largely one of experience or lack of experience and of biases largely attributable to this experience or lack of experience. On the one hand, we have the musical epicure or the musical purist who has so far cultivated a particular bent as to be ready to shut the door on the music that does not conform to that bent; on the other, we have the beginner who has yet to open a door that is as properly his to enter as it is the musical epicure's. The novice may be in the better position of the two, since he may contrive to retain what he has found behind other doors while advancing to new pleasures and benefits through the portal only now made available to him. He must learn through experience that chamber music is not music of the singer, the solo pianist or the solo violinist; that it is music very different from the music of opera and music of the symphony orchestra, though he will encounter some orchestral music of the effect and character of chamber music and some chamber music of the sound and suggestion of orchestral music.

Chamber music has been variously described, but several centuries of progress and change in the course of its evolution leave something wanting in all these definitions. It is music of the room and is best heard in a room, as distinguished from an auditorium. To reach the public it must be performed, ordinarily, in those halls where recitals and other musical events take place. In times gone by, it could be distinguished as "domestic" music, but those were the days when princely patrons had their own little musical organizations for personal and social entertainment and the question of public performance was a negligible one. Nor could all music of the room qualify as chamber music in the art-sense of the time. There was music for dancing and there was table-music to provide a background of agreeable sound while dishes rattled and the guests chattered. Chamber music is music for its own sake, not music for dancing, not a musical accompaniment for anything, whether a banquet, a theatrical act, a pantomime, a solo instrument or a voice. It is true that music adapted to some such purposes may have the character of chamber music and music written as chamber music may be put to such purposes. The circumstance remains, however, that true chamber music is music which exists for itself alone and not as handmaiden to, or co-worker with, any other art agency.

Layman and connoisseur alike think first of the string quartet when there is reference to chamber music. Since the time of Haydn and throughout a subsequent period of a century and a half, the string quartet has held this place of first importance in composition and performance of music of the room, and today it possesses a literature comparable to that written for the orchestra or the piano. Through the string quartet has largely been developed the form and character of all chamber music. Although various groupings of instruments have required individual treatment, quintets, sextets, octets and sundry works for chamber orchestra have been governed largely by the principles of design and interdependence of parts which commonly govern the string quartet. A composition utilizing fewer instruments, a trio, whatever the instruments employed, also partakes of the character of the quartet. With us, but not universally with foreign musicians, the sonatas and kindred music written for two instruments, such as violin and piano, 'cello and piano, clarinet and piano, come properly within the classification of chamber music. They are music for the room. They possess an interdependence of parts more to be likened to the relation between instruments in the string quartet than to that which obtains between instruments of the orchestra; and even less the relation of an instrument which provides an accompaniment for a solo voice or a solo instrument. Whether any solo instrument used singly can be thought of as presenting chamber music is doubtful, even though in some few compositions—notably the Bach Chaconne—there is an interplay of parts resembling that of chamber music. The Bach Chaconne, orchestrated, has taken its place in symphonic literature; played by two, three or four instruments, it might be considered chamber music. But as long as it remains a work for solo violin, its inclusion in this category is, to say the least, debatable. The piano is capable in many instances of achieving an interplay of parts that parallels what is achieved by a group of instruments; and the organ, with its multiple stops and its pedal mechanism, can extend this achievement into the domain of orchestral complexities. But neither the piano nor the organ is an instrument for chamber music in its solo capacity. The piano becomes a chamber music instrument only when it shares on something like equal terms the burdens of an ensemble embracing one or more other instruments. This quality of interdependence is basic in chamber music. Each instrument has its individual ends to achieve, but always in relation to the other instruments. This is distinct on the one hand from solo playing, in which one instrument is the principal and the others merely the support; and, on the other, from harmonic part-writing, such as may be found in choral and orchestral music that aims at a massed or united sound created by the merging into one of the several parts, with no independent movement or life for any of them. Each instrumental voice in chamber music is a separate and distinct voice, moving in co-ordination with the other voices but not absorbed or hidden by them. No one of these voices could be eliminated without destroying the design and the completeness of the parts. In true chamber music (although this is not literally lived up to in all works given by chamber orchestra) there are no additional instruments, several to the part; but only the number of players that there are parts to play. In orchestral and choral music, the common practice is to have additional players or singers for many or all of the parts, and there is much writing for mass effect, in which the parts become one harmonic entity, with no such individual movement distinguishing one voice from the others (the while they are co-ordinated in one common design), as is the rule rather than the exception in chamber music.

[284]

So it is that in chamber music something that goes beyond unity is required for a truly admirable performance. Unity is equally to be desired in orchestral and choral music—any music, in fact, where more than one performer is engaged; but chamber music requires give and take, with the leadership momentarily with one instrument, now with another, now devolving on two in perfect companionship, and shifting in delicate readjustments whereby new balances are obtained almost imperceptibly. This may be summed up in the word mutuality, implying an interdependence and close association for a common end, while retaining an independent life for all.

Another salient characteristic of chamber music is that of intimacy, naturally a quality of music for the room rather than the large hall. This quality of intimacy is to be found in all true chamber music, not excepting works for chamber orchestra. Though as many as twenty instruments be engaged in its performance, music for the chamber ensemble may still retain more of this distinguishing attribute than much music written for a single instrument. The piano, on occasion, may assert a stronger appeal and be heard to better advantage in a large auditorium than in a small one. Very rarely is power of expression or violence of emotion the goal of a composer of chamber music. Piano literature, however, often rivals that of the orchestra in seeking vehemence and energy in the piling up of sonorities. A century and a half of musical evolution has made little change in the acoustical character of chamber music. Originally music for the room, it still is lost in large spaces. Though there is often something of orchestral coloring in the chamber music of later times, this coloring, too, remains the coloring of intimate detail rather than of large blocks or masses. Undoubtedly, it is this intimacy of detail which gives to chamber music its particular charm for many musical epicures whose ears are weary of the larger and more obvious surges of orchestral compositions.

Because of limitations placed on sonorities by reason of the few instruments utilized, design becomes more important in compositions of the chamber type than in works which may depend for much of their appeal on the variety, the weight and the emotional stir of the large ensemble. The so-called purist in music is usually a lover of design and in the transparency of chamber music he is enabled to trace that design more readily and with keener satisfaction than in most orchestral writing. Moreover, the harmonic structure of chamber music reveals itself more readily to the practised ear and the unclouded natural tone-color of the several instruments has, for many, a virtue commonly sacrificed in a mixture of pigments for the purposes of orchestral color. Thus, we hear much of the pure color of chamber music, as compared to the impure color of orchestral music; largely a matter of hearing instruments singly, rather than in combinations.

All these considerations, added to that of the princely beginnings of chamber music in the salons of the nobility during a particularly courtly period, have given to this form of music a reputation for aristocracy which would seem to place it at the opposite pole from what is known as popular music. However, the basis of chamber music, quite as truly as of popular music, is melody. In innumerable instances, this melody is derived from popular or folk sources and the form in which it is cast is an art adaptation from popular dance forms, as in the suite and the symphony. In many compositions, there is use of the sonata form, with its structure erected on a first theme and a second theme, particularly in the first movement, but this is no more universally true of chamber music than of symphony. A layman need not begin his listening to string quartets intent upon identifying first and second themes and pursuing them through variation or development. The melodic material of string quartets, as of symphonies, will make its appeal if given fair opportunity. Thereafter, experience with many works—experience that should be pleasurable without any supplementary study or research—should gradually make the listener conscious of the essentials of design.

Certainly, he will come to note a difference between first movements, which commonly employ some modification of the sonata form, and succeeding movements, which may take on the characteristics of a minuet or other dance form, or present the extended melody of a romanza, or the caprice of a scherzo. Inevitably, he will become conscious, also, of the difference between the chamber music of the era of Bach and other composers antedating Haydn and Mozart, and the chamber music of these latter and all of their successors. The contrapuntal structure of the earlier composers will give him a very different feeling from that evoked by the melodic and the harmonic music of a composer such as Schubert. He will realize, too, that in the chamber music of such recent composers as Debussy and Ravel there is again a very different feeling from that of Beethoven and Brahms.

In the pre-Haydn chamber music, he will find no such "equal conversation" in the balance of the instruments as he will find in subsequent chamber music; but under a play of variously-assigned solo parts, running parallel to one another, will be an embroidered foundation also continually in movement. In due time he will identify this as the *Continuo,* one of the terms that may baffle him in his first reading of program annotations. With Haydn and with Mozart, he will come upon design in its most recognizable and authentic state. With Beethoven, particularly in that master's last quartets, he will note how musical content and emotional content threaten at times to overwhelm design; in

[288]

Brahms, how intricacy of rhythm gives new complexity to the use of thematic material quite as
melodious as that of the more straight-away Schubert;
and in Debussy and Ravel, how new harmonic nuances
bring a different character to a melodic expressiveness
that still retains an essentially intimate character. If
it is true that chamber music is likely to be the last
music to which the layman will become attached, it
is also true that, once attached to it, chamber music
is likely to be the last of which he will weary, however many the repetitions he may experience of those
works he most loves.

Josef Haydn (1732–1809) has been called the
father of the symphony, of the string quartet and
of instrumental music generally. All existed before
him. His service to the sonata, as the modern world
knows that form, was as great as his service to either
the string quartet or the symphony, which structur-
ally possess much that is sprung directly from the
sonata. But he approached perfection in the string
quartet, necessarily of a more limited horizon than
the symphony, which has been reaching into new
realms throughout the century and a quarter that
has elapsed since Haydn closed his eyes. What Haydn
achieved was a long remove from the seventeenth
century consort of viols. The world had meanwhile
learned the superiority of the Italian instruments developed as successors to the viols; Bach, Handel,
Corelli, Vivaldi, Gluck were but some of the figures

to whom Haydn could turn for examples of beautiful string writing. It is not surprising if at times he
wrote merely in four parts, as if for string orchestra;
what is amazing is that more often he devised a style
that gave the four instruments of the string quartet
their measure of interdependence, even if the first
violin assumed a place of more dominance than conforms to our later ideal of string quartet equality.
The quartet seems to have been Haydn's most natural
mode of expressing his feelings. The greatest of his
contemporaries, Mozart, was free to say that it was
from Haydn he learned how to compose quartets.

In the long life that began a quarter of a century
before Mozart was born and continued for nearly two
decades after Mozart's death, Haydn wrote no fewer
than eighty-four quartets, as compared to Mozart's
thirty-four. Many of them are never heard today,
except possibly where amateurs gather, but others
(possibly not the best) hold their places in the con-
cert-rooms and seem likely to live as long as any
quartets we know of, not excepting those of Mozart,
Beethoven, Schubert or Brahms. Their freshness,
their charm, their humor, their clearness and their
sweetness are matched by their manliness, their forthright strength. If, with Haydn, the progress of
chamber music assumed a definite course, this coin-
cided with the growth of what may be called the great
Viennese school. Its heyday was the Golden Age of
chamber music. Mozart, Beethoven and Schubert

built upon Haydn's quartets, as other later composers built upon theirs; Mozart dedicated some of his own to the beloved master; Beethoven and Schubert, though each was carried forward on new tides, showed plainly at the outset how much they were indebted to Haydn.

With the death of Schubert, there was a lapse in the great tradition of chamber music. Composers of the early romantic era were less in sympathy with this type of composition, since it was not the one most readily adaptable to their desire for a more personal form of musical expression than had prevailed in the classical period. As a striking instance, Berlioz left no chamber music. Chopin and Liszt are scarcely thought of in this connection, though Chopin left three unimportant compositions that come properly within the bounds of chamber music. Schumann remains, after Schubert, the most important chamber music composer until the ascendancy of Brahms. Mendelssohn, whose spirit was a blend of the classic and the romantic, contributed some pleasant works but it was with Brahms that the true renascence of chamber music was achieved. Here was a master who by temper, outlook and training, as well as power of inspiration, was the natural heir of Beethoven and Schubert. His chamber music stands beside theirs on the highest levels of workmanship; in wealth of ideas it meets any test that can be imposed. Dvořák, Smetana, Borodin, Tchaikovsky, Franck, Fauré, Debussy, Ravel, Bartok, Florent Schmitt, Hindemith and Schönberg are but some of the later masters in this sphere. The sonata for two instruments, the string quartet, the trio and the quintet that combine the piano or one of the wind instruments with strings have remained the most typical forms of chamber music expression. In some of their sextets, octets, etc., post-war composers in particular have found ways to reduce to small groupings music of an orchestral feeling that, for lack of a better way of classifying it, is chamber music.

A SCHUBERT TRIO

TWO compositions from the treasury of Franz Schubert (1797–1828) serve well to illustrate their kind. They represent the Golden Age. Unlike the two most celebrated Schubert Symphonies, the "Unfinished" in B minor and the C major of "the heavenly lengths," much of Schubert's chamber music was played in his time and no doubt in his hearing. Moreover, he had the satisfaction of seeing various of his chamber compositions in print.

No more melodious entrance can be made into the domain of chamber music than through the portals of the B flat major trio for piano, violin and 'cello, opus 99, composed in 1827, within a year of the composer's death. The same year brought forth a second trio, in E, opus 100, for the same instruments and equally beautiful, though for some reason never as popular. No layman, with half an ear for melody, need ever have to learn to like this music. Let him hear the records of the B flat trio by Cortot, Thibaud and Casals a few times and he will find he has much of it in his head.

But Schubert was more than a singer. His chamber music bespeaks genius in ways other than sheer beauty of melody. His inspiration went hand in hand with structural mastery, and while his music has its full share of individual devices and by no means duplicates in details of form what was written by those who preceded or followed him, it is not too much to say that the listener who comprehends the openly melodious B flat trio is well on the way to comprehension of chamber music generally. Other works may be more austere, more crabbed, more complicated, more obscure; less frank in what may as well be called tune; the structure may be quite different; the intellectual and emotional content may have little similarity. But a kinship remains, however, even as between Schubert and Bartok, or Schubert and Schönberg, not to speak of Schubert and Beethoven or Schubert and Brahms. To say that in this trio is chamber music of the most elemental appeal is perhaps to misrepresent the work, since it is of the highest inspiration and the most adroit craftsmanship. Universal is perhaps the word—universal in the sense that this is everyman's music as well as music for every Western land.

Let us try to follow a performance of this trio. At the outset, the three instruments unite in a precise enunciation of the first theme, one that sings as Schubert knew so well how to make his melodies sing. The piano marks the rhythm as violin and

VIOLIN

VIOLA

VIOLONCELLO

DOUBLE BASS

STRING INSTRUMENTS

'cello sweep along in companion runs. The theme is repeated higher by the two string instruments and passed on to the piano, which, in turn, carries it lower. The strings become the accompaniment. The instruments interchange ideas with an ease that makes all this a delightful play of sound within easily grasped design. The 'cello, over chords by the piano, begins the second theme, a truly Schubertian melody, and is soon joined by the violin. The development section follows, dealing with the first theme, then with the second, with a return to the opening theme, the piano now the singer.

The second movement is an Andante with a rhythm to suggest either a cradle song or a Venetian boat song—the old resemblance of the barcarolle and the lullaby. The piano begins the "rocking," the 'cello the singing. It is a dreamlike melody of rare softness and sweetness. The solo becomes a duet, as the violin takes over the tune and the 'cello continues on its lyrical way. The piano competes briefly with the strings in this contest of singers, then takes to scattering garlands, in the form of ornate figurations, along the path of the strings. The voices rise and fall in a richness of harmony as well as melody that only the dullest ear can fail to sense.

The Adagio is followed by a Scherzo, in which voices are interwoven with the most delightful play of fancy. Midway is a trio that is pure Viennese; the old Vienna of the waltz spirit that was to flower in its more popular form in the music of Lanner and the Strausses, father and son. All of the instruments are singers; all close to the popular heart.

The final Rondo at times suggests that themes have been thrown in helter-skelter, so impromptu is the effect of their succession. One instrument sings, another dances, with a turning and churning that brings no end of surprises; all with such momentum that the listener is swept ahead like a leaf in a strong wind. The close is a magical one and comes abruptly, after the ear has been prepared repeatedly for a conclusion that impishly failed to arrive.

A SCHUBERT QUARTET

THE Schubert String Quartet in D Minor, written about 1824, three years earlier than the B Flat Major Trio, carries the listener into quite a different world. The joyous, if wistful, Schubert of the trio had his opposite in the despairing, death-haunted Schubert of many of the songs. This quartet is the famous one that builds variations on the theme of one of these songs, "Death and the Maiden." These variations are found in the second movement, but the first already has conjured forth a vision of the struggle with death. The interplay of the four instruments, first and second violins, viola and 'cello, is such as to make this first movement one of the marvels of quartet writing. The thematic material is bold and significant. The working-out produces a unity, a sense of organic strength, such as only the greatest masterpieces have achieved. Instead of the usual two, there are no less than five main themes in this first movement.

Death comes as the "friend" in the theme and

variations. Schubert remains close to the original subject throughout this movement, achieving a remarkable range of poetic expression without carrying his variations out of a small frame and with but a single change of key. At least one of the instruments adheres closely to the melody in each of the variations. After the tumultuous fifth, there is a simple transition back to the original theme and mood that can only be regarded as a stroke of genius. The intensity and the poetic feeling of these variations, not their technical skill, is what has endeared the work to a multitude of chamber music devotees, but it is difficult to conceive of the variations being more expertly handled. Any further elaboration might have been at the cost of their direct emotional appeal.

"Death as the Demon Fiddler" is a designation given to the Scherzo, one of the most vigorous of Schubert's movements and also one of the most concise. It embraces a delicately embroidered Trio that leads back into the vigorous first part. The finale is regarded as still more definitely a "dance of death" and rushes forward with a dizzy, careening momentum, at once inexorable and intoxicating.

CHORAL MUSIC

CHORAL music in its several forms, not excluding that of the stage and the concert hall, owes its development chiefly to the church. Through most of the Christian era, it has been the most highly developed music in the common experience of the greatest number of inhabitants of the Western world. It had reached a high degree of complexity and, in a sense, finality, before instrumental music, either in solo form or ensemble, had made any important contributions to art. This development reached its apex in a religious age when a far larger part of the population regularly attended church than has since patronized the secular music of the concert hall. It is not surprising therefore, if choral music, and particularly that choral music which is associated with the church, troubles the musical layman less than instrumental music or vocal music for the theatre, though he may never have made any particular effort to comprehend its nature or its structure. The mass, the motet, the cantata and the oratorio have been taken for granted by multitudes of laymen, to a degree not true of the sonata, the concerto, the symphony, the string quartet, the opera or the music-drama.

Celebrants of the Roman Catholic church, in particular, have had the mass in the routine of their lives, week on week and year on year. Their fathers, grandfathers and more remote ancestors heard much the same music as they hear today at their church services. As a form the mass was complete by the early part of the sixteenth century, so that at least three centuries of listening may be said to be behind the comprehension of the ordinary communicant who hears a typical church composition in this form. It may be questioned whether—all religious associations aside—like multitudes of musically uneducated and even unmusical persons would listen with as little uneasiness to equally complex music for the symphony orchestra or the theatre ensemble. The mass may be regarded as an illustration of how long familiarity, even if of the more casual and generalized character, accomplishes for some music what study and analysis accomplish for other music. That many who are not quite certain how they stand with respect to polyphonic and fugal writing in the instrumental music of Bach, for instance, take in, unperturbed, the analogous writing for voices in the music of a church service, would seem to be beyond question. Transferred to the concert hall, this music may require a less passive kind of attention. At any rate, sufficient differences exist as between differing types of choral composition to justify, at least, their enumeration.

The great church masses, such as those of Palestrina, Josquin de Près, Vittoria and Orlando di Lasso are not often encountered in the concert hall. But some knowledge of their construction will aid any listener who hears a mass by Bach, Mozart, Haydn, Beethoven or some later writer that serves a concert purpose rather than a ceremonial one. The old masses divided themselves naturally into six movements: Kyrie, Gloria, Credo, Sanctus, Benedictus and Agnus Dei, settings of the Latin words of the unvarying part of the Catholic Liturgy, called the Ordinary. Since earliest Christian times it had been customary to sing portions of the Eucharistic service; the mass, as an art-form grew with the development of polyphonic music, but retained something always of the plain chant of the early church from which it sprang. The introduction of secular airs, such as the old French love-song, "L'homme arme," as subjects on which to build contrapuntal elaboration, influenced, but did not fundamentally alter, the character of the several movements. The usual plan of the Kyrie was that of contrapuntal elaboration of plain-chant melody. The Gloria was characterized by a less elaborate polyphony and was commonly divided into two parts, with the Qui tollis treated separately. The Credo, of more

modest fugal style, like the Gloria, also was sub-
divided, either at Et incarnatus est or Crucifixus;
with frequently another subdivision made of Et in
spiritum sanctum. Of more highly developed design,
like the Kyrie, was the Sanctus, with divisions frequently made of Pleni sunt coeli and Osanna. Solo
voices, two, three or four, prevailed in the Benedictus,
which frequently assumed the form of a canon, leading into a choral Osanna. The Agnus Dei was often
the movement of greatest contrapuntal ingenuity,
with the second of two sections given over to a
canon or complex fugue. In spirit, these successive
movements have been described as follows: Kyrie,
devout; Gloria, jubilant; Credo, majestic; Benedictus,
rapt; Sanctus, angelic; Agnus Dei, prayerful.

These divisions and their characteristics were developed before Palestrina (1525–1594) the greatest
composer of the Catholic church; his mission was
not so much that of either innovator or builder as of
purifier of a temple already established. He fixed
the style for what came to be recognized as the Golden
Age of Ecclesiastical Music. In his masses, number-
ing close to a hundred, he left supreme examples of
polyphonic architecture, in which artistic power is
subjugated to the demands of expression, according to
the ideals of the church he served. Vittoria and
Anerio of the great Roman school, Gabrieli and
Croce of the Venetian, Orlando di Lasso of the
Flemish, and William Byrd of the English were

among outstanding composers of masses that fulfilled the ideals of this age. Afterward came a period of decadence and when the mass again had masters worthy of its traditions, the rise of instrumental music and of music for the theatre had brought to it new characteristics that have since prevailed—characteristics that were less of the church and more of the world of art for its own sake, irrespective of the devout feeling engendered.

The Bach B Minor Mass, because of its excessive length and its elaboration of style, is unfitted for a church service. In form a mass, it has served the purpose of an oratorio or, as some have viewed it, a series of church cantatas under one cover. Its great fugal choruses, it airs and duets that approach the instrumental style, and its rich orchestral effects achieved by relatively simple means, all bespeak the need of resources beyond those of the churches of Bach's day or of any secular organizations of which we know anything. The question as to why Bach, a Protestant, should have turned to this form as a receptacle for so great an outwelling of his genius has never been satisfactorily answered; there is little to show that it could ever have been satisfactorily performed in his lifetime. But Bach poured equally great music into his Art of Fugue, which was not written for performance of any kind, but only as an exercise of his powers. The most utilitarian of all great composers—writing masterpieces among the cantatas he composed weekly for the churches he served—he also was the least practical in some respects; his visions and his technical gifts led him into the composition of much music that a later age, with far greater resources of performance than he could command, has been able to realize only by special study and heroic effort.

In the masses of Haydn are features of oratorio, in those of Mozart are similarities to the Mozart operas. Beethoven's Missa Solemnis has the dramatic implications of his symphonies; Cherubini, though perhaps closer in spirit to his Italian forerunners, shares this leaning toward drama in a manner foreign, of course, to religious writers of the Palestrina period. Nineteenth century Romanticism left its mark upon the mass as upon every other form of art. The great age of Vittoria and di Lasso was never to come again.

The Requiem Mass for the dead has had its special inspiration for several latter-day composers who have built on the historic past. Its form ordinarily embraces nine principal sections: (1) Introit—Requiem aeternam; (2) Kyrie; (3) Gradual and Tract —Requiem aeternam and Absolve, Domine; (4) Sequence or Prose—Dies irae; (5) Offertorium— Domine Jesu Christi; (6) Sanctus; (7) Benedictus; (8) Agnes Dei; and (9) Communio—Lux aeterna. A tenth section, Responsorium, Libera me, is sometimes added. Still another, Lectio—Taedet animam meam, is encountered. Palestrina, Vittoria, Anerio,

Vecchi and other famous Italians wrote requiems that represented their art at its highest. This was an art highly impersonal. Those later requiems that are best known in the concert hall were personal in spirit.

That of Mozart, written on his deathbed, was conceived by the composer as for himself. Commissioned under mystifying circumstances by Count Walsegg, who sent a funereal-appearing agent to Mozart, the work was viewed in a fantastic light by the composer, who never seems to have understood that Walsegg wanted it as a memorial for his wife, but recently dead. In his fever and weakness, the dying Mozart mistook the count's sombre but very mundane emissary as a visitant from another world. Mozart could not finish his task. The Requiem and the Kyrie were completely his; the remainder was filled in from Mozart's sketches by a pupil, Süssmayer, with some original composition also from his pen. Count Walsegg accepted the score, paid for it and tried to foist it on the world as his own. The secret could not long be hidden. In this pathetic document, the true composer is brought very close to those he addresses; the human submerges the churchly.

Cherubini wrote two important Requiems, the second of which is among the most dramatic of his achievements. The Dies irae from this work was formerly much sung separately as a stirring festival number; all thought of the church receded to a remote distance before the effect of this music in the concert hall.

More like an oratorio or cantata is the "German Requiem" of Brahms. The words are taken from Scripture but are not those of the traditional Latin service. The composer has employed an orchestra with all the richness of his symphonic scoring. His choral writing is sometimes of a complex fugal character, but not in the spirit of the old masters of liturgical music. The mood is one of reverie quite as much as of faith. The purpose of the work is to shadow forth the glories of the higher life that is to come, but the effect is more consolatory than jubilant. This is music that could only have been produced in the romantic era. Its outlook, as well as its style and technique, would have been strange, indeed, to Palestrina, Vittoria or Anerio.

The "German Requiem" gives forth a singular richness of tone in its opening section by reason of unusual scoring for the strings, without violins. The measured tramp of a great procession is suggested in the funeral march that follows. Two choral fugues of a highly individual character are found in the next division of the work. A magnificent crescendo intervenes. There is a melodious slow movement of a typical Brahmsian beauty, followed by a soprano solo and chorus in the fifth of the seven sections or movements of the work. The sixth, devoted to the resurrection of the dead, is of thrilling power, with fugal writing that conveys a feeling not paralleled among the works of Brahms's predecessors. In the concluding section there is a reminiscence of the first movement. The storm of the sixth section has given way in the seventh to a mood of calm, but it is a calm pervaded by pathos as well as by resignation.

Verdi's "Manzoni" Requiem, so-called because it was composed in memory of Alessandro Manzoni, the Italian poet and novelist who died in 1873, contains as its last movement, the Libera me, music that Verdi composed originally for a composite mass on which thirteen composers collaborated, each writing one number, at the time of Rossini's death in 1868. The names of the others who participated in the Rossini Requiem—Buzzola, Bazzini, Pedrotti, Cagnoni, Ricci, Mini, Bouchenon, Coccia, Gaspari, Plantania, Petrella, Mabellini—are virtually forgotten. Of all the important Requiems that choral organizations make use of today in the concert halls the "Manzoni" most suggests the theatre. It is in a world apart from either the traditional church mass or Brahms's "German Requiem." The fervor and sincerity of the work, however, have left their impress on multitudes of sympathetic listeners and doubtless will continue to do so in the face of the objections of those who find the prevailing mood that of dramatic rather than religious expression.

The motet was the form of composition most frequently employed by polyphonic composers from the

fourteenth century to the time of Bach. In its medi-
aeval beginnings it was essentially an embroidering of
a theme and a text. A host of beautiful motets were
written in honor of Our Lady, these including
Dufay's "Salvo Virgo," Arcadelt's "Ave Maria" and
Josquin de Près's "Ave vera virginitas"; while the
Lamentations of Jeremiah furnished the text for many
other such compositions. Countless motets were composed for great church festivals and others were written in laudation of princes and nobles. In the fif-
teenth and sixteenth centuries, the funeral motet became an important phase of music.

All the subsequent polyphonic schools, including
those of the Netherlands, Germany and Italy, developed the motet alongside the mass. Palestrina alone
wrote more than 300 motets. In Tudor England,
Tallis and Byrd were composers of works in this form.
The motet and the madrigal flourished side by side in
the Elizabethan era; Orlando Gibbons composed a set
of secular songs, published in 1612 under the title of
"Madrigals and Motets." In general, it can be said
that in its final form the motet was a short composition for voices, intended primarily for unaccompanied
singing and written in contrapuntal style on a Latin
text usually liturgical or quasi-liturgical in character,
but not invariably so. Bach and Handel were among
the last great masters of the form. Though composers
of subsequent eras have continued to write motets,
many are in reality sacred cantatas.

The early cantatas of the Italians were a by-product of opera; they were one-person dramas in the form of musical recitations or monologues. The aria then took its place in the cantata as it did in opera; as the form grew, recitatives and airs alternated. Carissimi and Alessandro Scarlatti brought this simple form to a high state of perfection. Handel, visiting Italy at a little later day, was moved to compose in similar style, and his "Apollo and Daphne" is one of the most beautiful cantatas of this period. With the introduction of the chorus in the cantata, a musical structure was evolved not always readily distinguished from that of the oratorio, though commonly on a much smaller scale.

The church cantatas of Bach and of some of his contemporaries, notably Telemann, occasionally possess choral numbers of gigantic proportions. After an opening chorus, ordinarily, works of this type presented airs and duets, in alternation with recitatives, and introduced chorales, the old Reformation hymn tunes of Luther's Germany. Sometimes there is an instrumental introduction and in despite of limited resources the orchestra plays an important part in many of these cantatas. Perhaps a majority of those by Bach were written to meet the specific requirements of church services on certain days. But he wrote secular cantatas also, like the "Kaffee Cantata," which has to do with a young woman's persistence in her favorite beverage in the face of parental opposition; and "Phoebus and Pan," a jovial satire that in recent years has been given stage dress and performed as opera. Bach, who wrote no music actually for the theatre, so far as has ever been disclosed, none-the-less designated some of his cantatas by the title, "Dramma per Musica." Though his is music that does not convey the thought of stage action, the contrapuntal impact of many of the choruses of the Bach cantatas is dramatic in the highest degree.

Oratorio may be described as a larger cantata, on the one hand, and opera without action, on the other. Some oratorios have been converted into operas, Handel's "Belshazzar" for instance. Among more modern works, Saint-Saëns's "Samson et Dalila" and Berlioz's "Damnation of Faust" lend themselves to treatment either as opera, with stage action, or as oratorio, without it. Operas, including such essentially theatrical works as Wagner's "Walküre" and Moussorgsky's "Boris Godounoff," sometimes are sung in concert-form, as if they were oratorios. The general distinction remains that in opera, dramatic and secular elements are uppermost; in oratorio, they are secondary. Common practice in oratorio has been to take the text from Scriptural or other sacred sources and to deal with religious events or the lives of religious spokesmen to the end that faith shall be glorified. In opera the conflicting destinies of individuals are depicted, with the emotional states engendered, for their own sake. Though there are secular ora-

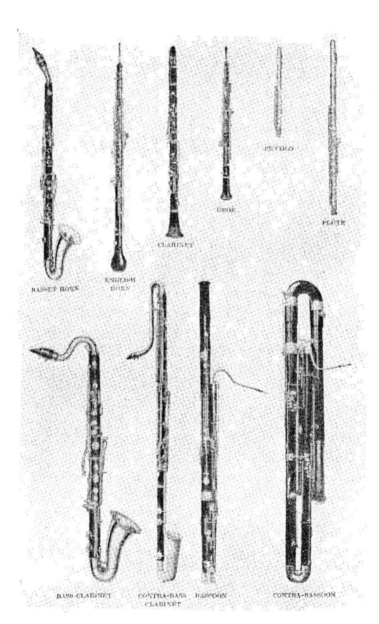

PICCOLO

OBOE

CLARINET

FLUTE

BASSET HORN   ENGLISH
HORN

BASS-CLARINET   CONTRA-BASS   BASSOON   CONTRA-BASSOON
               CLARINET

WOOD–WIND INSTRUMENTS

torios—a recent example being Stravinsky's "Oedipus Rex"—oratorio has been defined as "sacred art for art's sake," with its heroes and heroines "the ideal instruments and messengers of divinity." The great oratorios of Handel represent this conception at its apogee. His great Passions aside, Bach wrote nothing really similar to "Messiah," "Judas Maccabaeas," "Solomon," "Israel in Egypt," "Joseph," "Jephtha," "Saul," "Belshazzar" and others of the Handelian genus. Bach's so-called Christmas Oratorio is in reality a sheaf of cantatas, written to be performed separately on six holy days, beginning with Christmas and ending with Epiphany. The Handelian oratorio is often close to the stage. "Messiah" and others of his maturest works came after Handel's long career as an opera composer was ended by circumstances that bereft him of a theatre public, with the result that he was compelled to use the concert room. The difference between his opera airs and his oratorio airs often is a slight one. But the oratorios led him to the composition of huge contrapuntal choruses, whereas the operas had singularly little choral writing of any kind. The Handel oratorios quite generally make more prominent use of the orchestra than do the operas, the so-called "Pastoral Symphony" of "Messiah" being a case in point. Their successions of airs for various voices, usually with introductory recitative; and their opening, closing and intervening choruses proffer no new problems of form. In its larger aspects, oratorio is perhaps the most obvious of musical entities, though the separate numbers permit of intricacies as varied and ingenious as can be found in symphony, opera or chamber music.

Haydn's two great oratorios, "The Creation" and "The Seasons," bring into oratorio more of the symphony, thus enhancing the importance of the instrumental parts. "The Seasons" has much of that insight into Nature which was to become a characteristic of the romantic era after Haydn's death, and to develop new vistas of orchestral tone-painting. Beethoven's "Mount of Olives" pursues the symphonic phase of oratorio further and in Mendelssohn's "Elijah" is one of the happiest blends, so far as mere effect is concerned, of vocal and orchestral writing. Latter-day oratorio, with Elgar's "Dream of Gerontius" as typical, has retained the semblance of the Handelian form. This is true even of the Stravinsky "Oedipus Rex," though the sound and the spirit are quite something else.

The Schönberg "Gurrelieder," a relatively early work of this still perplexing master, is either a greatly expanded song cycle or a symphonic oratorio, according to the liberality with which one or the other of the terms is used. Stravinsky's "Symphony of the Psalms," with the chorus as important as the orchestra; Beethoven's "Choral Fantasia," which retains the general outlines of a piano concerto until it reaches its choral finale; Vaughan Williams's "Sea Symphony," and, most famous of all, the concluding movement of Beethoven's Ninth or "Choral" Symphony, present instances of choral writing in connection with other forms that retains something of kinship to the cantata and the oratorio and also to opera.

There remain the Passions of Bach. Handel and other composers wrote Passions, but for the world today the term suggests either the St. Matthew Passion or the St. John Passion of Bach. Among the predecessors and contemporaries of Bach in this form must be recognized Heinrich Schutz (1585–1672), "the father of German music," Johann Sebastiani (1622–1683), and Reinhard Keiser (1674–1739). The Passion as conceived by these men was a German transformation of the oratorio, imported from Italy. They took the sacred narrative of the Saviour's sufferings and death, treated it in recitative with intervening airs and choruses, introduced the German chorale, and thereby evolved a new type of work unrivalled for dignity, devotional expression and exalted pathos. The towering choruses of the Bach Passions are his most dramatic music. By the use of a narrator, whose mission it is to relate the gospel story—according to one or another of the Biblical witnesses—an easy intimacy is established with the listener. The airs and choruses provide effective contrast to this recitative. The chorales bring the whole closer to the heart of the listener, as if he himself were a participant in the performance. Congregations undoubtedly did sing the chorales in Bach's time.

"The Passion According to St. Matthew" is written for two complete choirs, each accompanied by a separate orchestra and organ. The instrumentation, like the choral writing, is highly polyphonic at times and rich in tone-painting that mirrors the words or the emotional moods. This, of course, is not the orchestration of Wagner or Strauss; nor yet that of Beethoven or Mozart. But it has remained amazingly fresh and ample for its purposes, with many a touch that was of genius at that time and remains of genius now. There have been no great examples of the Passion since Bach; and so completely did he sum up and surpass all that went before that there has been little incentive for antiquarians to bring to hearing in modern times the Passion music of his predeccessors. Though Bach was supreme in many branches of the musical art, perhaps no other form is so exclusively identified with Bach, for all time, as the Passion.

Only passing mention has been made of the madrigal, which, in its most cherished manifestations has come to be looked upon as a form of vocal chamber music, though the madrigal chorus has its place beside the madrigal group of four, five or six voices—sometimes only two. In Italy, Monteverdi was as celebrated a writer of madrigals as he was of operas and cantatas; Luca Marenzio and Gesualdo were Italian contemporaries of importance in this field;

Vecchi wrote a madrigal opera. However, it was in Elizabethan England that the madrigal flowered in its greatest beauty. One notable collection, "The Triumphs of Oriana," represented the collaboration of nearly thirty madrigal writers, each with one or more contributions—in praise of Queen Elizabeth. Orlando Gibbons, John Benet, Thomas Morley, John Wylbye, Thomas Weelkes, Michael Cavendish and Thomas Bateson were among the masters who wrote madrigals for this set.

The subjects of the madrigal were prevailingly secular, as those of contemporary motets were prevailingly sacred. The love song prevailed, with all the fantasy and poetic conceits of the period, but it was a love song in counterpoint, with an interplay of voices as complex as it was delicate. Beside the madrigal was the ballet or balletto, a dancing song, usually much more simple in its treatment and with a refrain to the syllables fa, la, la. Madrigal and balletto together passed out with their age. Today, they come to our ears as from a world that is lost to us, their charm that of a kind of music that will never be written again, save in imitation and then for the purpose of recalling the dead day.

SOME NOTES ON THE COMMON MUSICAL FORMS

THE SONATA

IN the Seventeenth and Eighteenth Centuries, any instrumental composition could be termed a sonata, as opposed to cantata, a vocal composition. In this early music there were two varieties, sonata da chiesa, church sonatas, and sonata da camera, chamber sonatas, the first being grave and dignified, the second lighter in character. In modern music, the sonata is an instrumental selection, usually of three or more movements; particularly a composition for the piano, or for piano and one other instrument, such as the violin or 'cello; having three or four movements with contrasted rhythms in related keys. The violin sonata, combining the violin and the piano, retains substantially the form of the piano sonata; so, also, the trio, the quartet, the quintet, all the various combinations of chamber music; and in an expanded state, the concerto and the symphony.

SONATA-FORM

The term commonly applies to first movements of sonatas, trios, quartets, concertos and symphonies;

with, however, many exceptions. In the Seventeenth Century the term sonata was applied to pieces for instruments characterized by what was then harmonic fullness. At the present time the term designates a composition almost solely for instrumental performance distinguished by the possession of two themes in different keys. The form, in brief, usually follows some such outline as this: (*a*) the exposition, in which the chief theme is followed by a subordinate theme in another key related to that of the chief theme; (*b*) a development, or working-out section, in which both themes are treated as the skill and fancy of the composer dictates, either singly or in conjunction; (*c*) a recapitulation, consisting of a return to the first theme and then to the second, not, however, in its original key, but in that of the first theme.

There are sonatas in which the sonata form applies only to the first of three or more movements. There are others in which there is some approach to this form in two or all movements. The same may be said of trios, quartets, concertos, symphonies—all music based, to some extent on the sonata.

The sonata of the seventeenth century was only a faint prototype of the highly developed compositions of Haydn, Mozart, and Beethoven. It was little more than a suite, containing, like the suite, a succession of varied and independent movements. That succession has remained, but independence of the movements is less characteristic of the modern sonata than structural unity.

In the three or four movements ordinarily employed, there is homogeneity as well as something of contrast. The themes of the different movements are much more fully elaborated and developed than was commonly true of the suite; there is much less of tune for tune's sake. The first movement, that which determines the sonata form, has no real parallel in the classic suite; the old overture served quite a different purpose.

Credit commonly is given to Haydn for fixing the form of the first movement. Later composers have followed his first movements as their basic model.

Though there is a marked similarity in the succession of movements of many sonatas, the composer who writes in this form is free to arrange in any order he pleases the movements which follow the first. Frequently an allegro of lively pace, this first movement may, in a given instance, be followed by a slow adagio, largo, or andante as the second movement; perhaps music of the romanza or aria type, suggesting a song form. Often the third movement is either a minuet or scherzo, the latter (though the term is much older) a development by Beethoven out of the minuet. The minuet or scherzo may be placed second and the slow movement third. The finale may be a second allegro, resembling the first movement in form, or it may be a rondo, or a theme and variations.

There are three-movement sonatas in which the minuet or scherzo is omitted. There are song-like middle sections which interrupt the main course of movements, called trios; and there are introductory and concluding passages, the former often of a slow, grave character, in contrast with the first allegro; the latter, an after-thought in the form of a gay or pensive coda, bringing in new melodic material. It must also be borne in mind that innumerable sonatas are to be found in which the Haydn principles do not apply. Beethoven was often unorthodox in his sonata structure, as in the first movement of the so-called "Moonlight" Sonata (op. 27, No. 2). The first movement of his Op. 49, No. 2, may be pointed to as having no middle part, so brief is the development. His Op. 26, though styled a sonata, might be termed a suite having an air with variations.

THE SUITE

The suite is probably the oldest of present-day musical forms calling for more than one movement. So variable is the relation of its parts, however, that it almost ceases, in some instances, to be a form. During the latter part of the middle ages, town bands are supposed to have brought the suite into being by stringing together a series of dance tunes which had no bond of similarity except that they were in the same key.

When serious-minded composers of the Seventeenth Century began to create music after this fashion, the composition often was called partie or partita. Such compositions continued to be based on dance tunes. For a time, there were four principal divisions: the allemande, the courante, the saraband and the gigue. Between the last two there were often interpolated others, called intermezzi. Among these were the bourrée, the branle, the gavotte, the minuet, the musette, the passepied, the loure and the pavane. As the form was extended, there no longer was adherence to a single key and other than dance forms were used. In later days, descriptive pieces, with programmatic titles, have been called suites; as have excerpts from operas, ballets and various other compositions; until, today, it might almost be said that a suite is any arbitrary group of relatively small pieces for which this title is a handier one than any other. The classic suite, of course, was another matter; but its own ancestor in the music of the town bands could scarcely repudiate these loosely assorted groupings of today.

From the first, the suite freely combined other musical ideas with its series of dance tunes. Often there was a prelude or introduction that merited the title of overture. Sometimes the suite finished with an air with variations, this movement consisting of a melody being given out first in its simplest and plainest fashion, and then repeated several times, each repetition introducing some variation of rhythm, harmony or melodic configuration. Virtually every instrumental form has made us of the air and variations; opera and oratorio have presented like elaborations in vocal music.

OVERTURE

In the most common sense, the overture is an introduction to an extended musical composition. Ordinarily it differs from a prelude in being of itself more extended, more self-sufficient and more positive in its form. But the form may vary with the character of the composition it precedes. The early overtures of Lully, as introduced by him in France in the Seventeenth Century, were of a slow and stately character. The overture of the Italian style which was developed later in the same century by Scarlatti, consisted of three distinct sections, the first and third lively and the second slow, with a marked contrast of accent or rhythm. This form was an ancestor of the symphony. Composers of the eighteenth Century elaborated the modern form of overture in conjunction with the sonata and the symphony, giving it a more concise and concentrated structure, with much less of the principle of development or repetition. In his own grand manner, Handel built boldly on Lully's foundations. Gluck, a little younger than Handel, gave more of dramatic char-

acter to the overtures of his operas and made them
more truly an introduction or preface to the drama.

Mozart wrote divine curtain-raisers in his overtures and at the same time contributed to the concert room compositions able to stand alone.

Beethoven eventually developed his own style in
the overture, as in the symphony, the sonata and the
string quartet. The third "Leonore" Overture (one
of four overtures written for his opera, "Fidelio,")
foreshadows and sums up the entire drama. He set
the style for most subsequent theatre overtures; and
to him is to be traced also the impetus to write overtures, as various later composers have done, which are
merely concert pieces to be played independently and
hence are not introductions to anything. Today,
there are overture-fantasias and fantasia-overtures
that might as well be called tone-poems, and are only
to be thought of as concert music; the while the true
overture has become a rarity among new works for
the theatre.

The concert overture usually boasts a title to indicate the nature or the purpose of the composition,
as in Mendelssohn's "Hebrides," Brahms's "Aca-
demic," Beethoven's "Consecration of the House."
Not infrequently a work of this order has a strong
likeness to the first movement of a sonata. Other concert overtures will be found to possess the nature of
the rondo.

At one time much attention was given to the oratorio overture as distinguished from the operatic overture. An instance of a latter-day overture written on the lines of the old French overture is that of the overture to Mendelssohn's "St. Paul." In his later work, "Elijah," Mendelssohn chose to write a single section in free fugal style. Some oratorio overtures borrow themes from the body of the work, which has long been the common, if not the invariable practice in operatic overtures.

THE CONCERTO

Many modern examples of the concerto would be undistinguishable from symphonies but for the presence of a soloist. Some older examples are close to the suite. Theoretically, the concerto, which is a composition for a solo instrument and orchestra, differs from a sonata, which it otherwise strongly resembles, in that the orchestra accompanies the solo instrument. But so much of the sonata's equality of parts is commonly achieved in the concerto that this distinction scarcely holds good. A Brahms concerto was ironically styled "a concerto against the violin" because of the importance of the orchestral parts. Irrespective of the avowed purpose of the concerto, as most composers since Mozart have treated it, to display the skill of the soloist, the orchestra demands the part of an equal. This, it has been contended, is only a fulfillment of the original meaning of the term; the participants work in concert, so to speak; hence the word concerto; but original meanings are no sure guide in music.

The concerto usually consists of three or four movements, much resembling those of the sonata. There are first and second subjects, often a third; frequently, but not invariably, these subjects are first given out by the orchestra, and then elaborated by the soloist.

The themes may be divided between orchestra and soloist, voice answering voice. As in the symphony there are episodes, digressions, bridge passages, the whole complicated structure of the extended sonata form when and where that form is utilized. concertos have been written for piano, violin, 'cello, organ, flute, clarinet, horn and still other instruments.

Some of the most important literature for both the piano and the violin undoubtedly is to be found in the concertos written for them. Those for the violin are commonly reduced to the status of sonatas by being played in recital programs, with the orchestra part entrusted to the piano.

CONCERTO GROSSO

The older form of concerto grosso, favored by composers of the time of Bach and Handel, was not a concerto for a single instrument (or, as in the Brahms "Double Concerto," for two instruments, violin and 'cello) and orchestra, but for a small group

of instruments treated separately from the other instruments of the orchestra. This favored small group,
called the *concertino,* was contrasted with the body
of the orchestra in alternating passages, styled *tutti,*
but became a part of the larger group in other parts
of the composition. The Bach Brandenburg Concerti
supply typical examples.

ARIA AND SONG-FORM

The aria, originally any vocal melody or tune in
the sense that the word Air is still used, has come to
represent specifically a type of formalized solo in
opera, oratorio or similar large forms, presenting, in its
classic examples, a contrast with the less formalized
Recitative, which partook of the character of a
sung speech. The typical Aria da Capo consisted of
a first section, a second of contrasting character and
a third that was a return to the first. The diminutive
of aria is arietta. Arioso was something between
an aria and recitative and in latter-day works, such
as the operas of Puccini, has come to mean a type of
melody approaching the aria in character but less
marked as to its divisions and possessing less the sep-
arable character of a set number.

Song-form, like dance-form, tends to follow a
regular rhythm of measures and, in general, can be
likened to verse-form in lyric poetry. The German
Lied and the French chanson correspond to the English song, though each has developed its own charac-

teristics, due partly to folk and dance beginnings, partly to the influence of poetry and the idioms of language. The strophic song or Lied is one in which the same music is used for successive stanzas of verse. The composed-through (*durchcomponiertes*) song is one in which the composer has given each stanza its individual music. The German Liederkreis is the English song cycle, in which a group of songs, sometimes the setting of a single long poem, are grouped together as one work.

VARIATIONS

Differing repetitions of a stated theme, by means of which the theme is presented in fresh guise with each repetition, often with longer or shorter notes, ornamentation, rhythmic alterations or changes of harmony; or with other devices so elaborate that the theme itself may virtually disappear, though some characteristic of it will remain. The Theme and Variations was a favorite form with composers of the classic period and was revived with particular effectiveness in the late romantic period by Brahms. His variations on themes by Handel, Haydn and Paganini are supreme masterpieces of their kind.

CHACONNE AND PASSACAGLIA

Any attempt to distinguish between these two terms invites dispute, based on historical grounds. Each is a musical form derived from an old Italian

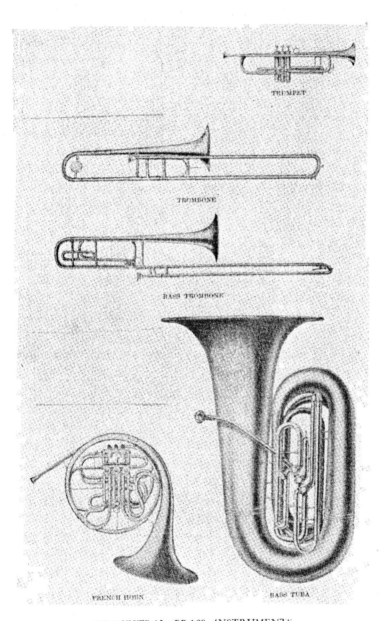

ORCHESTRAL BRASS INSTRUMENTS

or Spanish dance, of slow tread, the feature of which
is called a basso ostinato or ground-bass, by which a
theme is repeated throughout the work in the bass,
though in the passacaglia (some authorities say the
chaconne) it is sometimes transferred to another part.
Bach's violin chaconne and the passacaglia in the last
movement of Brahms's Fourth Symphony are two
of the most celebrated instances of the use of these
forms.

TOCCATA

This is a form of composition traditionally associated with a keyboard instrument, but subject, of
course, to transcription for orchestra, in which there
is usually a rapid, flowing and continuous succession
of figures or passages, often of a brilliant and showy
character.

ETUDE

Ordinarily an instrumental composition designed
to illustrate a problem or difficulty in the technique
of a particular instrument; literally, a study. It is
distinguished from an exercise in that it is a full-
fledged piece of music.

PRELUDE

Aside from the prelude or Vorspiel which is virtually an overture, or serves the purpose of an overture as an introduction to a larger musical work, the
literature of the piano has preludes that are inde-

pendent compositions, some of which might bear another title just as well. Bach's famous Preludes and Fugues represent an instance of the prelude in combination with another form.

IMPROMPTU

A work of irregular form, suggesting improvisation or spontaneous composition.

CAPRICE—CAPRICCIO

In modern usage, a composition in vivacious style, like a scherzo. In older times, one like a fantasia, free of style.

NOVELETTE

Schumann brought this name into piano literature to represent a freely constructed piece of instrumental music, romantic in character, suggestive, perhaps, of an adventure or a story.

NOCTURNE

Commonly an instrumental piece in lyric style, of dreamy or sentimental character; a night-piece.

ROMANCE OR ROMANZA

An instrumental piece of lyric character, like a song; originally a song or a ballad, in which sense the term also is still used.

RONDO

In instrumental music, a composition, or more frequently a movement of a composition, in which a theme, usually of dance character, is presented at the outset and repeated at intervals with episodes or digressive passages between. In the classical sonata the final movement was often a rondo. (Also, rondeau.) Originally the term referred to a tune adapted to a round dance.

FANTASIE, FANTASIA

A free composition somewhat like an overture or symphonic poem in some instances, but irregular and often capricious. At one time a contrapuntal piece of free construction. Still earlier a rather formless piece of impromptu character.

RHAPSODY

A free composition, generally of the order of a fantasy, though sometimes like a symphonic poem; Liszt introduced the term for compositions of this kind built on national themes, such as his Hungarian Rhapsodies.

DANCE FORMS

Among dances that are encountered in art-music may be mentioned Allemande (German), Bolero (Spanish), Bourrée (French), Chaconne (probably Spanish), Contredanse (French), Courante (old

Italian or French), Cracovienne (Polish), Czardas
(Hungarian), Écossaise (Scotch), Fandango (Span-
ish), Farandole (Provençal), Folia (Portuguese), For-
lano (Venetian), Furiant (Bohemian), Gaillard (old
French), Gavotte (old French), Gigue (probably old
English or Irish, jig), Habanera (Spanish, possibly
African), Hornpipe (old English), Jota (Spanish),
Ländler (Austrian precursor of the waltz), Lavolta
(Italian), Loure (old French), Mazurka (Polish),
Minuet (old French), Morris Dance (English), Ober-
tas (Polish), Passacaglia (Italian), Passepied (old
French), Pavane (old Italian), Polacca or Polonaise
(Polish), Polka (Bohemian), Polska (Swedish), Re-
dowa (Bohemian), Reel (Scottish or Irish), Riga-
doon (Provençal), Saltarello (Italian), Sarabande
(old Spanish), Seguidilla (Spanish), Siciliano (Sicil-
ian), Strathspey (Scotch or Irish), Tambourin (old
Provençal), Tango (Mexican), Tarantella (Italian),
Tyrolienne (Austrian), Zortiko (old Basque).

THE FUGUE AND FUGAL WRITING

The word fugue derives from the Latin *fugare*,
to put to flight. Thus the most highly developed
form of contrapuntal or polyphonic (many-voiced)
composition is conceivable as a flight or chase of melodies. A theme is sounded by one part, then by another, then another, until all have entered, each
apparently racing away from the one that follows.
Directly or indirectly each musical phrase is attached

to the initial motif or subject, and variety is obtained
by the manner in which these are jostled, combined
and modulated in their flight.

First is heard the subject or principal theme; next,
in a typical fugue, the answer, a repetition of the subject, given higher or lower; the counter-subject, a
counterpoint or second-subject, which combines
with the subject, and the stretto, which creates excitement by bringing subject and answer as close
together as possible. Episodes or digressions, developments which draw their material from the subject
or counter-subject, and serve to vary the work and
act also as transitions, will be found in most fugues.

The stretto is the climax of the chase. The pursuing entries crowd upon each other, overlapping in
effect, as if the pursuer were about to catch the pursued. Some fugues are without a stretto; others have
several. Often a coda is added.

There are double fugues, characterized by an interweaving of melodies, one or more of these acting as
"accompaniment" to others. Two principal musical
themes, announced separately, may proceed thereafter in unison. There may be three or four parts,
entering in the pursuit as in any other fugue. A contrast in both the rhythmical and the melodic treatment of the two subjects may make them recognizable whenever they appear. Mozart's Requiem
provides an example of what may be achieved in this
form. Bach, the greatest master of fugue of all

time, may be turned to endlessly for illustrations of every conceivable variety of fugal writing.

HARMONY AND COUNTERPOINT

Harmony has been described as the sounding together of two or more different musical tones. On this simple foundation has been erected a seemingly limitless structure of combinations and sequences. Each successive genius has contributed to it. Rules have hardened but never to the final exclusion of new contributions. Great composers are to be identified as much by their harmonic as their melodic personalities. Contemporaries differ, though not as greatly as harmonists a century or a half century remote from one another. The harmonies of Handel are not those of Bach. Much less are the harmonies of either Bach or Handel the harmonies of Debussy or Richard Strauss. Brahms and Wagner differ harmonically, one from the other; the same is true of Chopin and Liszt, of Rossini and Schubert, of Berlioz and Meyerbeer; but inevitably they are less unlike than Brahms and Stravinsky, Rossini and Hindemith, Chopin and Schönberg.

No layman need study, technically, either harmony or counterpoint to realize that counterpoint is a form of harmony—in that sounds are being combined— or to realize why there is a distinction between music of the great contrapuntal epoch, which may be

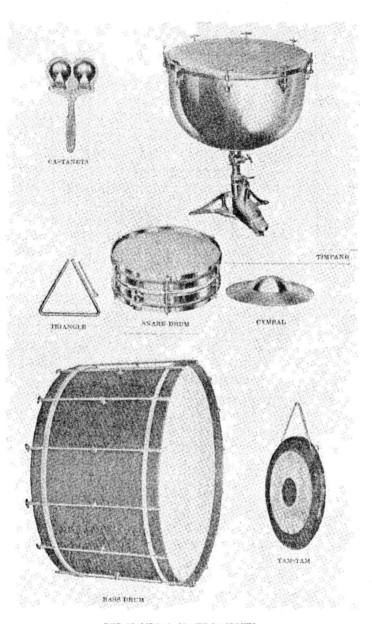

CASTANETS

TIMPANO

TRIANGLE   SNARE DRUM   CYMBAL

TAM-TAM

BASS DRUM

PERCUSSION INSTRUMENTS

said to have found its culmination in Bach, and the harmonic music thereafter.

As customarily defined, the difference between harmony and counterpoint is that between music conceived perpendicularly and horizontally. The harmonist looks at chords perpendicularly. The contrapuntist looks at melodic strands horizontally. The music of the former might seem meaningless or barren if each horizontal line were played separately. The contrapuntist's music would make sense if each of the separate voices were sounded alone. The harmonist moves from chord to chord, with each chord, in a sense, complete; the contrapuntist achieves no such sense of anything completed save at the end of a strand. Harmony tends to exalt and support one line, even though that be a line of chord effects rather than the line of a single voice; counterpoint tends to equalize several lines, each in separate, if correlated, motion as distinct from a unified motion.

A NOTE ON THE USE OF BOOKS

IF books on technical subjects—the voice, piano, violin, harmony, composition, orchestration and the like—are scarcely to be recommended to the layman who has had little or no musical study, there remains an embarrassment of riches in the form of books he can read for pleasure, while acquiring, incidentally, a background for his listening to music that will be of greater use to him than somebody's imaginings as to what this or that music "means." Particularly is this true of biography dealing with the great historic figures of music. Legends, of course, find their way into published lives of musicians as well as those of soldiers, statesmen, sovereigns and pugilists; perversions and assumptions of fact are perpetuated in every branch of biographical literature. Occasionally it becomes necessary for an Ernest Newman to sweep away an accumulation of untruths or half-truths regarding a composer or an artist, and what is then disclosed may tend to invalidate books of biography that have been widely read. However, secondary errors of fact and false conclusions drawn therefrom are of concern chiefly to the specialist; the average reader is not likely to remember, much less be guided by, details sufficiently debatable to be the cause of controversy among biographers and their critics. For this average reader, the perusal of such books results less in an accumulation of the specific than in the deposit of a residue of general information; he is in much the same position as the traveler who visits foreign lands without sojourning in any one long enough to become identified with its life; his horizon undoubtedly has been extended by the impressions gained in simply passing through. The traveler's recollections may not be altogether accurate as to any particular place in Italy or Spain. But he has made a beginning for any new contacts with the countries he has seen.

To read one of many lives of Handel, for instance, may be much less a matter of stowing away facts than of becoming familiar with his period and of subsequently hearing his music with some sense of the world in which he moved and wrote. There may be no truth in the story that Handel dangled a recalcitrant soprano from a window until she was ready to sing his music the way he wanted it sung, but any volume that gives an understanding picture of the composer in relation to the theatre of his day will contribute something to the listener's comprehension of music excerpted from the Handel operas. This is not to be construed as a recommendation for books that are careless of their facts or given over to the re-telling of dubious anecdotes. As between one volume that will withstand the most scrupulous investigation of its scholarship and another that can be shown to be an accumulation of fanciful tales, there can be no question as to which should be recommended and read. The point is that with new light continually being shed on details of the lives of eminent musicians, the disclosure of a misstatement here or a misconstruction there, does not, necessarily, make a book worthless for the layman making the acquaintance of a composer or an artist for the first time, unless there is such wholesale distortion or misrepresentation as to falsify larger aspects of the picture. In many, perhaps most cases, the latest biography, other things being fairly equal, is the one to be taken as a beginning, simply because the world is forever coming upon new material that alters the known facts and throws a different light on biographical subjects. But there are exceptions. Certainly, a serious work of earlier preparation is preferable to a shallow and sketchy one of later writing, even though some things in the older book may call for correction. It is to be assumed that the musical scholar will read and compare many works on the same subject. But we are not dealing here with musical scholars.

Given a limited number of biographies—slightly more than a score, let us say—the reader who has no interest in technical subjects but who has a real appetite for music and feels the need of knowing more about it than the music itself conveys to him, can cover handily most of the history of art-music, as he hears that music in the concert hall and the opera house. This need not be approached with the thought of getting a task over with and done. Instead, it can be regarded as reading for pleasure's sake; admitting that now and again there must be some buckling down to heavy-going. Where to begin, however, is a problem for any person approaching the bookshelves of musical biography for the first time. Literally dozens of books are available on the lives of some composers; while for others there is almost nothing that pretends to completeness. If a bewildering array of books on Wagner is at hand, a question remains as to whether any satisfactory volume on Schubert exists in the English language. With Bach or Handel the material is copious; with Gluck it is skimpy and difficult to find. Not to know something of Gluck's life, as it related to its period, is to lack something necessary to the perspective, not only with respect to Haydn and Mozart, who were to follow Gluck, but also Bach and Handel, who preceded him. Some familiarity with Schubert's life, brief as it was and commonplace as were most of its details, inevitably means a livelier appreciation of certain aspects of his music.

The purpose of this note on the use of books is chiefly to enable those who may feel the need of assistance, to make a choice of a first biography for a number of outstanding composers; and to correlate a series of such selections so as virtually to cover all great periods of music as an art. For such a series to be feasible, only books obtainable in English need be considered here. Moreover, the accessibility of their thought and their vocabulary for the layman, must play a part. Musical analysis may be reckoned of secondary importance to biographical narrative or to descriptions that tend to bring to life the composer, his associations and his times. With two or three exceptions, the several-volume "life" is to be avoided in favor of the single-volume one. In almost every instance, any choice ventured upon here has to be confessed a more or less arbitrary one, since other volumes might be substituted with equal reason. Moreover, it must be obvious that to stop with the works herein enumerated not only is to leave out certain monumental studies that can ill be spared, but also to ignore important composers and to slight certain periods, schools or countries. But to do justice to all these considerations would mean considering a hundred or more volumes, instead of between twenty and thirty. Happily, so inter-related were the lives of various composers that a good biography of one often brings others into the picture. Although only glimpses may thus be caught of incidental figures, these glimpses can be regarded as an enlargement of background. One of the pleasures of much reading of biographies is to find the chief character of the last previous one appearing in some subordinate rôle in its successor, the while the individual who was almost a supernumerary in the work that has been put aside becomes the protagonist of the one in hand. To encounter Mendelssohn while reading of Berlioz, and Berlioz when reading of Mendelssohn; to cross the path of Liszt in following the brief narrative of Chopin and to meet Chopin anew in surveying the pageant of Liszt—not only is there in this the pleasure of recognition, as of an old friend, but there is a rounding of the figures, an extension of the perspective.

Our suggested list begins with Monteverdi. There is an admirable volume by Prunières that is available in English. The splendor of the period when the madrigal was in its prime and when opera, cantata and oratorio were in their beginnings is pictured here against the princely days of Renaissance Italy. The reader may not remember the name of a one of Monteverdi's own operas, though there is good reason in Prunières's text to recall "The Coronation of Poppaea." But when he subsequently hears some Monteverdi madrigals, as sooner or later he surely will, something of Monteverdi's times will be in his consciousness, something of a vanished day in music that no miracle of art can recapture or restore, save as it is brought to life momentarily in the sound of music three centuries old.

Johann Sebastian Bach is the second world figure on this list, confined as it is to the few who can be regarded as representative of great epochs in the progress of the art. The relatively recent biography of Bach by Charles Sanford Terry is chosen in preference to Spitta's or Schweitzer's, not only because it contains new facts, but because it is much more compact and deals primarily with Bach's life, rather than with his music. This is not an easy book to read. For one thing, it is so studded with footnotes and cross-references as to entail a contrapuntal—even fugal—division of attention on the part of the reader. But all this is eminently worth while. These difficulties are not technical ones. So far as it treats of Bach's work, there is nothing the layman need have difficulty in understanding. The burdens are those of excess detail and documentation. The book so far transcends in value various more easily read lives of Bach that to recommend any other by preference would be to assume that the layman's lack of knowledge is only equalled by his lack of stamina. Terry's smaller book, "Bach, the Historical Approach," presents a supplementary human picture. For a less complete study of the life, but one combined with a description of the music, a handy Bach biography is that of Hubert Parry.

Any one of a half dozen or more Handel biographies might properly find place on this list. Admirable as these are, there remains reason to regret

that there has been no English translation of still another, the notable German study by Dr. Hugo Leich-
tentritt. As a sumptuous picture of the early Hanoverian era in England, in which Handel was a person
of a certain splendor all his own, the biography by
Newman Flower should interest even those to whom
music remains a mere incidental of general culture.
This is not to infer, however, that the volume lacks
value for the musician or the layman whose first
interest is music. Another Handel biography, that
of R. A. Streatfeild, ably parallels that of Newman
Flower, with a little less ornamental detail as to the
times, a little more attention to the music. It is a
particularly handy work for those who may have a
desire to know more about the Handel operas. As
with Bach, the temptation must be resisted to name
various other Handel biographies, including two or
three that were "standard" in an earlier era, since our
rudimentary cause is amply served by either Newman
Flower or Streatfeild.

For the period immediately succeeding Bach and
Handel, Terry's biography of one of Bach's famous
sons, John Christian Bach, for a time regarded as
Handel's successor in the opera world of London, and
Ernest Newman's biography of Gluck may be suggested. The Bach volume is not lacking in the human-
interest qualities that make good reading of the Handel biographies named; this London Bach's career
affords the biographer much the same opportunity to

reconstruct the Hanoverian period, if of a slightly later day. In it we meet the child Mozart, playing duets with Johann Sebastian Bach's middle-aged son, from whom, as he was afterward to admit, Mozart learned much that pertained to vocal style. Newman's "Gluck" is an early work of that author and is neither so detailed as to facts nor so thorough-going in its conclusions as later biographical works from his pen, but it bridges nicely the gap that otherwise would exist before Haydn and Mozart. There are many German and Austrian books on Haydn, but he does not appear to be a tempting subject, today, for English or American biographers. A life by J. Cuthbert Haddon, if by no means as detailed as could be wished, will meet the requirements of the reader who is in no sense a specialist but stands in need of something more than he will find in Grove's Dictionary or other lexicons.

With Mozart, a rather difficult problem is presented. Obviously, Otto Jahn's several-volume biography fits better into the scheme of a reference library than it does into a plan of general reading. But Jahn is difficult to replace with any single volume available in English. There are various and sundry literary pictures of Mozart's life and work—compact and convenient ones are the biographies by Ghéon and Sitwell—which either leave something to be desired in the soundness of their musical opinions or stray into a semi-fictional style and treatment of material. In considering these, the reader who already knows something about Mozart needs to be on his guard. What then of the completely uninformed person who turns to one of these books for his first enlightenment? Better, it would seem, a plodding familiarity with Jahn, even though his biography is not to be read at one, two, or fifteen sittings (and is without the benefit of some recent revelations in the form of published letters from the pen of Mozart), than a quick assimilation of dubious background derived from volumes devoted to questionable small talk and equally questionable opinion.

Beethoven, like Mozart, tempts to more detailed treatment than the one-volume study. The English edition of Alexander Wheelock Thayer's monumental biography is in three volumes, and, like Jahn's Mozart, is not for rapid reading. To substitute for it any one of many less expansive works is to raise serious questions. To refer to but two, there are books by Schauffler and Specht that afford lively biographical reading. Thayer is heavy-going, but well repays the additional effort for those whose interest is proportionate to the task. Perhaps only Wagner presents a more bewildering array of supplementary reading, irrespective of what book is to be considered first. There is Beethoven biography that is almost pure fiction. And there is Beethoven biography that is almost pure psychology. Newman and Rolland have given us valuable studies of the man.

Schubert, as has already been said, stands in need of some such English biography as Dahm's German one. Oscar Bie's translated "Schubert the Man" may serve as a point of departure for further reading; so, too, a concise volume by Ralph Bates; but in lieu of any really comprehensive biographical study for English readers at this writing (1935) the extended article in Grove's dictionary from the pen of Sir George Grove himself is an equally promising springboard. For the Italy of about the same time, either of two relatively recent Rossini biographies, one by Francis Toye, the other by Lord Derwent, can be read with pleasure as well as profit. Turning to France, but by no means to the exclusion of its neighbors, the reader of musical biographies will find in Hector Berlioz's own Memoirs one of the most fascinating and illuminating books likely to be encountered in a lifetime of reading. Some of it requires the proverbial grain of salt. But Ernest Newman has taken care of that in his skillful editing of a recent new edition. This is a book of background-plus. Mendelssohn, no such interesting subject, today, as Berlioz, can conveniently be viewed through the eyes of Schima Kaufmann, whose conversationalized biography of recent date gets over the ground easily; probably what most readers will want to do in this case. Far more interest abides in Chopin, Schumann and Liszt. Basil Maine has a convenient small biography of Chopin; Huneker and de Pourtalès have spread more color on a larger canvas. Murdoch's recent volume is thorough and factual.

With Liszt, the reader may have need to know that he is on controversial ground. Ernest Newman's "The Man Liszt" is largely an assault on what he regards as the legends, the untruths, the injustices and the misconceptions perpetuated in a long succession of earlier biographies. But read alone, rather than as a corrective or intended corrective of other works, it scarcely fullfils the purpose of a separate and independent biography. Again, Huneker and de Pourtalès are among those whose Liszt biographies suggest attention; so, too, Sacheverell Sitwell, whose recent volume only slightly antedated Mr. Newman's and tells the Lisztian tale in an attractive way. Perhaps Sitwell or de Pourtalès, plus Newman, is the best recommendation today for those intent upon background rather than the literary stimulus of such writing as Huneker's.

Of the making of books about Wagner there is no end. But at least two more are urgently needed. At this writing only the first volume of Ernest Newman's projected three-volume life has been issued. If the other two are as eminently readable as the first, and packed with the same scholarship, (and there is every reason to believe they will be), there need be no hesitation in leaving other Wagner biographies out of consideration in making up any such list as is here formulated. But in lieu of the second and third volumes of this work, several single-volume works, from among the many, can be recommended to the English reader. That of de Pourtalès is not only admirable but quite recent. W. J. Henderson's is older but subsequent revelations have not impaired its value.

Of composers since Wagner, some have written interesting memoirs or autobiographies like Massenet and Rimsky-Korsakoff; some, like Bruckner and Mahler, have had the solicitude of propagandists who also were biographers (Gabriel Engel has written small biographies of the two composers named and to Cecil Gray must be credited a valuable if strong-opinioned book on Sibelius); others, like Richard Strauss, have not always been fortunate in what has been said about them by biographers who either lacked sympathy or possessed an excess of it. Léon Vallas has given us a study of Debussy that is unusual in the extent to which it quotes the newspapers and magazines for contemporary record and contemporary opinion. Toye's "Verdi" and John Tasker Howard's "Stephen Foster," Niecks's "Schumann" and Niemann's "Brahms" come naturally into the list, paralleling Wagner in some parts of his career and preceding Strauss, Debussy and others of the group just named. Biographies of living composers are commonly so tentative as to serve little better than current magazine articles. The life stories of Stravinsky, Schönberg, Hindemith, Bartok and other contemporaries can wait. Historically, their background is largely the layman's own. Our suggestions here are concerned primarily with the past. Let it be emphasized again that various other volumes would serve the purpose in much the same way as the ones that have been named. At best, they represent only a beginning. But they are a beginning.

Printed in the United States
48436LVS00004B/123

9 781417 992027